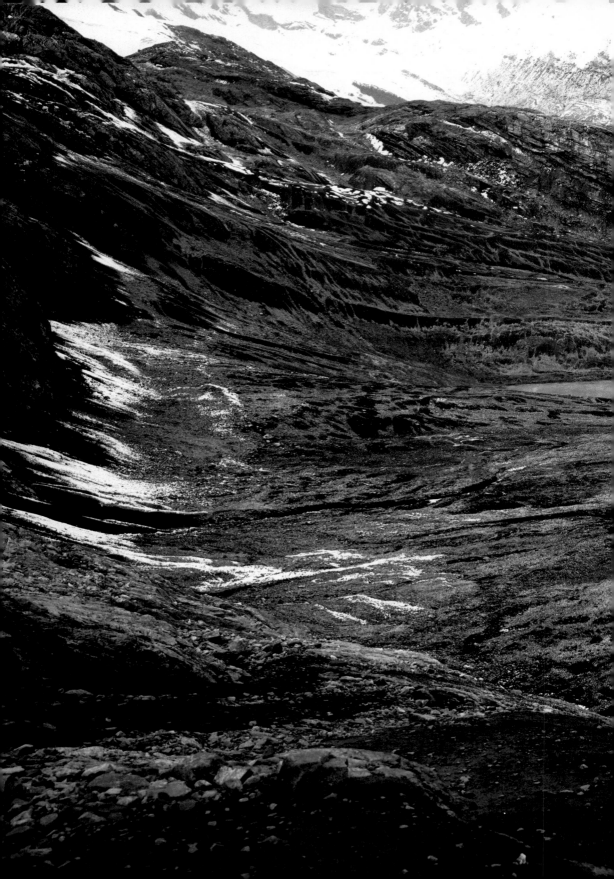

Opening Images: A History of the Future
Susannah Sayler & Edward Morris / The Canary Project

A History of the Future consists of a set of photographic images, all landscapes, showing places around the world where scientists are observing the impacts of climate change. In this case, the images portrayed where all taken in Peru. Sayler and Morris struck a different bargain between illustrating the facts of climate change (which is always contingent on captioning and context) and laying bare a state of disorientation and collapse of scale that seemed the only reliable opening into the trauma of climate change.

# MCHAP WELCOME
## Dirk Denison

This publication began in connection with the 2016 Mies Crown Hall Americas Prize (MCHAP), which recognized the best work of architecture in the Americas during 2014 and 2015. A lot has changed since then. The last year has made it impossible to ignore the pervasive ecological, climatic, social, and economic forces that shape our lives. At this inflection point, I wish to reaffirm our commitment to the prize as a vehicle for celebrating excellence in the quest for new architecture in a new world.

MCHAP exists within the College of Architecture at Illinois Institute of Technology (IIT), a school on the threshold of teaching and practice that provides the opportunity to expand the boundaries of what we consider education today.

Even before COVID-19 forced classes online, our notions of education were rapidly changing. Information is gathered and disseminated at a breakneck pace through new models of interaction and access. The promise of today's technology is discovering and understanding the world around us in a more holistic, integrated way. But discover and understand what, exactly? Who is creating and sharing knowledge, and with whom?

With acceleration and interconnectedness come occasions for observation, comparison, and sharing. We believe that looking out to the world, as MCHAP does, and devoting our careful attention to architecture that is performing well is not a luxury—it is fundamental.

Where we look is important. The Americas is comprised of thirty-five countries with diverse cultures, geographies, densities, and histories that have long formed dynamic contexts for architecture to engage. By looking at North and South America together, MCHAP reinforces a unique North-South axis that creates the potential for urgently needed cross-cultural learning at a moment of global change and crisis.

Just as crucially, we believe the information and insights gathered by MCHAP shouldn't be accessible only to students or those within our immediate circles. It is for this reason that we do not merely grant a prize but ask MCHAP jury members and winners to teach, speak at lectures and symposia, and develop research for publication; these contributions are, in an important sense, the actual prize. MCHAP conversations are catalysts for other conversations that focus on what excellence in architecture means, using the highest quality examples to reveal the highest potential of what we can contribute. MCHAP is unabashedly optimistic in its belief that we can learn from this exercise and improve our communities.

The MCHAP award process involves the collaboration of a global network. In the early months of each MCHAP prize year, nominators throughout the Americas—architects, curators, editors, visual artists—submit built works of formal, social, and technical accomplishment, broadly defined to include architecture, landscape architecture, and works of urbanism and infrastructure. An expert jury conformed by practitioners, educators, writers, and editors gathers in Chicago to review the nominations in January, which is the first step in uncovering the prize cycle's key insights.

Then, in the Spring, the Prize for Emerging Practice is awarded to a work by a practice in its first ten years of operation. In 2016, Emerging Practice finalists included Haffenden House, a suburban home in Syracuse, New York, by PARA-Project; CID, a public facility in the Chilean desert by Emilio Marin & Juan Carlos Lopez; the San Francisco Building, an apartment complex in Paraguay by Jose Cubilla; OZ Condominiums in Winnipeg by 5468796 Architecture; and the winning project, a temporary pavilion in the historically-charged site of Mexico City's Zocalo, by the firm PRODUCTORA. Each of these projects rethought existing associations through an intelligent engagement with their types or sites. While these works are not featured in this volume, it is important to note this facet of the prize: a close look at young practices' approaches is of particular interest to us in an academic setting. The winning Emerging Practice gets invited to teach at IIT and continues research toward an MCHAP-sponsored publication that will carry these lessons forward.

In the summer, the Americas Prize timeline picks up pace: the jury visits all the finalist projects on-site to see the projects first-hand and to meet the architects, the design teams, and the clients—the persons best equipped to share insights into a project's performance. The jury not only examines how each project met its objectives but its contributions beyond the brief. In each location, MCHAP also organizes conversations with local leaders and designers. In 2016, these took place in Lima, Toronto, Mexico City, São Paulo, Los Angeles, and New Canaan, CT, near the finalist projects: the UTEC Campus, by Grafton Architects; the Pachacamac Museum, by Llosa Cortegana; the Fort York National Historic Site Visitor Centre, by Patkau Architects/ Kearns Mancini Architects; Tower 41, by Alberto Kalach; the Weekend House, by Angelo Bucci; Star Apartments, by Michael Maltzan; and that year's winning project, Grace Farms, by SANAA.

In October, the cycle's jury, architects, and clients met again in Chicago for a series of events that served as a form of conclusion and a platform for new beginnings. A full day was spent in formal proceedings with students, faculty, and practitioners in Crown Hall, Mies van der Rohe's seminal work of universal space and expressive structure. Diverging, international perspectives came together to uncover what they could learn from one another and project visions for the future of architecture.

Once the prize is awarded, MCHAP invites the author of the winning project to Chicago to lecture, collaborate in studios and workshops with IIT students and faculty, and produce a publication of their research. After the 2016 prize was granted to Grace Farms, SANAA worked with a group of IIT students to develop "Lake 33$^{rd}$ Bronzeville," an installation that presented their vision for the neighborhood surrounding IIT featured in the 2017 Chicago Architecture Biennial. Through this interaction, fourteen IIT students had the opportunity to work closely with Kazuyo Sejima; two of these students traveled to Japan to work on the project at SANAA's office, and a third one was eventually asked to join the firm's staff. A publication is currently in development.

Meanwhile, MCHAP also commissioned the book you are now reading to synthesize the themes uncovered in the prize cycle. The book aims to mark and define the moment and present jury findings while supporting reflection and new scholarship. The Americas books are artifacts of the juries' excursions into the world, experiences fundamental to the character of the prize.

The 2016 MCHAP jury, whose observations come together in this volume, was comprised of Stan Allen, jury chair, professor and former dean of Princeton University's School of Architecture and principal of Stan Allen Architects; Wiel Arets, under whose deanship at the IIT College of Architecture MCHAP was established in 2012; Ila Berman, then director of the School of Architecture at the University of Waterloo; Jean Pierre Crousse, partner of the Lima-based firm Barclay & Crousse; and Florencia Rodriguez, founder and former director of PLOT in Buenos Aires.

The six finalist projects presented the jury with a rich array of what excellence in architecture means and how it can be accomplished. They embody strong thinking and demonstrate a positive impact. In the Weekend House and Tower 41, an intensive urban condition is inverted, with nature and architecture seemingly invading one another towards a refreshing effect. In the Star Apartments and Grace Farms, the 2016 Americas Prize winner, sculptural forms are carefully calibrated to its environment—one urban, one pastoral, and suburban—to enrich a specific community. At UTEC and Pachacamac, the architects created contrasting forces, vertical at UTEC and engaging the horizon at and Pachacamac; the architecture is a symbol, signaling a place for gathering around knowledge. To witness each project's effectiveness and engagement with its context in person was a great privilege.

In the deliberations that surrounded the project visits, Stan Allen drew out each juror's perspective while formulating a framework from which a consistent theme emerged: the specific but hybrid conditions of material, ecology, and culture in each location. These conditions not only informed the relationship between form, space, and site in the projects but also generated terms to reflect on what is shared across the Americas. As editor of this volume, Florencia Rodriguez was tasked with pulling the lens back even further, assembling new thinking around each finalist project, and giving form, both visual and written, to these wider reflections.

As the jury traveled from southern winter to northern summer, we passed around a book published earlier that year: Andrea Wulf's "Invention of Nature: Alexander von Humboldt's New World." Wulf finds in Humboldt a captivating, startlingly relatable subject who, through research, travel, and an indefatigable desire to draw connections, underwrote much of our current thinking about the natural world. Today, we are embedded in the fragility of the connections Humboldt identified. We face an acute need to remake the human-made environment, especially in cities, for the better. The six finalist projects teach us how we might begin to meet this fundamental responsibility with sensitivity and intelligence.

Beyond the work of our dedicated juries, collaborators, and amazing anonymous nominators, MCHAP would not have been without the visionary efforts of Professor Wiel Arets, during his deanship, then Associate Dean for Research Professor Vedran Mimica, then IIT's Provost and subsequently President Alan Cramb, and would not continue without the support of Dean Reed Kroloff and current Provost Peter Kilpatrick, as well as the faculty and students of the College of Architecture and our sponsors: IIT, the Alphawood Foundation, Kohler Co., the Mies van der Rohe Society, and our individual patrons. I am grateful for the impassioned collaboration underlying this book between our guest editor and juror who experienced the expedition and territories of MCHAP firsthand, Florencia Rodriguez; the extradentary designer of this volume and indeed the entire MCHAP publication program Edwin van Gelder; MCHAP Coordinator and my partner in this multi-faceted initiative Sasha Zanko; MCHAP Fellow Andrew Jiang, who works tirelessly to keep the MCHAP community connected; and to Jayne Kelly, for invaluable editorial counsel. Finally, I thank the architects and the clients who have created the extraordinary work we have the privilege to shine a light on and to everyone in the international MCHAP network for sharing our conviction that when we give excellence our attention, we uncover ways to improve the world.

# INTRODUCTION
### Florencia Rodriguez

*And we never retain the integrity of the constant flow of information. Indeed, the trip provides an opportunity to broaden the five senses: smell and hear more vividly, look and see more intensely, taste or touch with more attention: the shuddering body, in tension and willing to new experiences, records more data than habit.*

*(...) Emotion, affection, enthusiasm, amazement, interrogation, surprise, joy and stupefaction, everything is mixed in the exercise of the beautiful and the sublime, of the change of habits and of the difference.*

*— Michel Onfray, Travel Theory*

Some time has passed since we began planning this book, but the changes between our first round of conversations in 2016 and our current moment made it all the more pertinent. The last several years have confronted us with phenomena that have urged inquiry about the ways in which we inhabit the world. As a result, these types of reflections are (fortunately) impacting academic programs, biennials, and all forms of media and cultural production. We can see them expanding narratives and canons, integrating previously silenced voices, and foregrounding critical issues.

The Mies Crown Hall Americas Prize resonates with those priorities. Its defining quality is that it builds on the architecture of The Americas, a continent determined by a North-South axis, and one that was once was optimistically represented as a new world but later became evidently complex and characterized by contrasting realities. The Prize and all that goes with it—the trips, discussions, books, studios, symposia, exhibitions, and new friendships it inspires—have made it a vehicle to explore commonalities and differences within this vast territory, and beyond. MCHAP is a platform to theorize and think critically about contemporary architecture on a broader scale. Today's conjuncture enhances a dialogue and speaks to the need to learn from one another.

In that context, this book aims to expand upon the types of references, themes, and texts that usually circulate, and does so with the understanding that each cycle of the Prize has had its own particular identity, one defined by the timely production it reviews, the values of its jury, the discussions prompted by the nominated projects.

On the occasion of the second MCHAP cycle, which involved work completed between 2014 and 2015, the jury members were: Stan Allen as its president, Wiel Arets, Ila Berman, Jean-Pierre Crousse, and myself. After a couple of intense meetings at IIT to review the nominations, the jury selected the finalist projects to later visit them during June 2016, together with Dirk Denison (MCHAP Director), and Sasha Zanko (MCHAP Program Coordinator). The expedition lasted twelve days. I travelled

from Buenos Aires to São Paulo, where I joined the group. Then we went to Lima, Mexico City, Los Angeles, New York, New Canaan, and Toronto.

As Dirk Denison describes in his welcoming text, in each city, the group met the architects, clients, and other actors involved, enabling us to learn about and experience each specific context. Long conversations, sounds, smells, surroundings, the texture of each city and its spaces, weather conditions, foods, and nature, all formed part of the intellectual and experiential dissection of each building, its history, and its impact.

Questions were raised, and the conversations about the production and project methodology intrinsic to each place, the idiosyncrasies and particular modalities of each group of people, the specific relations to the built environment, technology, collective, and nature, were profound and extensive. The MCHAP experience is a dynamic mode of research that takes as its focus the specificity of the culture of architecture throughout the Americas, and the potential contributions to the discipline in each selected case and place.

'MCHAP 2 The Americas, Territory & Expeditions' intends to reunite part of those reflections and expand on them through a selection of invited essays, interviews, short texts, and photographs. It is both a logbook of the

trip and a reader—and its subtitle responds to that double role. The 2016 MCHAP cycle was traversed by discussions about the ideas of nature in design, geography and geology, the future of the built environment, and a certain polyvalence implied in the majority of the finalist projects.

The book is structured into three chapters: Territory & Expeditions, Projects, and Post Scriptum. The first chapter has two parts. It begins by providing historical readings of the intricate construct that defined the Americas and its architecture in the twentieth century with Patricio Del Real's 'Good Morning Buildings: How MoMA Invented Latin American Culture'; Barry Bergdoll, 'Learning from The Americas: Gropius and Breuer in the New World,' and Beatriz Colomina's 'Towards a Global Architect' on Le Corbusier and air travel; Sanford Kwinter comments on competitions, books, and criticism in 'Other Criteria.' The second part features contributions by Enrique Ramirez, Mason White, Uriel Fogué, and Sol

Camacho, inspired by the finalist projects, though not limited to them; these essays open possible relations, lineages, and networks, and encapsulate something about the state of the arts. To finish, two texts illustrate research on specific pieces of territory from the Americas. The first one is co-authored by Ciro Najle and Lluís Ortega, and the second one by Susannah Sayler and Edward Morris.

The 'Projects' chapter opens with the 'Notes on The Second Edition' by Stan Allen. It features the six finalist works and is organized according to the order in which they were visited. Each is represented with a project description and photographs accompanied by a jury member's commentary. The chapter also provides information related to the nominated and outstanding projects, and the MCHAP.emerge.

The first stop was São Paulo. The Weekend House by SPBR, the firm created and led by Angelo Bucci, explores the possibilities of the eccentric. This directly alludes to the location of this vacation house in the middle of the city and how it integrates landscape and architecture, dissolving binary relations. As Jean Pierre Crousse expresses in his comment, the project transcends the Paulista tradition and inverts the usual predominance of the program above site. The house is diluted in the garden and vice versa; the spatial sequence unfolds in an integrated manner that involves a very sensitive understanding of nature.

Leaving Brazil, the jury departed for Lima to visit the New Campus for the University of Engineering and Technology by Grafton Architects and the Pachacamac Museum by Llosa Cortegana Architects. The building designed by the Irish practice created by Yvonne Farrell and Shelley McNamara experiments with renewed forms of matter, resolving the more visible façade of the project with a porous and monumental juxtaposition of open terraces that create a brutalist cliff. Ila Bergman comments on how this is a topographical project, "as the geological infuses this layered yet highly-articulated built landform with continuity and a monolithic consistency reminiscent of the matter out of which the earth is made," making it permeable to its urban context.

The second Peruvian project shares the built landform analogy but dissolves into the landscape. Patricia Llosa and Rodolfo Cortegana designed a museum characterized by an ambiguous relation between mimesis and heterotopia. The new building's references to the pre-Hispanic period and its precise location establish a subtle tension with the Pachacamac Sanctuary; the project permits a radical openness to history, nature, and experience. It is heterotopic because its spaces juxtapose discourses about things other than themselves in a delicate and sophisticated manner.

Leaving Peru, the jury visited the Tower 41 office building in Mexico City by Taller de Arquitectura X / Alberto Kalach. Kalach, as a designer, is a rebel with no fear of imagination. In cheating typologies and canons, he searches for the unexpected, creating new experiences of architecture. When walking through Tower 41, a certain familiarity interlaces with surprising design decisions evocative of magical realism. Stan Allen expands on this by comparing Kallach to contemporary Mexican film-makers Alejandro González Iñárritu and Guillermo del Toro: "What they all share is a sense of a place where absolute precision coexists with the irrational and the inexplicable." A strong understanding of all that takes part in design is what makes this possible.

That provocative use of imagination also resonates when visiting Star Apartments in Los Angeles, by Michael Maltzan Architecture. This case is based on the need to respond to the complex urban issue of homelessness through architecture. Michael Maltzan, together with his client, the Skid Row Housing Trust, worked on a new model to provide permanent housing and support to those in need. In order to disarm what can be an urban battlefield and transform it into a space of care, Maltzan looks for social integration, functionality, and efficient use of technology, without compromising the aesthetic and formal outcome.

The last building visited by the jury happened to be the winner of the Mies Crown Hall Americas Prize: SANAA's project for Grace Farms Foundation in New Canaan, Connecticut. This "River" building, as the architects describe it, presents a paradox between a succession

of non-figurative spaces and a radical form. Separate programs in different volumes are put together by a continuous and fluid roof. Even as it seems dominant in plan and
aerial photographs, it tends to loosen its presence when
walking through the building. This form responds to the
contingencies provided by the topography and pre-exis-
tent trees. As Wiel Arets writes: "This is a project born out
of multiple readings of the site; readings with no beginning
or end, without hierarchy."

Together with the outstanding works, these
buildings talk as much about the Americas as they do about
the global changes that are affecting architecture. Many of
them look beyond an opposition between the project of

autonomy vs. architecture with a social agenda. They are
contributing to a more integrated understanding of the
capabilities of design.

Following that journey, the Post Scriptum puts
together time-dispersed conversations and emailed instant
reflections that, from a distance, add voices to the critical
thinking of architecture, planetary culture, and nature,
among other issues. These afterthoughts represent a symbolic opening of the discussions in this book to a broader
community of designers following MCHAP's prompt to
build a collaborative platform based on dialogues.

In that section, the late Jean-Luc Nancy corresponds with Florencia Rodriguez about the world, nature,
religion, and a certain *fièvre rationaliste*. Isabella Moretti
and Magdalena Tagliabue talk with Graciela Silvestri about
landscape roots, travel, and Guaraní knowledge. When

interviewing David Harvey, Mariano Gomez-Luque and Daniel Ibañez inquired about capital and urbanization. After those dialogues, Juan Pablo Corvalán, Jeannette Sordi, Rodrigo Kommers Wender, Paul Preissner, Pedro Aparicio, Juliana Ramirez, Ana Rascovsky, and Todd Palmer email MCHAP to share some intimate thoughts and profound reflections distributed throughout the Americas.

A group of photo-essays by The Canary Project, David Sisso, Pablo Gerson and Miguel de Guzmán are organized as a parallel visual narrative that interrupts the

reading and invites us to rest on these landscapes and complement the written discourses.

Imagination, nature, artifice, ecology, environment, beauty, meaning, urbanity, care, and responsibility are part of the glossary that guided this editorial process. Some of these concepts feel like forgotten old friends who are returning, transformed and grown, to re-affect and question the ways in which we think and produce architecture.

I would like to thank Dirk Denison for his commitment to MCHAP and tireless work to make this book happen. Also, Dean Reed Kroloff for supporting this endeavor. I am personally grateful to Isabella Moretti, as her steady work was key to the process of this book; and to Sasha Zanko, Andrew Jiang, Edwin van Gelder, and Pablo Gerson. We are all indebted to the contributors who have generously shared their thoughts and work magnifying the MCHAP network.

# TERRITORY & EXPEDITIONS

This book is the result of travels and projects, and the discussions they inspired. One that is an inherent part of the MCHAP is the geographical and socio-political construct of the Americas. To read through it, Patricio del Real writes about how MoMA worked with the idea of a specific architecture from Latin America, and Barry Bergdoll elaborates on an intriguing triangle of influences involving Europe together with North and South America. Beatriz Colomina explains how Le Corbusier was the first global architect and how air travel affected his understanding of space and the world. After that, Sanford Kwinter reflects on critical criteria, competitions, and books.

25

For the second part of this introductory chapter, the contributors were invited to reflect on some prompts inspired by the jury's debates. Particularly about territories, new conceptions of nature, openness, architecture, and urban models for the future.

Enrique Ramirez, Mason White, Uriel Fogué, Sol Camacho, Susanne Sayler and Edward Morris from The Canary Project, and Ciro Najle together with Lluís Ortega, wrote about the physical limits of architecture, the Posthumanism turn, urban 'black boxes,' porosity and experience, geography, and the agricultural economy of space. These voices and explorations also resonate in the captivating visual essays by David Sisso, Pablo Gerson, and The Canary Project.

# "GOOD MORNING BUILDINGS:" HOW MOMA INVENTED LATIN AMERICAN ARCHITECTURE
## Patricio del Real

*We are challenged to build here in this hemisphere a new culture which is neither Latin American nor North American but genuinely inter-American. Undoubtedly it is possible to build an inter-American consciousness and an inter-American culture which will transcend both its Anglo-Saxon and its Iberian origins.*

*— Henry Wallace, Vice President of the United States, 1939*

In a moment of crisis, the United States turned south to Latin America to imagine its own future. The dawn of the Second World War saw the emergence of a new Western Hemisphere, imagined in US political and cultural circles as a united American continent, inheritor to and defender of Western civilization.[1] Culture was mobilized to make evident a common geography of universal values, and modern architecture was enlisted in these efforts. A "Latin American" modern architecture appeared out of political urgency of the historicity of architecture's maps of the Americas. In the mid-twentieth century, modern architecture in Latin America crystalized into an identifiable style, distinct yet at the same time part of modern universal Western culture. So claimed US architecture historian Henry-Russell Hitchcock, for whom architects across the region had produced a recognizable idiom, a "Latin American architecture," that successfully and elegantly negotiated its early formal inheritance, which he attributed to Le Corbusier; embraced local customs and idiosyncrasies; and, most importantly, was open and receptive to postwar developments exemplified by the work of Mies van der Rohe in the United States. In short, architects in the region had reached maturity, he argued, being both responsive to local tasks and open to the world that is, to the United States. The proof was the works he included in the exhibition "Latin American Architecture since 1945," which opened at MoMA in 1955. In the ten-year period covered by the exhibition, Hitchcock found the forms of a definable architectural aesthetic that gave evidence of the existence of Architecture. "We have an architecture still," he had claimed in 1932.[5] This was also the case in 1955. That this had happened in Latin America was to be noted, celebrated and contained. There is much to be said about this; my interest here, however, is to highlight the institutional character of the mid-Twentieth Century idea of Latin American architecture, which has much to do with the mechanisms of Pan Americanism of the interwar period.[6] Born in the throes of the Great Depression, the fires of the Second World War and the hopes of the postwar, Latin American architecture was

26

# In the dialectic between diversity and difference, architecture shifts between being a tool for geo-cultural constructions and a site of cultural debate. It is therefore critical to ask: which 'Americas' is being invented through architecture today?

war.[2] The Mies Crown Hall Americas Prize continues this hemispheric project, testifying to its endurance and renewed political valence by threading contemporary architecture practices to an imagined community called the Americas.[3] Does the positive fact that these practices happen to be in a particular geography make them of "the Americas" that is, part of and advancing a unique worldview that undergirds this geo-cultural category? The stability and usefulness of this concept is challenged by the tremendous diversity it aims to capture. Diversity—cultural, social, and architectural—holds together this imaginary called the Americas only by smoothing and muffling difference, that is, the pressing imbalances and contradictions the category unfolds, drawing alternative maps. In the dialectic between diversity and difference, architecture shifts between being a tool for geo-cultural constructions and a site of cultural debate.[4] It is therefore critical to ask: which 'Americas' is being invented through architecture today? I aim to shed light on this question by looking at the Museum of Modern Art (MoMA) and its engagement with Pan Americanism between the two world wars, and expose

part of a project to imagine the Americas as a family of nations. Nelson A. Rockefeller championed this imaginary and advanced it through the Office of the Coordinator of Inter-American Affairs (OCIAA), which he directed from August 8, 1940 to August 25, 1945. Supporters of all things modern didn't hold back their excitement; Rockefeller's close ties to MoMA meant that his Washington DC appointment had doubled his power.[7] In 1940, a cultural war had begun.

In the OCIAA, the celebration of an American continent of equal nations went beyond ritualized forms of Pan Americanism to mobilize cultural relationships under the Good Neighbor Policy.[8] The OCIAA was envisioned as a tool for economic development. Culture, however, became part of its tool kit to bring the continent together. Competing with the State Department's Division of Cultural Relations, the OCIAA's Cultural Relations Division, chaired by US architect Wallace K. Harrison, launched and enabled diverse projects at multiple levels and varied sites. The management of culture was a major point of contention between the two US government agencies.[9] In

Rockefeller's office the notion of *reconocimiento*—the need to know and to acknowledge in the United States the achievements of the "other American Republics"—was a key concept guiding its initiatives with a section dedicated to inter-American activities in the United States. The will to know the region was inflected by the awareness that difference had to be controlled so that culture could be properly disseminated. The OCIAA

and enlisted the Mexican worker for the Allied cause.[12] Although larger Latin American nations such as Venezuela, with its rich oil fields—and its links to Rockefeller family interests—demanded the attention of US political and economic circles, smaller nations, especially those in Central America close to the strategic Panama Canal, were not disregarded. Through its various departments, the OCIAA engaged a vast hemi-

Born in the throes of the Great Depression, the fires of the Second World War and the hopes of the postwar, Latin American architecture was part of a project to imagine the Americas as a family of nations. Nelson A. Rockefeller championed this imaginary and advanced it through the Office of the Coordinator of Inter-American Affairs (OCIAA), which he directed from August 8, 1940 to August 25, 1945. Supporters of all things modern didn't hold back their excitement; Rockefeller's close ties to MoMA meant that his Washington DC appointment had doubled his power. In 1940, a cultural war had begun.

27

managed a vast array of formal and informal cultural technologies. It renewed and revamped Inter-American understanding and collaboration by identifying and celebrating "Latin American civilization." In the idea of Latin American architecture, the notions of civilization and culture managed by the OCIAA played out in the dialectic between an international and local expression of architectural modernism. The Museum of Modern Art was brought into the fold of official Pan Americanism early on with informal and formal connections with OCIAA's cultural and information projects. Rockefeller drew from his experience at MoMA and from its personnel. John E. Abbott, MoMA's Executive Vice President and member of its Board of Trustees became head of the OCIAA's Art Division and Monroe Wheeler, MoMA's director of publications, of Publications Division.[10] Before this, in the early 1930s, MoMA had engaged the artistic culture of Mexico, primarily painting. These first steps were fundamental in the development of the modern cultural projects and its proclivities to construct cultural geographies. With the help of Rockefeller's Washington office, MoMA was able to extend beyond Mexico, bringing forth a new cultural geography and aesthetic world from which the idea of "Latin American" architecture emerged.

With the OCIAA, a clear hierarchy appeared in the "family of nations" that made up the Western Hemisphere. Brazil, with its immense size, apparently inexhaustible natural resources and strategic military importance came to the forefront of US economic and political interests. Zé Carioca, Donald Duck's South American friend, led the Latin American parade. Panchito Pistoles, the sombrero-wearing, gun-slinging friendly rooster, however, was never far behind.[11] The historic relationships with Mexico, its natural resources and labor force so close to the United States, brought both nations into a symbiotic friendship. The 1942 Bracero Program effectively mobilized

sphere. It instituted programs in every independent Latin American nation. The Museum of Modern Art, working primarily within the field of modern culture, had to be selective, and focus its resources on initiatives that could operate at multiple levels, within national, Inter-American and international registries.

Contrary to the image advanced by official US-Pan Americanism, this cultural geography was not frictionless, but was rather a charged and contested politicized field in which regional powers produced their own local and Inter-American cultural projects. Argentina's government, for example, remained officially neutral during the world conflict and mobilized alternative visions of regional unity that challenged the cultural imaginaries of US-led Pan Americanism. Initiatives such as the 1942 *Primer Congreso de la Cultura Hispano-Americana* (First Congress on Hispano-American Culture) celebrated not only cultural ties with other Latin American nations but also closer relations with Fascist Spain. In Brazil, the Ação Integralista Brasileira (Brazilian Integralist Action) had, in the early 1930s, established close ties with the Government of Benito Mussolini.[13] The dictatorship of Getulio Vargas and the Estado Novo, broke Integralist's nationalist dreams but fascist and authoritarian tendencies persisted. In the region, culture was highly charged with political and social debates over the nature of a national and trans-national Ibero-American culture. Architecture, both as practice and discipline, was not immune to these forces, and framed within the confrontation between a vital colonial tradition and the new architecture, it became enmeshed in the period's cultural battles. In US political circles, the idea of Latin America served to counter the rise of nationalism.[14]

With MoMA, modern architecture was brought into the fold of US cultural politics. The museum's formal and informal links to the OCIAA exposed the political nature of its cultural project, intertwining it with official Pan Americanism. The Modern's curatorial projects have consistently drawn cultural geographies. The 1932 exhibition, "Modern Architecture: International Exhibition," and its parallel book, *The International Style*, is a key example of the worldviews advanced by the museum's curatorial projects.[15] These worldviews were not frictionless, neither were they singular or left unchallenged—even within the museum itself. Yet, these imaginaries advanced by curators and diverse projects were all part of the museum's drive to define itself through modern art and architecture. In all,

intertwined with the modern aesthetic culture crafted at MoMA. The Modern was the key site in the construction of Latin America because this museum had been imagined early on as an international stage in which cultural questions developed abroad could be focused and entangled with U.S. cultural and political concerns. The Modern established an international assembly line that had its final station in New York. Exhibitions and related projects were produced there to tell a story of modernism to local, national, and international audiences. The projects were then being exported back

The idea of a "Latin American modernism," helps unravel MoMA's institutional project. It reveals that the idea of Latin America was there from the start, integral to the creation of the museum as a center of international culture in New York. The modern architecture of the region was a late addition to this project. It nonetheless helped renew the centrality its Architecture Department had claimed in 1932.

28

they gave shape to a project called MoMA. With the OCIAA, the endeavor called MoMA was woven into the political relations between the United States government and the states of Latin America. The idea of a "Latin American modernism," helps unravel MoMA's institutional project.[16] It reveals that the idea of Latin America was there from the start, integral to the creation of the museum as a center of international culture in New York. The modern architecture of the region was a late addition to this project. It nonetheless helped renew the centrality its Architecture Department had claimed in 1932.

As examples of the region's modern architecture started to travel through professional and popular cultural circuits, inflected and propelled by Pan Americanism, it was made to speak 'Latin American.' Reaching a crescendo after the war, modern architecture in the region appeared regularly in the international stage. Architectural journals, historians and critics outside the region noticed specific buildings and pointed to the contours of a Latin American modern manner, not as homogeneous but as a positively identifiable style. The circulation of the region's modern buildings in the mechanism of international exposure was undergirded by the idea of a "Latin American manner."[17] The notion of style, explicitly named or implicitly assembled through published and exhibited examples, was critical for it allowed this architecture to transcend its national context and imagine the region as a whole. Style enabled a geo-cultural reading of this architecture. The contours of a Latin American style seemed to crystalize in the 1950s. For architectural historians, it has served to define an alternative modernism, revealing the primacy of geographic imaginaries operating within modernism. These condemn us to think "diversity" by abandoning "difference." As Edward Said points out, cultural formations presume a world map that has been drawn by imperial power.[18] Latin American modernism was a concept deployed from the United States, born from the historic conditions of Pan Americanism and

through formal and informal chains of cultural production, in the form of new, enhanced visions of modernity with the promise of a new world to come. MoMA was certainly not alone but, being the first in the United States to incorporate a Department of Architecture within a museum of art, it played an unparalleled role in the formation of a comprehensive modern culture. It is relevant to highlight that the museum's proselytizing activities started with the 1932 "Modern Architecture: International Exhibition," which circulated widely in the United States as "International Exhibition of Modern Architecture." Many challenged MoMA's cultural project, and although fraught with conceptual contradictions and internal divisions, it not fail to provoke fears of internal and external cultural imperialism.

The situation coalesced in January 1943 with the exhibition, *Brazil Builds*. MoMA's cultural capital was immediately recognized by political and cultural leaders such as Brazilian Education Minister Gustavo Capanema, and by architects.[19] Soon after the closing in New York of the Brazilian exhibition, Mexican architect Carlos Obregón Santacilia expressed his desire for MoMA to "do something similar about Mexico."[20] Obregón Santacilia was well aware of MoMA's cultural influence and the Pan American web extending from New York. He had written Nelson Rockefeller on the absence of modern architecture in the 1940 exhibition "Twenty Centuries of Mexican Art," which MoMA had co-organized with the Mexican government.[21] The culture wars in Mexico had created an embattled and fragmented cultural field; unification required a strong message.

By the mid 1930s, signs of Mexican architectural building traditions had been incorporated in buildings that gave evidence to a growing capitalist market. In the main façade of the Hotel Reforma (1936), for example, Obregón Santacilia and Mario Pani incorporated *tezontle* stone as a vertical counterpoint to the horizontal reinforced-concrete bands of floors, weaving together tradition and modernism.[22] Experiments that sprung from radical functionalist positions, such as Enrique Yañez's building for the Sindicato Mexicano de Electricistas (Mexican Electricians's Syndicate, 1939) that incorporated David Alfaro Siquerios extraordinary *Retrato de la burguesía*, continued the muralist tradition. Debates on functionalism had early on galvanized the public sphere with the Pláticas de Arquitectura (Architecture Conversations), organized in 1933 by the Mexican Society of Architects, (SAM). Tensions between the proper way to represent the nation and build the revolution undergirded Mexican architecture. The use of the neocolonial style in the 1938 Petróleos Mexicanos (Mexican Oil) Building, which celebrated the expropriation of the foreign owned oil industry under President Lázaro Cárdenas, revealed that the question of *mexicanidad* (Mexicanness), in architecture was still unresolved. At the same time, President Cárdenas' support of the Polytechnic University, and in 1938, an official invitation to former Bauhaus director Hannes Mayer to teach there, was clear evidence of the consolidation of the government's emerging administrative bureaucracy, which challenged the figure of the artist-architect supported by the National University and the SAM. The search to produce a synthetic *mexicanidad* in architecture did not receive international acclaim until the early 1950s with the Universidad Nacional Autónoma de México (UNAM) campus—although its critical reception was mixed.

In the late 1930s, Mexican modern architects had been left out of official cultural management in Mexico. With the creation in 1939 of the

MoMA's *Twenty Centuries of Mexican Art* hid the confrontations between different cultural projects by celebrating diverse artistic productions and tying them to a single force that expressed and encompassed the inner national force of *mexicanidad*. Mexico's artistic productions—vital and heterogeneous—were, nonetheless, the heritage of conquest and revolution. Violence undergirded *mexicanidad*. In the early 1940s, *mexicanidad* could fan the fires of nationalism, and it needed to be harnessed and adapted to the rhythms of Pan Americanism. At a distance, *Twenty Centuries of Mexican Art* was the poster child for a new era of official collaboration between Mexico and the United States. However, the U.S. Government did not officially sanction the exhibition. At MoMA, Nelson Rockefeller was playing cultural broker for the "other" American Republics, prefiguring his role in the OCIAA.

John McAndrew, who was responsible for the Mexican show at MoMA, acknowledged the need and made efforts to include modern architecture. However, there was no cohesive and coherent discourse in Mexico that fit his own views and could be mobilized to meet the overall demands of the show. When Obregón Santacilia wrote Rockefeller to express his concern about the absence of modern architecture in the MoMA show and to propose a follow-up exhibition to be called *Twenty Centuries of Mexican Architecture* in 1940, it was clear that the museum had closed its chapter on Mexican modern culture. MoMA was moving to greener, more fecund pastures. With the Brazilian Pavilion on display at the 1939 New York World's Fair, a

29

Installation view of "Brazil Builds." January 13, 1943–February 28, 1943. The Museum of Modern Art Archives, New York. Ph. Soichi Sunami.

Instituto Nacional de Antropología e Historia (INAH, National Institute of Anthropology and History), *mexicanidad* was placed in the hands of historians, archeologists and anthropologists. Architects had not been entirely excluded, but modern architecture was.[23] The official narrative of *mexicanidad* proved a considerable obstacle for the inclusion of modern architecture.

new center of gravity in modern architecture culture had appeared. It also happened that Alvar Aalto and Sven Markelius had emphatically advanced the cause of modern architecture with sophisticated non-heroic national pavilions. MoMA's 1941 exhibition *Sweden Builds* attempted to draw attention to both the architecture of Scandinavia and the plight of a war torn Europe; yet, these efforts were swept by the tide of Pan Americanism. In the early 1940s, it was critical for all departments at MoMA to engage in the production of a Western Hemisphere. In the United States, Brazil's national pavilion was mobilized to manifest a transnational region called "Latin America" as part of a defensible Western Hemispheric geography. Its architectural forms were imbued with a "Latin American spirit."[24] By 1940, it was clear that *Mexico Builds* was an impractical enterprise. Mexican modern culture was too particular and exclusionary. Grafted to a relentless and too visible national discourse founded on the Revolution, *mexicanidad* could not be ambiguous enough to represent the Latin America called forth by Pan Americanism.

The Second World War fueled a need in the United States to construct a regional category capable of negotiating cultural differences within a unified Pan American geography. Undergirded by isolationists' principles in the United States, this rhetoric of a united hemisphere of peace separated from the war-tossed world developed into the regionalism of the postwar. Pan Americanism demanded a relational geography and comparative methodology. It called for simultaneous

gravity in architecture that corrected the asymmetries of the International Style as argued by MoMA in 1932 by insisting on a new cosmopolitanism of modernism.[28] *Brazil Builds* articulated this shift in the cultural geography of modernism, but Lucio Costa and Oscar Niemeyer had emphatically announced it to the world first in New York in 1939. This war inflected cosmopolitanism found its full potential in Brazil because the forms of its architecture and the images it advanced offered an idealized space and time, a universality that sprung from the local as an alternative path to the postwar future.

The Latin American geo-cultural imaginary that unfolded at the New York World's Fair went beyond Pan American rhetoric. The Brazilian pavilion formulated a new synthetic spatial construct capable of mediating the tensions between organic and geometric abstractions in art and architecture. This capacity to mediate contradictory forces went beyond pure formalism; the pavilion was able to address larger social questions, as noted by critics, such as the excessive influence of commercialism that had galvanized cultural conversations in the United States. Its spatial lan-

30

The Second World War fueled a need in the United States to construct a regional category capable of negotiating cultural differences within a unified Pan American geography. Undergirded by isolationists' principles in the United States, this rhetoric of a united hemisphere of peace separated from the war-tossed world developed into the regionalism of the postwar. Pan Americanism demanded a relational geography and comparative methodology. It called for simultaneous double readings: national and regional, local and universal, traditional and modern within a specific geographical marker.

double readings: national and regional, local and universal, traditional and modern within a specific geographical marker. For long, Brazilian intellectuals, constructing their own brand of exceptionalism, had argued that Brazil and *brasilidade* (Brazilianness) had nothing to do with Latin America.[25] Yet, "Brazil Builds" was conceived as MoMA's first Latin American survey.[26] It manifests the period's Pan American cultural strategy; the hermeneutic demand of comparative readings of images, forms and ideas in a fuzzy geography that facilitated transnational crossings that defanged cultural nationalism. Simply put, in the context of 1940s US culture, Brazil had to represent Latin America. Pan American demands articulated a soft geography based on centuries of discursive and visual tropes on the nature of the tropics and a Latin American ethos.[27] In architecture, this soft geography was possible because Brazilian modernism, with its sensuous organic forms, had the capacity to be ambiguous and operate both as a national and a regional marker. At the same time, however, this capacity for Latin American ambiguity was possible because Brazilian modernism claimed universality. Brazilian modernism created a new center of

guage operated within a critical present time, offering a positive road towards the future. Form and space advanced an imaginary that operated as a territorial and temporal mental construct and an ideal place and time. This complex alignment of architecture culture with politics was replayed and enhanced at MoMA with "Brazil Builds."

It took more than the dramatic emergence of Brazilian modernism into the international scene to make it speak 'Latin American.' The presence of tradition—a highly charged concept at the time—had to be addressed. "Brazil Builds" brought it to the forefront of architectural modernism with a section dedicated to the "old architecture" of Brazil. Modernism in Brazil, it was argued, offered a new language of modern architecture that incorporated tradition and offered a clear and distinctive roadmap beyond both early rationalism and mid-1930s European forays into vernacular imaginaries. The discourse on tradition and the vernacular developed in Brazil enriched that being articulated at MoMA by John McAndrew and Elizabeth Mock with projects like "What is Modern Architecture?" and US-American focused exhibitions such as the 1944 "Built in the USA: 1932-1944." The growing influence and continued life during the postwar of "Brazil Builds" as evidenced by the mounting circulation of Brazilian architecture through journals and magazines signaled the complex temporalities at play—the tensions between the past, the present, and the future—in the accelerating time of postwar modernity. Brazilian modernism became a productive category. The Carioca modernist school, the modern architecture developed in Rio de

imaginary was constructed by the OCIAA and its Pan American networks.

In the 1940s, the images and stereotypes of Latin American encountered not only a new context but also a new institutional and intellectual authority in the United States that incorporated scholarship on art and architecture. The idea of a Latin American modern style in the United States was empowered by the growth of intellectual, economic, social

Installation view of "Latin American Architecture Since 1945." November 23, 1955 – February 19, 1956, The Museum of Modern Art Archives, New York. Ph. Ben Schnall.

Janeiro, was bestowed with a national condition: *brasilidade*. Yet, this Braziliannes was constructed both in Brazil and abroad—*brasilidade* was dependent on a general Latin American ethos. MoMA's *Brazil Builds* helped create both a national Brazilian architecture and the prototype of what historians and critics saw as a Latin American manner. These double construct—the national and the regional—cannot be separated or severed from the international networks that created it as a promise for the future. The realization of this promise was staged at MoMA in 1955 with "Latin American Architecture since 1945."

The national discourse of *brasilidade*, mobilized within Brazil to highlight that country's difference with the rest of Spanish (Latin) America, served in the United States to highlight precisely the opposite: the country's similarity with Latin (Spanish) America. The rhetoric of Pan Americanism demanded a unified geography: a Western Hemisphere. The imagery of tropical landscapes and natural settings—a discourse already well established in the U.S. in the early twentieth century—helped surmount political national markers. At the same time, the imagined unified cultural geography of Latin America did not need to be simplistic and homogeneous; national identities did not need to be dissolved, but rather operate within a Pan American discourse that emphasized unity and similarity, enabling both positive national idiosyncrasies and constructive regional commonalities. And this complex

and cultural studies under the rubric of "Latin American Studies," which set the foundation for the development of Area Studies.[29] The drive to establish a Pan American political and economic alliance, spearheaded by Rockefeller's OCIAA, was accompanied by the intellectual project to articulate a Western Hemisphere and continued in the postwar.[30] Latin America was to be not only identified but also celebrated as a culturally-recognizable region with its own contribution to Western civilization.[31] Modern architecture in the region became both a culturally recognizable image of Latin America and a universal Western ideal. This was clearly stated by Philip Goodwin, who organized the 1943 exhibition, when he proposed the architecture in "Brazil Builds" as a model for European reconstruction.[32]

"Brazil Builds" developed from the overwhelming lack of knowledge of the architecture of the region; from the need to surpass Mexican muralism as the key artistic domain of Latin American modernity (as the 1940 MoMA exhibition "Portinari of Brazil" made clear); and by the incorporation of tradition, as both history and ethos, to the narrative of architectural modernism. These were not just guided by a dominant Pan Americanist discourse but, more importantly, by desires for peace and progress—which set the stage for a polyvalent exhibition of Brazilian architecture.

This could not be invented from thin air. In Brazil, MoMA encountered a cultural infrastructure that incorporated modern architects within the state apparatus of cultural management. In the Serviço do Patrimônio Histórico e Artístico Nacional (SPHAN, National Historic, Artistic and Patrimony Service), created in 1937 within the Ministry of Education and Health headed by Gustavo Capanema, modern architects like Lucio Costa found the institutional framework and mandate to incorporate diverse traditions to

Secretary of State Cordell Hull. Exit strategies and transference of projects from Washington to New York had to be planned. The slow liquidation of the OCIAA and the survival of Rockefeller's Inter-American project has to be read in conjunction with the conservative political turn in the United States against New Deal programs and its attacks on modernism; with Nelson Rockefeller's own flirtations with Washington politics;

# Latin America was to be not only identified but also celebrated as a culturally-recognizable region with its own contribution to Western civilization. Modern architecture in the region became both a culturally recognizable image of Latin America and a universal Western ideal.

their developing architectural views. SPHAN enabled the creation of a Brazilian tradition, developing a cultural hierarchy in which the Baroque period and its architectural and artistic production became the key signifier of *brasilidade*. Without this, "Brazil Builds" would not have succeeded.

The Pan American cultural strategies of the 1940s reached fruition in the 1950s when postwar politics and Cold War agendas emphasized and capitalized on regional constructs. The 1955 exhibition "Latin American Architecture since 1945" made evident this regional crystallization, announcing a new future for the entire region. MoMA's cultural products were far from naïve and embraced economic contradictions and political imbalances identified early on by Rockefeller's OCIAA. Developmentalist attitudes grounded on social and economic modernization strategies found their place in MoMA's Department of Manual Industries created in 1944 and headed by René d'Harnoncourt. He also served as MoMA's Vice-President of Foreign Activities, being responsible to maintain cultural relations with the "other" American Republics —d'Harnoncourt double appointment was the clearest extension of the OCIAA at MoMA. Here the development of local industries connected to international economies found a brief interlude, exposing the economic instrumentality of the museum's cultural projects. At the same time that "Brazil Builds" circulated throughout the United States, imagining a fully realized modern region, d'Harnoncourt's projects were addressing the imbalances of modernity in the region. The Department of Manual Industries at MoMA sprung from the OCIAA and Rockefeller's concern over the region's future after the war. Rockefeller's Pan American project was short-lived. Official U.S. government postwar policies for the region started in February 1943, when President Roosevelt ordered the staggered dismantling of the OCIAA and the immediate transfer of all its cultural programs to the Division of Cultural Relations of the State Department.[33] Unbeknownst to most everyone, the preferential treatment given to countries in the region had ended before the end of the war. This meant that when the much-acclaimed "Brazil Build" ended its showing in New York and was about to start its five-year tour of the United States, the postwar world was being organized. Tensions arouse between Rockefeller and

with Rockefeller family economic ties to the region, and with the early rumblings of the Cold War. Nelson Rockefeller's creation of the International Basic Economic Corporation (IBEC) in 1947, had the region as its prime laboratory and was an offshoot of his time in Washington. The creation in 1948 of the Comisión Económica para América Latina (CEPAL, United Nations Economic Commission for Latin America), brought in full force the management of economic and technical modernization under state control that Rockefeller's IBEC aimed to both counter and guide.[34]

In 1945, René d'Harnoncourt toured Latin America. His was a double mission; one was cultural, to encourage the development of MoMA member centers and thus strengthen modern culture in the region. The other was political, a fact-finding mission for the US State Department to gage the political temperature of the region. Under the cover of culture, d'Harnoncourt traveled Latin America as a spy for the State Department. As a scout for the US Government, he aimed to solidified MoMA's cultural infrastructure in the region and the cause of modernism. It was Nelson Rockefeller, then Assistant Secretary of State for the Western Hemisphere who sent d'Harnoncourt to the Latin America.[35] D'Harnoncourt's trip tested the grounds for IBEC, for private investment as a tool for development, and prefigured MoMA's international projection, which will be institutionalized in 1952 with the creation of the International Program.[36]

In the late 1930s, a Latin American ethos had been mobilized around the Brazilian Pavilion as a positive force, as an "infectious spirit" that had made even New York architects turn to modern architecture. By the late 1940s and early 1950s, and in the weakened Pan American web, this architectural language of soft geometries became a warning against a growing corruption that threatened postwar modernism. The promise of Brazilian modernism had transformed—in the views of some—into a mannerist lack of vitality that made it recognizably Brazilian. Critics argued that this exuberant modernism revealed a negative pathology deep within Latin American culture as a whole. The formalism developed in Brazil was accused in postwar European and the US architectural circles of formal degeneration and capricious license. Oscar Niemeyer was the focus of these attacks: his unrivaled

32

mastery of form; his vitality as one the youngest members of the United Nations design team; his professed communism and developing international practice, pressed against the postwar restoration of the old geo-cultural order of modernism. Denunciations came from many quarters. They coalesced in concerns over the dangers of a baroque ethos. Although Hitchcock had emphatically stated that the Baroque was a dead style, there was, he argued, something "certainly Baroque …[if] one does not use too historical a definition" in the use of curves in plan so characteristic of a Brazilian style. Many joined the fray. The aim was to re-center international architecture culture back in Europe and the United States.[37] This baroque impetus—although ill-defined, ambiguous and problematic—was an important thread that wove together a postwar Latin American architecture, modulating earlier Pan American drives through a new postwar emphasis on leisure and exoticism with a Latin temperament.

This Latin American ethos was part of the culture wars in the United States. MoMA's 1948 symposium, "What is Happening to Modern Architecture?," captured this moment of inflection. The rise of consumer culture, formal and technical experimentations in architecture and—as already mentioned—an internationally active Niemeyer, who was projecting buildings

Swiss designer Max Bill and Italian Architect Ernesto Rogers attempted to re-orient the international cultural map and the values of postwar modernism.[38] Accusing and warning against the "utter anarchy in building, jungle growth in the worst sense," which he saw in Brazilian architecture, Bill led the charge by calling for unfaltering decency.[39] Rogers also saw caprice and license; this, however—he pointed out—was appropriate for Brazil. The issue, for him, was one of locality, of recognizing another modernism but containing it to its place. Both positions advanced the imperative of cultural order in postwar modernism that resonated with political positions of Cold War warriors and the idea of Containment advanced by George Kennan in the late 1940s. Kennan recognized the power of artists to create a "credible civilization" and the need for cultural exchanges in the Cold War.[40]

With "Latin American Architecture since 1945," the idea of Latin America crystalized at the Museum of Modern Art. This was a counterpart to ongoing parallel efforts on art. Now there was a complete aesthetics on the region and companion to economic development policies. The Latin American exhibit, organized by Henry-Russell Hitchcock—who had also organized the seminal "Modern Architecture: International Exhibition" in 1932—managed the negative turn against Brazilian modernism. Highlighting key

33

Installation view of "Latin America in Construction: Architecture 1955-1980." March 19, –July 19, 2015, The Museum of Modern Art, New York. Ph. Pablo Gerson.

at all scales in the United States, brought to the foreground the need for normativity. This *rappel* à l'ordre was the fundamental mission of the 1949 exhibition "From Le Corbusier to Niemeyer: 1929-1949." If concerns had been voiced at MoMA's 1948 symposium, the critics had not doubted the significance and vital presence of the Brazilian, and growing Latin American, contribution to modernism. In 1953, calls for the restoration of the old international order came to the fold in the context of the II São Paulo Biennial. Masked by preoccupations on the social character of architecture,

Brazilian contributions, the show emphasized their foundational character but advanced a mature postwar modernism that had surpassed these early developments. Against those who, like Max Bill, fixed on the dangers of formal exhibitionism, Hitchcock noted the sensibleness and sophistication of works being produced throughout the region. Niemeyer's lyricism was but the conclusion of a formal tradition that had emerged from the region's first encounter with modernism. Those who pointed at exuberance—tying it to reinforced concrete, Le Corbusier and a 'Latin ethos'—

missed the tremendous shift manifested in postwar buildings such as Aquiles Capablanca, 1952-54 Tribunal de Cuentas (Comptroller's Office) in Havana, Cuba, and Jorge Machado Moreira's 1953 Instituto de Puericultura (Children's Clinic), in Rio de Janeiro, Brazil, where Hitchcock saw elegance, restraint and masculinity as the signs of a postwar Latin American idiom. For Hitchcock, these buildings revealed other modernist traditions. The bold and lyrical work of Carlos Raúl Villanueva, with all but a marginal debt to Le Corbusier, supported his assessment and gave evidence of the move away from Brazilian modernism and its founding tradition.[41] For Hitchcock, the shift away from what had been the center of architectural production in the region was clear; but for those who doubted, he offered Niemeyer's 1943 São Francisco Church, which introduced the show and the catalogue. The elegant reinforced concrete vaults Niemeyer deployed at Pampulha marked the synthesis of technical reason and formal lyricism in the architecture of the region; dispelled the threat of formalism and made the exhibition go back to "Brazil Builds" as its point of departure to correct the narrative it had generated.

"Latin American Architecture since 1945" was the second survey of the region—that is, the snapshot of a process that had been first surveyed in 1943. At mid-century, Latin American modernism was the conclusion of a tradition initiated by Brazilian modernism, then ending, and the birth of a new, vital and, for the first time, synthetic Latin American style. It showed new materials and programs, but more importantly, it underscored the maturity of architects who, in Hitchcock views, professed a common postwar

could negotiate this postwar order. If, before the war, cultural cross-fertilization in Latin America had engaged Europe—producing an embattled cultural subjectivity, more national than Latin American—after the war, with its cross-fertilization with the United States, it reached regional consciousness. The works on display illustrated the sphere of influence and positive effect of the United States as leader of postwar Western civilization: the growing use of steel and an emerging Miesian language adapted to the region; the presence of US led international commerce as illustrated by numerous tall office buildings; a liberalized and cosmopolitan architectural practice as revealed by the work of US firms throughout the region; the secularization of society, as exemplified by the almost complete absence of prominent religious buildings; the modernization of the family which had become nuclear. The geo-cultural order was clear, and Arthur Drexler powerfully staged it with a decontextualized architecture in photos and drawings that floated in a white background—a similar strategy was used in the catalogue—under a continuous luminous dropped ceiling used in US corporate architecture. Only the exhibition title grounded the architecture of the exhibition in region. Deprived of any specific context, the works encountered by visitors inhabited an imagined geography that reinforced the idea of Latin America as culturally unified, if not homogeneous, certainly illuminated by a common postwar condition.

Political disruptions of this bright order proved the pressing need for cultural constructions. In 1954, President Eisenhower enlisted MoMA in the cultural Cold War, casting the museum as a stage of

Installation view of "Latin America in Construction: Architecture 1955-1980." March 19, –July 19, 2015, The Museum of Modern Art, New York. Ph. Pablo Gerson.

optimism. In all, Latin American architecture was firmly secured in a postwar geo-cultural order under US hegemony.[42] This did not curtail aesthetic independence. The exhibition advanced the figure of the cosmopolitan Latin American architect as a subject who

freedom. That year in Guatemala, Colonel Castillo Armas had deposed the democratically elected president Jacobo Arbenz with the help of the CIA.[43] As Special Assistant to President Eisenhower, Nelson Rockefeller, a member of the National Security Council and head of the Planning Coordination Group, underscored the overwhelming negative effects of the coup in the region and how it had compromised the image of the United States as a progressive democracy-defending nation.[44] A "psychological action program" was suggested, with a hero's tour of the United States for the Colonel and his wife, including a visit to MoMA.[45] The architecture displayed at MoMA was evidence of the possibilities of modernization as the path of US-led development. In the United States, faith in modern architecture enabled a common space in which

national architecture and a Latin American modernism, the 1955 show helped invent both a Latin American modernism and a US-American modern architecture.

Exhibitions like "Brazil Builds" and "Latin American Architecture since 1945" were instruments to imagine and organize the postwar world. They were intertwined in the culture wars first and foremost because there was "good modern building." In the early 1940s, MoMA's Department and Architecture and Design set out to find "good modern building" in the region.[49] Differences regarding what this was emerged

Today, as the Mies Crown Hall Americas Prize sets to discover exemplary contemporary buildings in the Americas, cultural and political circles in the United States claim "America" as a proprietary white-racial construct. The turn to the Americas as a productive category gains new urgency. If it is to have a future, we must ensure that Americanity is transformed from an instrument of power to a powerful instrument wielded by many—not against an 'other,' but against those who willfully erase our shared transnational American histories.

the private and governmental management of culture could meet. "Latin American Architecture since 1945" served to actualize the promise of *Brazil Builds* as a threshold for the entire region and a showcase for decolonizing nations in the developing world. Although the exhibition had a limited run, its ideas and images reached the world. In the bi-polar world of the Cold War, however, clear unambiguous messages were essential. The cultural approach promoted by the OCIAA had to be repurposed under the overarching idea of information management and the preeminence of sending messages rather than receiving them.[46] Hitchcock voiced this uni-directionality of Cold War culture when he confessed that the work he was doing for MoMA "might well be of more interest to people down there [in Latin America] than up here [in the United States]."[47]

"Latin American Architecture since 1945" helped shake loose the geo-cultural order under the banner of a Western Hemisphere established by the war by articulating a positive and unthreatening difference between the United States and Latin America. The museum's efforts paid off. "They live better down there," expressed a visitor.[48] From the United States there was a unified Latin America that made possible to speak of the Americas that is, of two Americas. As important as the exhibition's ability to manifest a "down there," was its ability to reinforce the "up here" which Hitchcock and Drexler had drawn in the 1953 exhibition "Built in the U.S.A.: Postwar Architecture." One encounters an entangled history that constructed Latin America as ambiguous, yet recognizable, to make 'America' unmistakable and recognizable. In 1955, an 'American' architecture—an architecture proper and specific to the United States—operated within "Latin American Architecture since 1945" to define the region. As "Brazil Builds" had created the image of a Brazilian

and left traces in the exhibitions. Yet, it all rested on this category: "good modern building." MoMA could not have imagined Latin America, if there were no excellent works to imagine it. Only then did modern architecture become an object of political power and contribute to the invention of Latin America and of America. Today, as the Mies Crown Hall Americas Prize sets to discover exemplary contemporary buildings in the Americas, cultural and political circles in the United States claim "America" as a proprietary white-racial construct. The turn to the Americas as a productive category gains new urgency. If it is to have a future, we must ensure that Americanity is transformed from an instrument of power to a powerful instrument wielded by many—not against an 'other,' but against those who willfully erase our shared transnational American histories.[50]

35

1          For a history of the emergence of the idea of the Western Hemisphere caught in the wake of the ideology of the unity of Western civilization in the Americas: Arthur Preston Whitaker, *The Western Hemisphere Idea: Its Rise and Decline* (Ithaca N.Y.: Cornell University Press, 1954). For a key text that established the irreconcilable difference and confrontational stance between the United States and Latin America: Roberto Fernández Retamar, "Caliban: Notes Towards a Discussion of Culture in Our America," in *The Massachussetts Review* XV, no. Winter-Spring 1, 2 (1974).

2          As Mauricio Tenorio-Trillo has recently argued, by now, the idea of Latin America should have become extinct. It is outside the scope of this essay to examine if it endures in the present ideas of the Americas. Mauricio Tenorio-Trillo, *Latin America: The Allure and Power of an Idea* (Chicago: University of Chicago Press, 2017).

3          Benedict Anderson, *Imagined Communities: Reflections on the Origin and Spread of Nationalism* (London; New York: Verso, 1991).

4          On the vicissitudes of architecture and culture and the dynamics of cultural diversity and cultural difference: Gülsülm Baydar, "The Cultural Burden of Architecture," *Journal of Architectural Education* 57, no. 4 (2004). Baydar draws from: Homi K. Bhabha, *The Location of Culture* (London; New York: Routledge, 1994)

5          Henry Russell Hitchcock and Philip Johnson, *The International Style* (New York: Norton, 1966), p. 95.

6          The concept of Latin America, as Tenorio-Trillo argues, is an institution formed by governance bodies and the structure of knowledge production in the US. Tenorio-Trillo, p. 164.

7          Paul Rosenfeld, "High Brazil," in *The Nation* 151, no. 17 (October 26, 1940), p. 402.

8          There was of course still much unilateralism in the Good Neighbor Policy as this attitude had been institutionalized in the late 19th Century.

9          It is not possible here to give a full account of the extraordinary dynamics between the State Department and the OCIAA on the question of cultural relations with the 'Other American republics.' These are presented in: United States. Office of Inter-American Affairs, *History of the Office of the Coordinator of Inter-American Affairs* (Washington,: U.S. Govt. Print. Off., 1947).

10         As close confidant of Nelson Rockefeller, Wallace K. Harrison played several roles at the OCIAA. From 1940 to 1943, Robert G. Caldwell, Dean of Humanities at MIT, was director of the OCIAA's Cultural and Educational Activities Division, with Scholarship, Literary, Publications, Music and Art sections. These sections and their heads varied throughout the life span of the OCIAA. See: United States. Office of Inter-American Affairs, *History of the Office of the Coordinator of Inter-American Affairs* (Washington,: U.S. Govt. Print. Off., 1947), p. 91. On Harrison's chairmanship, p. 95. On Inter-American Activities in the U.S., pp. 105-114. On the OCIAA also: Gisela Cramer and Ursula Prutsch, "Nelson Rockefeller's Office of Inter-American Affairs (1940-1946) and Record Group 229," *Hispanic American Historical Review* 86 (November 2006): 785-86. The terms "reconocimiento," "other American Republics" and "Latin American civilization" come from the Inter-American field. See: William Rex Crawford, "Cultural Relations," in *Inter-American Affairs 1942, an Annual Survey*, ed. Arthur Preston Whitaker (New York: Columbia University Press, 1943) and Earl Parker Hanson and Raye R. Platt, *The New World Guides to the Latin American Republics. Sponsored by the Office of the U. S. Coordinator of Inter-American Affairs. Earl Parker Hanson, Editor in Chief; Raye R. Platt, Editor, Rev. 2d Ed.; Associates: Antonio Colorado, Natalie Raymond [and] Dorothy Teall* (New York: Duell, 1943). On John E. Abbot and Monroe Wheeler see the December 4, 1940 OCIAA Organization Chart in *History of the Office of the Coordinator of Inter-American Affairs*, Face p. 150.

11         These characters appeared in Disney's 1944 animated film *The Three Caballeros*.

12         The OCIAA had nothing to do with the Mexican Farm Labor Program Agreement (1942-64), known as the Bracero Program, which fell within the jurisdiction of the U.S. State, Labor, Agriculture and Justice departments and Mexican Foreign Labor Division headed by Minister Ezequiel Padilla.

Anna Bartnik, "The Bracero Program," *Ad Americam. Journal of American Studies*, no. 12 (2011), p. 24. Also: Ronald L. Mize and Alicia C. S. Swords, *Consuming Mexican Labor: From the Bracero Program to Nafta* (Toronto: University of Toronto Press, 2010). On the OCIAA and Brazil: Antonio Pedro Tota, *The Seduction of Brazil: The Americanization of Brazil during World War II*. (Austin: University of Texas Press, 2009).

13         On the 1942 congress: *Primer Congreso de la Cultura Hispano-Americana* (Buenos Aires: Optimus, 1942). On architectural and technical relationships between Germany and Argentina: Fabio Grementieri and Claudia Shmidt, *Germany and Argentina: The Modern Building Culture* (Buenos Aires: Larivière, 2010). On Fascism in Argentina: Federico Finchelstein, *Transatlantic Fascism: Ideology, Violence, and the Sacred in Argentina and Italy, 1919-1945* (Durham [N.C.]: Duke University Press, 2010). Also: Daniel Gunnar Kressel, "The Hispanic Community of Nations: The Spanish-Argentine Nexus and the Imagining of a Hispanic Cold War Bloc." *Cahiers des Amériques Latines*, no. 79 (2015): 115-33. On Brazilian connections to Fascist Italy: João Fábio Bertonha, "The Cultural Policy of Fascist Italy in Brazil: The Soft Power of a Medium-Sized Nation on Brazilian Ground (1922-1940), in Museu de Arte Contemporânea, Universidade de São Paulo, online: http://www.mac.usp.br/mac/conteudo/academico/publicacoes/anais/modernidade/ Also: Marcos Tognon, *Arquitetura Italiana No Brasil: A Obra De Marcello Piacentini* (Campinas, S.P.: Editora Da Unicamp, 1999).

14         Tenorio-Trillo builds this idea throughout his book and specifically in Chapter 8. Tenorio-Trillo.

15         For the differences between the exhibition and the book see: Barry Bergdoll, "Modern Architecture: International Exhibition," in David A Hanks, Ed., *Partners in Design: Alfred H. Barr Jr. and Philip Johnson* (New York: The Monacelli Press, 2015). On the International Style: Terence Riley and Stephen Perrella, *The International Style: Exhibition 15 and the Museum of Modern Art* (New York: Rizzoli/CBA, 1992).

16         Esther Gabara advances the notion of ethos to recover modernism and produce a "Latin Americanism out of place" intertwined to the production of "Americanness." Esther Gabara, *Errant Modernism: The Ethos of Photography in Mexico and Brazil* (Durham: Duke University Press, 2008), p. 18.

17         "The Latin-American Manner," *The Architectural Review*, vol. 118, December 1955.

18         Edward W. Said, *Culture and Imperialism* (New York: Vantage Books, 1993), p. 199. As Vikramaditya Prakash argues, the persistence of "other modernisms," flattens historical specificity and maintains the asymmetry of universality. Vikramaditya Prakash, "Third World Modernisms, or Just Modernisms: Towards a cosmopolitan reading of modernism," in Duanfang Lu, *Third World Modernism: Architecture, Development and Identity* (New York, NY: Routledge, 2011).

19         For Capanema's views on the "valuable publicity" of *Brazil Builds* see his letter to Alfred Barr in Mauricio Lissovsky and Paulo Sérgio Moraes de Sá, *Colunas da Educação: A Construção do Ministério da Educação e Saúde, 1935-1945* (Rio de Janeiro: Ministério da Cultura Fundação Getúlio Vargas, Centro de Pesquisa e Documentação da História Contemporânea do Brasil, 1996), p. 170. On Lucio Costa's surprise on Philip Goodwin's use of his ideas on Brazilian architecture in *Brazil Builds* see: Lauro Cavalcanti, *Moderno e Brasileiro: A História de uma Nova Linguagem na Arquitectura (1930-60)* (Rio de Janeiro: Jorge Zahar Editor, 2006), p. 167.

20         Carlos Obregón Santacilia to Philip Goodwin. March 27, 1943. Registrar Exhibition Files. A&D Exh. 213. Museum of Modern Art Archives, MoMA, New York.

21         Carlos Obregón Santacilia to Nelson Rockefeller. May 24, 1940. Folder 1354, Series L, Box 138, Record Group 4, NAR Papers, Rockefeller Archive Center (RAC), Tarrytown, New York.

22         For the background of the hotel see: Patrice Elizabeth Olsen, *Artifacts of Revolution: Architecture, Society, and Politics in Mexico City, 1920-1940* (Lanham, Md.: Rowman & Littlefield Publishers, 2008), pp. 153-58.

23         On INAH: Olivé Negrete, Julio Cesar, and Cottom, Bolfy. *INAH: una Historia* (México, D.F.: Consejo Nacional

36

para la Cultura y las Artes: Instituto Nacional de Antropología e Historia, 1995). Architect Ignacio Marquina was an important figure in INAH; his interests, however, were in pre-Columbian architectures.

24    F.A. Gutheim, "Buildings at the Fair," in *Magazine of Arts* 32, no. 5 (May 1939).

25    See the section I.6: Does Brazil Belong to Latin America? in Mari Carmen Ramírez et al., *Resisting Categories: Latin American and/or Latino?*, vol. 1, Critical Documents of 20th-Century Latin American and Latino Art (Houston: Museum Fine Arts Houston, International Center for the Arts of the Americas, 2012).

26    Arthur Drexler states this in the introduction to the catalogue. Henry-Russell Hitchcock, *Latin American Architecture since 1945* (New York: Museum of Modern Art, 1955), p. 8. Drexler was curator of the Department of Architecture and Design from 1951-55 and its director from 1956-86.

27    The tropes and images upon which such interpretations rested had been deployed in the nineteenth century, the tropical being perhaps the most recurring. Alexander von Humboldt was the key figure in the construction of the modern idea of the tropics. Humboldt's views were laudatory of the tropics: Felix Driver, "Imagining the Tropics: Views and Visions of the Tropical World," *Singapore Journal of Tropical Geography* 25, no. 1 (2004).

28    On the notion of the asymmetries of modernism see: Vikramaditya Prakash, *op. cit.* On cosmopolitanism: Kobena Mercer, *Cosmopolitan Modernisms* (Cambridge, MA: MIT Press, 2005). Also: Mariano Siskind, *Cosmopolitan Desires: Global Modernity and World Literature in Latin America* (Evanston, Illinois: Northwestern University Press, 2014).

29    The problem of clear regional delimitations engaged new specialized disciplines such as Human Geography that developed in the Social Sciences in the Unites States under the Cold War. For a period article on this problem see: Edward L. Ullman, "Human Geography and Area Research," *Annals of the Association of American Geographers* 43, no. 1 (1953). Also: Vicente L. Rafael, "The Cultures of Area Studies in the United States," *Social Text*, no. 41 (1994) and Neil L. Waters, *Beyond the Area Studies Wars: Toward a New International Studies* (Middlebury, Vt; Hanover, NH: Middlebury College Press; University Press of New England, 2000). For a perspective from the region that examines Latin American Studies in the US and Latin America see: Daniel Mato, *Estudios y otras prácticas intelectuales en cultura y poder* (Caracas: Consejo Latinoamericano de Ciencias Sociales (CLACSO) Universidad Central de Venezuela, 2002).

30    A clear attempt was to address the perceived difference between the United States and Latin America by reexamining the inheritance of the Enlightenment in the Western Hemisphere: Arthur Preston Whitaker, *Latin America and the Enlightenment* (New York, London,: D. Appleton-Century company, 1942).

31    As a cultural construct, the idea of Latin America deployed by Pan Americanism celebrated difference by eliminating confrontation. The complex and varied cultural traditions of the Americas as a whole were mobilized to celebrate common and shared values. This was imagined as a mosaic of cultures.

32    Philip Goodwin cited in MoMA Press Release: "Brazilian Government Leads Western Hemisphere in Encouraging Modern Architecture Exhibit of Brazilian Architecture Opens at Museum of Modern Art," January 12, 1943. Exh. 213. Curatorial Exhibition Files, MoMA Archives, NY.

33    Nelson Rockefeller, *Memorandum on Post-War Planning for the Hemisphere*, February 23, 1943. Folder 63, Box 8, Series O, CIAA, Record Group 4, NAR Papers, RAC, Tarrytown, NY.

34    On the attacks on modernism: George Dondero, "Americans Take Notice—School of Political Action Techniques," in *92 Congress Record* (79th Congress 2nd Session, House of Representatives, Tuesday, June 11, 1946) (Washington DC: 1946), p. 6701. On IBEC: Wayne G. Broehl, *The International Basic Economy Corporation* (Washington: National Planning Association, 1968). On IBEC in Brazil: Elizabeth Cobbs Hoffman, *The Rich Neighbor Policy: Rockefeller and Kaiser in Brazil* (New

Haven; London: Yale University Press, 1992).

35    Nelson Rockefeller to René d'Harnoncourt. September 29, 1944. Folder 1325, Series L, Box 135, Record Group 4, NAR Papers, RAC, Tarrytown, NY.

36    On MoMA's International Program: Helen M. Franc, "The Early Years of the International Program and Council," in *The Museum of Modern Art at Mid Century at Home and Abroad*, Studies in Modern Art (New York: Museum of Modern Art, 1994).

37    Henry Russel Hitchcock, "Latin-American Architecture," in *Journal of the Royal Society of Arts*, no. March (1956), p. 354. On the baroque and modernism: Gillo Dorfles, "Edizioni Per Gli Architetti," *Domus*, no. 318 (1956) and *Barocco nell'architettura moderna* (Milano: Libreria editrice politecnica Tamburini, 1951). Juan M Borthagaray, "Gillo Dorfles, *Barocco Nell'aarchitetura Moderna, nv: Nueva Visión* enero, no. 2/3 (1953). Also: "Crítica de las ideas arquitectónicas," *Arquitectura México* XIV, no. 62 (June, 1958). On the Italian reception and interpretation of the region's architecture: Clelia Pozzi, "Latin America Made in Italy," *ABE Journal* 7 (2015).

38    Walter Gropius et al., "Report on Brazil," in *Architectural Review* 116, no. 694 (1954).

39    Ibid. p. 238.

40    George F. Kennan, *International Exchange in the Arts* (New York: International Council, MoMA, 1956). n.p.

41    Henry Russell Hitchcock, *Latin American Architecture since 1945* (New York,: Museum of Modern Art, 1955). On Capablanca, p. 73; Moreira, p. 84. Villanueva, p. 94.

42    Jorge Francisco Liernur, "Un Nuovo Mondo per lo Spirito Nuovo: Le Scoperte dell'america Latina da parte della Cultura Architettonica del XX Secolo / A New World for the New Spirit: Twentieth-Century Architecture's Discovery of Latin America," *Zodiac*, no. 8 (1992 Sept.-1993 Feb.), pp. 107-09.

43    The idea of covert intervention had been considered as early as 1953. See: Memo, C.D. Jackson to President Eisenhower, April 2, 1953. Folder 4, Box 1, Sub Series 9, Recently Declassified, Series O, Record Group 4, NAR Papers, RAC, Tarrytown, NY.

44    Rockefeller returned to Washington D.C. in 1953 as Chairman of Eisenhower's Advisory Committee on Government Organization. He became Under-Secretary of the Department of Health, Education and Welfare in April 1953, an appointment he resign in December 1954, to become special assistant to the President on Cold War Strategy.

45    "Memorandum for the Operations Coordinating Board, by J.W. Lydman: EMU. Subject: Some Psychological Factors in the Guatemalan Situation," SECRET, DRAFT. September 30, 1955. Folder 91, Box 3, Sub Series 9, Recently Declassified, Series O, Record Group 4, NAR Papers, RAC, Tarrytown, NY. The visit to MoMA was cancelled due to Mdme Castillo Armas' illness. Memo, James White to Mrs. Mellon, Nov 3, 1955. Rene D'Harnoncourt Papers, III.19, MoMA Archives, NY.

46    Ninkovich, *The Diplomacy of Ideas: U.S. Foreign Policy and Cultural Relations, 1938-1950*. p. 117.

47    Henry-Russell Hitchcock to Shippen Goodhue. December 12, 1954. Hitchcock Papers, Box 6, Correspondence G, 1954, Archives of American Art, Washington D.C.

48    Arthur Drexler to Henry-Russell Hitchcock. December 19, 1955, Folder 4744, A&D Exh. 590. MoMA Archives, NY.

49    Memo, Janet Henrich to Elodie Courter, cc. Mr. Wheeler. Re: South American Architecture, January 15, 1942. Exh. 213 REG, MoMA Archives, NY.

50    Recently, Fox News TV anchor Laura Ingraham claimed the idea of "America" for a white population in nostalgic racist terms: "the America that we know and love doesn't exist anymore." See: https://www.youtube.com/watch?v=z0WV-QUHkNmc (Accessed August 29, 2018). On the concept of Americanity: Anibal Quijano and Immanuel Wallerstein, "Americanity as a Concept, or the Americas in the Modern World-system," in *International Social Science Journal* 44, no. 4 (1992), pp. 549-57.

# LEARNING FROM THE AMERICAS: GROPIUS AND BREUER IN THE NEW WORLD [1]
## Barry Bergdoll

The fascination of the European architectural avant-gardes with the United States as a brave new world has been a mainstay of the historiography of modernism for generations, even if Walter Gropius's publication of American grain silos in the *Werkbund Jahrbuch* in 1913 in fact included more (unacknowledged) Argentine examples–four in fact–than United States examples.[2] Yet the accompanying text is entirely an ode to the United States, for Gropius a land of frank invention, of *Sachlichkeit*, of no-nonsense problem solving. No mention is made of Buenos Aires, one of the most vertiginously growing cities and economies anywhere in the world at the time. By the time one of the Argentine images masquerading as an United States one had been doctored by Le Corbusier and recontextualized in *Vers une architecture* of 1923, the Buenos Aires grain silos, actually the design of German engineers, had been moved further north to Francophone Canada. America and the Americas were more places of ideological projection than engage-

chitecture to the United States by the exiles and emigres from Hitler's Germany as a phenomenon largely centered on the east coast of the United States in such powerful institutions, old and young, as Harvard's venerable Graduate School of Design which was going through major changes under Joseph Hudnut and the upstart New York Museum of Modern Art (MoMA), whose first guest book seems a veritable register of influential names recently arrived from Europe: Marcel Breuer, László Moholy-Nagy, Herbert Bayer, Mies van der Rohe.[4] Yet other geographies begin to emerge if we follow other *Bauhäusler*. In 1936 one of the few US students actually trained at the Bauhaus, the New Yorker, Michael Van Beuren, who had studied under Hannes Meyer and Mies van der Rohe was on his way to test his professional fortunes in Mexico City—where he would remain for the rest of his life and have a great impact on the aesthetic of the modernist middle-class Mexico City domestic interior. Van Beuren took time to offer advice to his former professor Mies van der Rohe to take more seriously the wooing of the Armour Institute of Technology than that of Harvard University. "It would be better for you in Chicago than in Boston. The people in Chicago have more initiative; they get more naturally and directly to the point of things. At Armour you could do what you want…"[5]

Certainly, the obscuring from view the networks of Bauhaus influence being laid in Mexico and South America was in part this association in the

38

America and the Americas were more places of ideological projection than engagement. In the decades before the great transatlantic emigration unleashed by the rise of Hitler in Germany and Central Europe, little distinction was made between North and South, and for the most part, before Le Corbusier's 1929 visit to Argentina, Uruguay and Brazil, South America remained terra incognita, nowhere to be found in the Bauhaus publications on modern architecture, totally absent even in 1932 from the so-called international style book and exhibition.

ment. In the decades before the great transatlantic emigration unleashed by the rise of Hitler in Germany and Central Europe, little distinction was made between North and South, and for the most part, before Le Corbusier's 1929 visit to Argentina, Uruguay and Brazil, South America remained *terra incognita*, nowhere to be found in the Bauhaus publications on modern architecture, totally absent even in 1932 from the so-called international style book and exhibition.[3] Yet if we look only to Mexico and Brazil we can see that the American curators missed out on a decade of important work in Latin America. Neither the work of Juan O'Gorman in Mexico City nor the early work of Lucio Costa or Gregori Warchavchik in São Paulo and Rio de Janeiro were represented.

No less well established is the notion of the transfer of the European avant-garde project in ar-

north with powerful institutions. In autumn 1938 the "Bauhaus 1919-1928" exhibition was opened in a shop-front in the concourse of the newly completed Rockefeller Center, then serving as the temporary home of the MoMA. If politically, it was a retort to the Nazi's "Degenerate Art" show in celebrating the school five years after its definitive closure. It was also the tenth anniversary of Gropius and Breuer's departure from the school in Dessau. If in Weimar and Dessau Gropius had built an institution–even if it prided itself on being an institution like no other–in the United States he knew how to align himself with existing institutions, famously rewriting the history of the Bauhaus as an institution centered on his own vision of it. This was notably found in the MoMA exhibition, which treated the institution from its founding in Weimar in 1919 until the departure of Gropius and his closest allies: Marcel Breuer, Moholoy-Nagy, and Herbert Bayer—all of whom were in the United States in 1938 – to the exclusion of the other two directors, Hannes Meyer who took over in 1928, and Mies van der Rohe, who directed the school from 1930 until its closure was negotiated with the Nazis in 1933. By 1938 the Bauhaus was flying the Swastika, and Gropius was at work crafting the exhibition at the MoMA as a presentation of his depoliticized version of his Bauhaus as 'the one and only' Bauhaus. The other directors were in part marginalized by this coopting of the Bauhaus by its founding

Massachusetts. In New York, the United States was celebrated as the sole heir to the Bauhaus.

Equally well known is the work of Town Planning Associates after 1945, the firm founded by José Luis Sert and Paul Lester Wiener in the great chapter of the hemispheric exportation of US expertise— and along with it CIAM urbanism—to the newly defined 'developing world' of Central and South America.[7] Here is where the internationalist vision of CIAM met the Cold War hemispherical politics of Washington. The relationship was celebrated in the MoMA show "Two

If the war had created whole new supply lines for resource exportation between Latin America and the theatre of war, it had interrupted the flow of young designers to the schools in Paris and Madrid. By the early 1950s a whole network was developing. We might propose that the extended influence of the US Bauhaus masters would happen via networks more than institutions after the war.

39

director. The third director, Mies van der Rohe, had arrived in Chicago to take up his position at the Armour (now Illinois) Institute of Technology and Hannes Meyer had arrived in Mexico, where the revived project of the Mexican Revolution under President Laszlo Cardenas seemed to offer a promise for his conviction that architects were offers of technological and planning expertise rather than form givers, and that that expertise had the potential to alter not only social conditions but even consciousness. Supported by a group of enthusiastic recent graduates from the National University's School of Architecture, chief among them Enrique Yáñez, Meyer would help create the *Instituto de Urbanismo y Planificación del Instituto Politécnico Nacional* which became an influential body for rethinking the large-scale interventions of the fast-growing Mexican capital.

Even before their emigrations, the three men had been competing for ownership of the Bauhaus in part through rival exhibitions in Europe. Gropius, Breuer, and Bayer—all of whom had left the Bauhaus as the directorship passed to Mayer in 1928— worked under the auspices of the Werkbund in mounting the German section at a great exhibition organized in Paris in 1930, but the prominent place of the model of the Bauhaus building in Dessau and Breuer's tubular steel furniture first designed there led to the immediate confusion of the show as an official representation of the Bauhaus. At the same time, Hannes Meyer had organized a very different exhibition to represent the shifting look and ethos of the Bauhaus under his direction.[6] By the end of the decade they were competing globally to establish spheres of influence in Cambridge, Chicago and Mexico City. At the MoMA, Gropius showed the work from a variety of US-successors to the Bauhaus including the work of the Harvard students, of the short lived Laboratory School of Industrial Design in New York, and the work he and Breuer had done in England, and now in New England, including the Hagerty House recently completed at Cohasset,

Cities: Planning in North and South America," in 1947, which featured the Cidade dos Motores, a town for automobile and military production in Brazil, and Walter Gropius's Michael Reese Hospital in Chicago. Soon that project was to find a base at Harvard's Graduate School of Design. Indeed, as Gropius was worried in 1951 over his successor at the Graduate School of Design, he wrote to his biographer Reginald Isaacs, "I think I told you already recently that I have been seeing José Sert and that I pressed him hard that he should think twice and accept if he should be asked to come to the GSD. On account of the large commissions for South America, he was very doubtful, but to my pleasure he just writes me that he has decided to accept the job, if it should be offered to him."[8]

Less well known is the profound nexus of north-south relationships that had developed in the the nascent Cold War years between the ex-Bauhaus masters Marcel Breuer and Walter Gropius as well as in the growing number of Latin American architects starting their careers in their native countries after some years of training in the United States. If the war had led to the well documented migration of European architects toward the New World, it had also changed the patterns of architectural education for Latin Americans. Those who had the means to study outside the schools of architecture in their home countries turned increasingly to US schools. If the war had created whole new supply lines for resource exportation between Latin America and the theatre of war, it had interrupted the flow of young designers to the schools in Paris and Madrid. By the early 1950s a whole network was developing. We might propose that the extended influence of the US Bauhaus masters would happen via networks more than institutions after the war. No sooner had the armistice been announced in 1945, than the young Venezuelan architect Tomás José Sanabria—who would later stamp the face of Caracas—transferred from the Central University of Venezuela to Harvard to complete his studies in 1947.[9] By 1955, when the MoMA mounted an exhibition surveying the post-war decade of Latin American architecture, Henry Russell Hitchcock, the guest curator, noted:

> A very considerable portion of the best Latin American architects,… particularly those under 40, owe at least the final stages of their professional education to the architecture schools of the United States. It is not alone the more famous and old established schools, or even those that have been headed by the world-famous architects like Gropius and Mies… It is a tribute to our schools that they have given to Latin Americans a training so broad that it could readily be applied under very different local conditions. Even the influence of the great masters, Wright and Gropius and Mies, are rarely very noticeable; which is the more surprising since no single Latin American architect has yet, except Niemeyer, established so sharply personal a style that his influence on his colleagues is worthy of comment. In a sense, there is in present day Latin America—outside Brazil and Mexico at least—something approaching, Gropius's ideal of an impersonal anonymous architecture…[10]

If the influence becomes difficult to read visually or formally it is precisely because now it comes in an emergent triangulation between three continents, rather than a North Atlantic transfer between two. Take for instance the case of the Austrian born Harry Seidler, who found his way to both the Harvard Graduate School of Design of Gropius and Breuer and to Black Mountain College for a spell under Josef Albers.

Before he decided to follow his parents to Sydney, where he would emerge as the most recog-

nizable Australian architect of the 20th century, Seidler worked as Breuer's very first assistant in his tiny nascent Manhattan practice (1946-48), and then in 1948 for a few months with Oscar Niemeyer in Rio de Janeiro. The time with Niemeyer was perhaps an astute apprenticeship in an architecture for the temperate zones of the Southern Hemisphere. Seidler's earliest architectural works after arriving in New South Wales

Ruins of the Ariston Club. Mar del Plata, Argentina, 2020. Ph. Daniel Weisswein.

respond as much to what he witnessed at Harvard—as in the Rosa Seidler House (1948-50) for his mother, a late and distant addition to the then current 'Harvard Box' and built of wood—as well as to Niemeyer, as in an early apartment house that paid unmistakable homage to Niemeyer's Obra de Berco in Rio de Janeiro, or the Williamson House (1949-50), a few hundred feet away from the Rose Seidler House, that reworks the free form parabolic vaults of Niemeyer's chapel in Pampulha in Brazil.[11] Seidler's work announced not only the internationalization of practice but the international flow of forms, thoughts, experiments, images that would break the uniform flow of influence much the way air travel was rapidly retracing new nodal points of exchange.

Already during the war, but especially in the immediate post-war decade when public attention was much more on the United States' involvement in the reconstruction of Europe through the Marshall Plan, a politics and practice of intercontinental exchange was developing quietly in the New World in which Breuer and Gropius were to play significant roles. But the roles were not to be simply in terms of providing models. Rather, the two former Bauhaus masters were framing sets of interests, investigations, commitments, and methods.

The experiences of Latin America would have a decisive role on the development of Breuer's post-war work. Indeed, with post-war material restrictions still in effect, Breuer's house practice was slow to take off. In 1947, he considered moving to Argentina to accept the invitation of a former Harvard

40

pupil, Eduardo Catalano, to give lectures and to help start, as dean, a new architecture school in Buenos Aires. He also had pending an invitation from the Colombian government to consult on aspects of the master planning for rapidly growing Bogotá. A double issue of the Argentine magazine *Nuestra Arquitectura* in 1947 was dedicated to Breuer's work to prepare the way for South American reception, declaring that although "Breuer does not believe in the existence of the International Style," he nonetheless offered an "architectonic language" which "opens up new horizons and serves to confirm the natural simplicity of men with positive values."[12] Although the rise of Peron's government probably contributed to the abandonment of Breuer's possible return to academia, the Argentine invitation opened a bi-continental exchange of influence that can be traced in both South American and in Breuer's North American work in the 1950s, not the least in the thin shell parabola vaults developed along with Catalano for the Hunter College Library in the Bronx (1957-60). These vaults bear homage not only to Catalano's direct involvement in the project, but also to the transfer of the fascination of thin shell masonry as a new means of spanning spaces and creating continuity between support and span from the south to the north.

Breuer left behind his first building on foreign soil, the Ariston Club at Mar del Plata, a clover-leaf shaped dance hall and bar clad in wood and cantilevered off a rectangular base, finished by Eduardo Catalano and Francisco Coire in 1947-48. Although it was taken up as a pavilion project, Breuer and his English partner in the mid 1930s, F.R.S. Yorke, had imagined the Concrete City of the Future a decade earlier. Now it was built in a hybrid of materials expressing a dialogue between technological and manual labor, between machine made and crafted, which would become one of the main themes of the debate on modern architecture in many Latin American countries. Today the Ariston Club is abandoned and slowly falling into ruin, almost a metaphor for Breuer's first trip to South America it would seem.

The exchange was by no means unidirectional. In 1951 a student group at Harvard invited Amancio Williams to help stage an exhibition of Argentine architecture. Williams visited Harvard and Gropius's studio in 1955 on a trip organized by the State Department in conjunction with the exhibition at the MoMA and was to remain in touch with Gropius for the rest of his life. On his return he gave a lecture

Contact was not limited to Argentina. In a list of works submitted to MoMA curator Peter Blake in 1949, Breuer included planning proposals for Bogotá that he had completed during his stay in the Colombian capital in December 1947.[13] Among them were a hospital city with a medical center and 3,800 beds; an 1,110 unit, low-cost housing project with shopping center and schools, food markets with "a smooth floor surface and the least possible number of walls and columns;" and an administrative center with government offices and a presidential palace. It is possible that the food market was an early design for the supermarkets that the Rockefeller family would begin introducing during this time in Colombia and Venezuela.[14] Breuer's master plan for Bogotá began with optimism and the seeming support of the Ministry of Public Works, who never brought him a contract which was "a complete lack of government responsibility."[15] By 1950 Le Corbusier and then Paul Lester Weiner would become involved in the Bogotá master plan, in turn also abandoned. The subsequent planning history of Bogotá was to include palimpsests of both visits, Breuer's less celebrated one and Le Corbusier's recently extensively studied one.[16] Breuer's connections with Colombia would continue for some years, but questions of influence were no longer possible. Certainly, the tree-like piloti of German Samper's 1960 SENA building in Bogotá are easy to juxtapose with those that Breuer developed for the library of St. John's Abbey and College in Minnesota.

Most important, without a doubt, was the input of the long-standing interest in developing methods of pre-fabrication for housing that had been the central preoccupation of Gropius and Breuer since the Bauhaus days in Weimar. This had been translated to Harvard, both to the curriculum—Breuer worked on his proposals for a system of reinforced timber developed with Monsanto Products with GSD students, who produced the study model prototype of the Plas-2-Point House in 1943—and to their joint practice in Cambridge—Breuer and Gropius had attempted, unsuccessfully, to bring their research to the US Defense Housing, notably in the built project at New Kensington, Pennsylvania.[17] After the war their efforts were to dissipate: Gropius eventually disillusioned with the General Panel System he worked on with Konrad Wachsmann, and Breuer abandoned efforts to move beyond patent applications to applications for his various systems developed in the office. But it was to be one of Gropius and Breuer's students who became the link between these industrialized systems for the first

41

If the influence becomes difficult to read visually or formally it is precisely because now it comes in an emergent triangulation between three continents, rather than a North Atlantic transfer between two.

on Modern Architecture in "Los Estados Unidos de Norteamérica" in Buenos Aires reporting on what he had seen on his ten-university journey in 1955. Together Williams and Gropius would study the project for a new German embassy in Buenos Aires in 1968.

world and systems that could be applied to what was just being requalified as the 'developing' or 'third world.' The key figure is the understudied Leonard Currie, who received his M.Arch from Harvard in 1938 and joined the office of Breuer and Gropius, where he stayed for two years. After military service during the war, Currie returned to Harvard as an assistant professor of architecture from 1946-51, and was one of the designers in The Architects' Collaborative (TAC) Six Moon Hill development in Lexington, Massachusetts. Currie's real impact, however, was not to come from design but from policy administration, carrying the Gropius notion of the architect as a designer of collaborative frameworks into the US cold war involvement in housing in Latin America. In 1952 he travelled to Bogotá to serve as the founding director of the Cento Interamericano de Vivienda (the Inter-American Housing and Planning Center) better known under its acronym CINVA. "Our center is slowly getting organized and promises to be really successful... We are still working on our plans for a new building," he wrote to Gropius as he began working for CINVA.[18] There a group of Harvard graduates were to take on key roles, notably Currie's relative the economist Lauchlin Currie, a graduate not only of Harvard but of Franklin D. Roosevelt's New Deal which was the key background to CINVA's financial and architectural models. Currie joined forces with

aid during the rest of the Cold War. Latin America was to become a battleground not only for arms supplies, as the USSR and the United States competed for influence, but also for techniques of the architectural politics of 'development,' with the United States becoming the largest promoter of self-help schemes, and the USSR the advocate of large scale industrial approaches.

After Gropius reluctantly retired from the GSD in 1952, his attention became emphatically global. He and his wife Ise Gropius travelled extensively during the next few years to Japan, to Australia, and above all, to Latin America, where they not only cultivated a network of former students but also offered advice both sought and volunteered. Already during his last years as the head of the Department of Architecture, Gropius had traveled, on the invitation of former students in the region, to Mexico and Cuba and provided designs for the paper factory buildings in the Container Corporation of America, then moving on to Colombia, notably with factories in the Cauca valley and Cali, both designed in 1945. In 1950, on Gropius's urging, a Cuban delegation had been granted

42

Latin America was to become a battleground not only for arms supplies, as the USSR and the United States competed for influence, but also for techniques of the architectural politics of 'development,' with the United States becoming the largest promoter of self-help schemes, and the USSR the advocate of large scale industrial approaches.

Harvard trained Colombian architect Alvaro Ortega, who had studied at McGill before obtaining a M.Arch degree at Harvard in 1945. By the early 1950s he was involved, along with Gabriel Solano, in studies of pre-fabrication, both heavy pre-fabrication in key projects such as Barrio Quiroga in Bogotá and, most importantly, in the studies of low-tech pre-fabrication for poor rural communities and the growing urban fringes throughout Latin America. While Ortega focused on heavy pre-fabrication elements such as the "vacuum concrete" roof sections (about 1.5 inches thick) that could be craned into place and which were heavily employed at Quiroga, CINVA turned to developing technologies that could be employed by low-skilled individuals, most famously, the CINVA-Ram for the production of modified adobe type bricks. The ram is operated manually by applying pressure on a long lever arm as it produces blocks that can be either hollow or solid. As the company literature for the product, which is still in production over a half century later, notes: "The machine weighs only 140 pounds... Three men, doing all of the work, including processing, mixing, molding, etc., should make 300 blocks a day. Five workers can make 600 per day by dividing the jobs."[19] Here the Bauhaus dream of pre-fabrication had moved from the factory to the field in ways that no one could have predicted in Dessau in 1928, or even in Cambridge in 1945. These were key experiences for the construction of US government

membership in CIAM, and key actors were Mario Romañach, who had developed a friendship with Gropius and would later work in TAC after he left Castro's Cuba; and the former Harvard student Frank Martinez, who brought Albers to lecture in Havana in Spring 1952, and then Gropius a few months later. Martinez hoped to change the architectural education at the Universidad de la Habana, having written to Gropius with no sense of irony in 1951, "Things at the University are running the same and will not change until the old Professors have gone away", and then continued, "The Government is now talking about making economic dwellings for working class and also about City Planning—you cannot imagine how bad we need our Mr. Gropius around here."[20]

By 1953 Gropius was emerging as something of a negotiator for world architecture, taking a break from commuting between Cambridge and Paris where he was heading the committee charged with naming the architects for the new UNESCO headquarters to undertake his first trip to South America. Having been awarded a prize at the second São Paulo architectural biennial in 1953, Gropius was invited by the Brazilian government to come to Brazil to collect his prize. He left in January 1954, extending his return trip via Peru. For the next two years, Gropius was a sort of roving diplomat commenting on the great initiatives of Latin American republics, asserting their presence on the world architectural stage.

In Brazil, he stepped into a minefield created by the previous winner of the prize, another ex-*Bauhäusler* Max Bill, now the director and figurehead of that other post-Bauhaus outpost, the Hochschule für Gestaltung in Ulm. Bill had begun his studies at the Bauhaus in the final months of Gropius's directorship and had been reunited with his mentor in 1938, helping to gather materials for the MoMA Bauhaus show. But now Gropius was eager to take some distance from the hornet's nest that Bill's acceptance speech of his 1951 prize had caused. As we would say today in social media terms, Bill's words had gone viral, speeding from the daily press in Brazil to the professional press around the world. Bill offered his thoughts on what he saw in Brazilian architecture during his travels in Rio and São Paulo. He thought it urgent to lecture Brazilian architectural students on the ideological and formal flaws of their architecture. This for him was urgent as students flocking to Brazil's architectural schools would "fashion the look of the cities of tomorrow,"[21] and Brazilian influence was on the rise. Niemeyer's work in Pampulha, and in particular his own house at Canoas, were attacked as "love of form for the sake of form," and for cultivating a capricious individualism, something all the more dangerous as Brazil was seen as "the boom-province of the Modern Movement." In São Paulo, Bill said:

> I saw some shocking things, modern architecture sunk to the depths, a riot of anti-social waste, lacking any sense of responsibility towards either the business occupant or his customers… Here is utter anarchy in building, jungle growth in the worst sense… One is baffled to account for such barbarism as this exemplifies being able to break out in a country where there is a CIAM group, a country in which international congresses on modern architecture are held, where a journal like *Habitat* is published and where there is a biennial exhibition of architecture. For such works are born of a spirit devoid of all decency…[22]

The British *Architectural Review* used the occasion of Gropius's review to reprint Bill's remarks and solicit responses in a "Report on Brazil" from Ise and Walter Gropius, Ernesto Rogers, and Peter Craymer, a young British architect working in Brazil. As Ise Gropius writes:

> In Rio we were taken by Niemeyer to his new house which he has built on a slope in a gorge between two mountains with a fantastic view on to the sea. The air was still full of Max Bill's accusations which have made the rounds in South America. We did not think them quite justified and Niemeyer can anyhow only be understood if one knows Rio. There one can do the craziest things unpunished. Everything flourishes and grows, everybody seems to live on air and no-

body ever presents the account. […] One can criticize the construction; but mistakes are not very deadly here, as they would be in our climate, and it is not justifiable to measure them by a Swiss yardstick. We were most impressed by Reidy's Pedregulho… A new housing estate for state employees built with government support; it is not quite ready yet but already quite delightful and most successful from an aesthetic technical and social point of view. Flats, schools, stadium, library, health care, swimming pool, market, nursery, and kindergarten, a model for the world. […] All in all, I think one can really stress the point that the Brazilians have developed a modern architectural attitude of their own and that they have a great many genuinely gifted architects who carry the ball. I do not believe that this is just a passing fashion but a vigorous movement.[23]

Pedregulho indeed seemed to correspond to that neighborhood multi-functional planning that was increasingly the centerpiece of Gropius's own stakes in the post-war debates about community planning. Gropius took up some of the same themes in his speech to the Institute of Brazilian architects. Rino Levi served as translator for the speech, and Gropius diplomatically reminded the Brazilians, whose cities were on the brink of transformation with the proliferation of skyscrapers, of the need for the mechanisms of planning.

From Brazil Gropius travelled to Lima where he was invited by the group who had formed the modernist think tank Espacio to offer his thoughts on the current state of a Peruvian architecture and city planning as the profession and the country were grappling with explosive urban growth and a housing crisis. US-trained architect Fernando Belaunde Terry, later to serve as President of the country, had coined the operative term of the "unidad vecinal," a direct translation of the "neighborhood unit," a core concept borrowed from Gropius's 1943 article "A Program for City Reconstruction," in the *Architectural Forum,* and taken over in the Peruvian housing plan of 1945.[24] In February 1954 Gropius was given a tour of some of the projects underway which were beginning to apply that notion, and gave an address at the National University under the title "Personal message to the graduating students in architecture."

No less indirect was Gropius's influence in Mexico, where in parallel to the teaching of Hannes Meyer, Gropius was a frequent correspondent with the German emigre architect Max Cetto. Cetto, who had worked with Hans Poelzig in Berlin and alongside Ernst May in the Frankfurt housing office in the 1920s, emigrated in 1938 to Mexico via the United States. His own house built in the newly developing garden suburb of El Pedregal has striking parallels with the mixed steel frame and structural masonry architec-

43

ture that Gropius and Breuer developed in New England. One might compare the 1949 Cetto House in Mexico with the Hagerty House at Cohasset by Gropius and Breuer of a decade earlier. Cetto had a sustained correspondence with Gropius at Harvard and the letters reveal both a professional association and a growing personal one. Perhaps encouraged by the enthusiasm of Josef and Anni Albers for Mexico, where they vacationed regularly from the 1930s,[25] Gropius first visited Morelia in 1946. On that occasion Gropius met Cetto. The two of them were already in touch through John McAndrew, who had curated at the MoMA both the Bauhaus show and the 1940 Show "Twenty Centuries of Mexican Art."[26] Their correspondence in German was wide ranging, often focused on the challenges of an architecture that could widen its scope to the whole of human living. For instance this exchange: "If I understand you correctly, the lesson that we should derive from this decade, above all, is to grasp human life in its 'totality,' and to make that the foundation of our planning and to protect us from (probably methodologically unavoidable in the 20th century) to follow the direct path of a single factor, either exclusively practical-technical or social or economic or political or aesthetic or hygienic or geological-climatic or any other.[...] Recently I have once again read through what Adolf Loos around 1900 spoke into the void and it seems to me—especially in today's Mexico—just as prophetic as ever. Loos is most certainly too little understood in his proper meaning and I would like, as soon I find the time for it, to translate a few of his essays and to publish them in a contemporary architectural magazine."[27]

Cetto had tried to convince Gropius to stop in Mexico in 1954 on his return from Brazil and Peru, but the first visit came a year later, when Gropius offered a somewhat critical appraisal of the new campus just inaugurated for UNAM, the National University, although it was a startling act of diplomacy in comparison with Sybil Moholy-Nagy's critique published two years earlier (1953) in *Progressive Architecture*.[28] Gropius found here, to an extent, the project of TAC taken to the national level:

> Entering the CU [Cuidad Universitaria] I was impressed by the bold courage of its creators in trying to tackle such an enormous planning and building task as an organic entity, carried out in one stroke. The vigor and vision in leadership, and the enthusiasm of architects and engineers to cooperate with each other have started a trend toward a common denominator of form expression characteristic of contemporary democratic spirit. Such an attempt at finding architecture unity among a large number of various individual designers represents certainly a most desirable trend in design which should be highly welcomed.[...] However in my opinion, the architects have miscalculated the physical dimensions of their

campus plan. An important criterion of judging architectural achievement lies in the success or failure to bring the scale of the building masses and the open spaces between them into a harmonious balance. Walking through the campus, I felt that the enthusiasm of the designers must have carried them away when the scale of the overall-all plan was established. Its hugeness reminds me of the megalomaniac planning dimensions with which the might of the Roman Caesars was glorified. In contrast, the scale of buildings and open spaces in a democratic society should not intimidate the spirit by sheer size, but rather attract and invite people by enchantment. Human scale is achieved when there is a tangible harmony in the relationship of the architectural setting and the living performance enacted against its background. A plaza should, therefore, be only barely large enough to accommodate the expected peak-hour traffic. The main plaza of the CU, however, is six and one-half times larger than the famous Piazza San Marco in Venice and can hardly ever be filled. Its dimensions are out of proportion to the potential size of the activities taking place in it. It will always appear too empty and make passing humans appear insignificant in their relative size. The horizontal dimensions being over-extended to the detriment of the pedestrian, the space effect of the plaza—its architectural confinement—suffers simultaneously from the relatively low height of the surrounding buildings compared to the great length and width of the plaza.

And he continued to praise one design in particular:

> An example of balanced scale—in spite of its huge size—is the Stadium. Its undulating rest line—result of the ingenious planning: a circle superimposed on the oval of the arena—blends beautifully into the dramatic silhouette of the mountains. The large exterior reliefs of Diego Rivera fit masterly the scale of the gigantic surrounding Stadium walls and are equally remarkable from the point of view of new techniques used. Highly developed stone techniques for masonry, pavements and incrustations, the most characteristic Mexican craft since Aztec times, prevail all over the campus of the University.

Ever the diplomat, and always on the lookout for applications of his own belief that the future practice of architecture lies in team work rather than autographic

44

design, he concluded on a positive note that "The real importance of the Ciudad Universitaria for our time, I see in the fact that the people of Mexico in a period of intellectual confusion and contradictory aims have been able to give the world an example by mobilizing the necessary creative, financial, and administrative forces for concerted action on a cultural task of this large order."[29]

These lines were to have enormous impact, not only because they came from Gropius, but because they are paraphrased almost verbatim a few years later in 1961 when Cetto published his bilingual *Arquitectura moderna en México,* which would remain the only synthetic account for many years.[30] There he sought to take distance from the followers of Hannes Meyer in the school, any of which would later be named after the great masters of Mexican Modernism: Villagran, Cetto, and Meyer. Cetto proclaimed in citing Villagran:

> Those who have called our movement functionalist—and by that mean that we have forgotten the aesthetic in the service of social requirements and the utilitarian—fail to recognize the scope of the doctrine advanced by our school of architecture and also, it must be added, the parallel doctrine propounded, although in a different form by European functionalists such as Gropius.[31]

And there he tries to direct Mexican architecture away from the grandeur of those who sought to fold the planning of pre-Columbian complexes such as Teotihuacan or Monte Albán into a Mexican version of CIAM. Just as Max Bill had been used in part as a proxy

Indeed, it seemed that influence was poised to begin flowing more emphatically in the other direction. Certainly, this was the message in 1954-55 as Henry-Russell Hitchcock was undertaking the photographic mission that would result in the influential 1955 exhibition at MoMA "Latin American Architecture since 1945." In the catalogue Hitchcock noted "Modern Architecture in Latin America has come of age and this major flowering has much to contribute to the rest of the world... Because of the quantity of current Latin American building exceeds our own, the appearance there of predominantly 'modern' cities gives us the opportunity to observe effects which we ourselves still only anticipate."[33] Hitchcock was in London completing work on his seminal contribution to the Pelican History of Art, "Architecture: Nineteenth and Twentieth Centuries", first published in 1958 and the first English language survey of architectural modernism ever to incorporate Latin American material as a natural part of the sequence of the unfolding of modernism seen in the perspective he had been developing for a half century since his *Modern Architecture* of 1929. Telegrams went back and forth, and Hitchcock presented a lecture on Latin American modern architecture to the RIBA. In recompense Drexler wrote to him on December 29, 1955: "during the Christmas Holiday week it has been filled with visitors. The general reaction among architects is almost one of relief on discovering that Latin American work does not impose on them the need to abandon whatever they have been doing and declare themselves followers of still another revolution. The general public, however, seems

45

Overshadowed by the progressive disengagement of the United States from Latin America in the 1970s in the period of political and economic turmoil, the departure of many key designers from Argentina in particular, and the waning of the United States attention to Latin America as a vision of a modernist as opposed to a dystopic future, left also in deep shadow an intense period where influences with a lingering Bauhaus tinge can be traced along the new lines of Pan American dialogues.

opening up in the internal debates between Rio, São Paulo and the group around Lina Bo Bardi in Brazil in the early 1950s, so in the late 1960s Cetto would seek to enlist Gropius to reinforce his position in the emerging debates in Mexican architectural practice. Cetto is eager for Gropius to give a lecture in Mexico on "Das Bauhaus und sein Einfluss" (The Bauhaus and Its Influence). There is even talk of an exhibition, which as Cetto admits would be "a good influence and useful for the Mexicans (who have become half wild), indeed necessary."[32] Clearly that very influence was at once part of a complex set of international networks that would shape the architectural discourses of the postwar decades and a strangely rearguard action. The Bauhaus had long since become a pliable concept, useful as a tool in debates, but increasingly far from any historical definition and blunted in its usefulness.

to regard the exhibition as proof that life is richer and more beautiful down there: "They live better."[34] John McAndrew, the Harvard trained architect who had taken over MoMA's architecture department after Philip Johnson left in disgrace in the mid-1930s due to his involvement with right wing politics, reviewed the show in an article entitled "Good Building by Good Neighbors," in *Art News,* where he noted:

> It is particularly surprising for us to be outdone by 'quantity' of anything new outside our own borders. But we sometimes forget that our Latin neighbors are growing twice as fast as we are both in numbers and in wealth. Mexico City, now two million, has more modern buildings than any other city in the world, and has had for the past ten

years. Caracas, expanding at an explosive speed, is building more than any three cities in the United States even in Texas. While there are few parts of our country, even in California where most of the building is carried out in the living architectural language of today, there are scores of cities in Latin America where it is exceptional to use anything else…

And he concludes,

Another field where our good neighbors have particularly distinguished themselves is in their publically commissioned buildings. Officials are less afraid of modern art and architecture is their perhaps the most respected modern art. It is certainly more of an art and less of a business than it is with us.[35]

In the following years Gropius and Breuer would seek commissions in these countries, Breuer with unrealized projects for Venezuela—here his project for a real estate development to be called El Retiro—and Gropius with his project for the German Embassy in Buenos Aires, where the key concepts came from

German Embassy and Residence in Buenos Aires, project by Amancio Williams and Walter Gropius. Courtesy of the Amancio Williams fonds, Canadian Centre for Architecture, Gift of the children of Amancio Williams. Special thank you to Martin Huberman and Galería Monoambiente.

Amancio Williams. But the analysis of those flows of influence still remains to be undertaken, and they are anything but uni-directional. Overshadowed by the progressive disengagement of the United States from Latin America in the 1970s in the period of political and economic turmoil, the departure of many key designers from Argentina in particular,[36] and the waning of the United States attention to Latin America as a vision of a modernist as opposed to a dystopic future, left also in deep shadow an intense period where influences with a lingering Bauhaus tinge can be traced along the new lines of Pan American dialogues.

1    What follows is just a sketch, impressions gathered on travels in the seven years of research in preparation for the show "Latin America in Construction, Architecture 1955-1980" at the Museum of Modern Art (2015). It was assembled for the inaugural "Gropius Lecture" in April 2015 at Harvard University's Graduate School of Design, and underscores in particular Harvard-Latin American connections. It offers, I hope, some lines for further research and discussion.

2    Walter Gropius, "Die Entwicklung Moderner Industrie-Baukunst," *Jahrbuch des Deutschen Werkbundes,* 1913, pp. 17-32. On Americanism see especially Jean-Louis Cohen, *Scenes of the World to Come: European Architecture and the American Challenge, 1893-1960* (Paris: Flammarion, 1995). For the identification of Le Corbusier's images as in fact Argentine examples see Jorge Francisco Liernur, *La red austral: Obras y proyectos de Le Corbusier y sus discípulos en la Argentina (1924-1965)* (Buenos Aires: Universidad Nacional de Quilmes, 2008).

3    Neither the catalogue of the Museum of Modern Art's first architectural exhibition, "Modern Architecture: International Exhibition," nor the book that appeared at the same time authored by Philip Johnson and Henry-Russell Hitchcock, included a single example from Latin America, despite the fact that photographs of Juan O'Gorman's studios for Diego Rivera and Frida Kahlo at San Angel in Mexico City were sent to them at the museum (these are still conserved in the files of the Department of Architecture and Design).

4    On MoMA's guestbook see Cammie McAtie in *Mies in America* (New York: Harry N. Abrahms with the Canadian Centre for Architecture, Montreal and the Whitney Museum of American Art, New York, 2001), pp. 132-191 and Barry Bergdoll "*Memento Mori* or Eternal Modernism? The Bauhaus at MoMA,1938," in Mark Stocker and Philip Lindsey (eds.), *Tributes to Jean-Michel Massing: Towards a Global Art History* (London: Harvey Miller Publishers, 2016), pp. 15-32.

5    See Ana Elena Mallet, *La Bauhaus y El México Moderno: El Diseño de Van Beuren* (Mexico City: Arquine, 2014). Michael van Beuren, excerpted from two letters to Mies, November 6, 1936; Mies van der Rohe Archive, Museum of Modern Art, New York.

6    See Barry Bergdoll "Bauhaus Multiplied: Paradoxes of Architecture and Design in and after the Bauhaus," in Barry Bergdoll and Leah Dickerman, *Bauhaus 1919-1933: Workshops for Modernity* (New York: The Museum of Modern Art, 2009), pp. 40-61.

7    Eric Mumford, *The CIAM Discourse on Modernism, 1928-1960* (Cambridge, MA: the MIT Press 2002).

8    Reginald Isaacs, *Gropius, An Illustrated Biography of the Creator of the Bauhaus* (Boston: Bulfinch Press, 1991), p. 267; quoted in Joseph M. Rovira, *José Luis Sert, 1901-1983* (Milan: Electa, 2000), p. 315.

9    He was only one of a generation that deserves to be studied—if it has not been already—which included Eduardo Catalano from Argentina, Frank Martinez and Max Borges from Cuba, Gabriel Solano Mesa from Colombia, Carlos Guinand also from Venezuela.

10    Henry-Russell Hitchcock, *Latin American Architecture Since 1945* (New York: Museum of Modern Art, 1955), p. 21.

11    On Seidler's work see Vladimir Belogolovsky, *Harry Seidler Lifework* (New York: Rizzoli 2014). See also Helen O'Neill, *A Singular Vision: Harry Seidler* (Sydney: Harper Collins Australia, 2013), pp. 111-13.

12    *Nuestra Arquitectura* 9 (Buenos Aires: September 1947). The Spanish original reads: "Breuer no cree en la existencia del Estilo Internacional," and "abre nuevos horizontes y sirve para confirmar la sencillez natural de los hombres con valores positivos."

13    See project "Bogota Master Plan" in Breuer archive, Syracuse University. Available online at http://breuer.syr.edu/project.php?id=252

14    Since this lecture was written a study has appeared: Shane Hamilton, *Supermarket USA: Food and Power in the Cold War Farms Race* (New Haven: Yale University Press, 2018).

15    Letter of Ortega to Breuer, June 13, 1948, Breuer Archives, Syracuse University. Available online.

16    María Cecilia and O'Byrne Orozco (eds.), *Le Corbusier en Bogotá* (Bogotá: Universidad de Los Andes, Facultad de Arquitectura y Diseño, 2010).

17    On Breuer and prefabrication see Barry Bergdoll and Peter Christensen, *Home Delivery: Fabricating the Modern Dwelling* (New York: The Museum of Modern Art, 2008, esp.), pp. 86-89.

18    Leonard Currie to Walter Gropius, Handwritten letter dated "Easter Sunday, 13 April 1952," Gropius Papers, Houghton Library, Harvard. HOU b MS Ger 208/617.

19    Inter-American Housing and Planning Center, *Cinva-ram: portable block making press* (Bogotá: Scientific and Documentation Exchange Service, Inter-American Housing and Planning Center, 1957).

20    Typewritten letter from Frank Martinez to Ise and Walter Gropius, 26 February 1951, Gropus papers, Houghton Library, Harvard University, HOU b MS Ger 208/ 1172.

21    Max Bill, "Report on Brazil." In *Architectural Review* (October 1954), pp. 238-239.

22    Ibid.

23    Ise Gropius, "Report On Brazil" in *Architectural Review* (October 1954), p. 236.

24    Walter Gropius, "A Program for a City Reconstruction" in *The Architecture Forum*, 79/1 (1943), p. 81.

25    Albers, Anni, Josef Albers, Jenny Anger, Kiki Gilderhus, Heinz Liesbrock, Brenda Danilowitz, *Anni and Josef Albers: Latin American Journeys* (Ostfildern, Germany: Hatje Cantz, 2008).

26    See Keith L. Eggener, "John McAndrew, the Museum of Modern Art, and the 'Naturalization' of Modern Art in America, ca. 1940" in *Architecture and Identity*, Peter Herrle and Erik Wegerhoff (eds.) (Berlin: Lit, 2008), pp. 235-42., Barry Bergdoll, "Good Neighbors: The Museum of Modern Art and Latin America, 1933-1955, a journey through the MoMA Archives" in *Urban Modernity, México*, (DOCOMOMO, 2012) and Mardges Bacon, *John McAndrew's Modernist Vision: from the Vassar College Art Library to the Museum of Modern Art in New York* (Princeton: Princeton Architectural Press, 2018).

27    Letter from Max Cetto to Walter Gropius, 26 September 1946, Gropius Papers, Houghton Library, Harvard University, HOU b MS Ger 208/ 567. Original in German: "Wenn ich Sie recht verstehe, zieht die Lehre, die dieses Jahrzehnt erteilt haben sollte, in erster Linie dahin, das Menschliche Leben in seine TOTALITÄT zu erfassen und zur Grundlage unserer Planungen zu machen und uns davor zu hüten (was vielleicht in den 20er Jahren methodisch unumgänglich war) ausschließlich praktisch-technischen oder sozialen oder ökonomischen oder politischen oder ästhetischen oder hygienischen oder geologisch-klimatischen oder sonstwie isolierten Richtlinien zu folgen. [...] Diese Tage habe ich mal wieder einiges von dem durchgelesen, was Adolf Loos um 1900 ins Leere gesprochen hat und es schien mir-besonders in diesem Mexico von Heute – noch so prophetisch wie je. Loos ist sicher viel zu wenig in seiner Bedeutung gewürdigt und ich möchte, sobald ich dazu Zeit finde, ein paar Aufsätze von ihm übersetzen um in einer hiesigen Architektur Zeitschrift herausbringen."

28    Sybil Moholy-Nagy, "Mexican Critique" in *Progressive Architecture*, vol. 34 (November 1953).

29    Typewritten manuscript of a lecture "Ciudad Universitaria" by Walter Gropius, dated March 1955, Gropius papers, Houghton Library, Harvard University, HOU b MS Ger 208, pp. 1-2.

30    Max Cetto, *Arquitectura Moderna en Mexico / Modern Architecture in Mexico* (New York: Frederick A. Praeger, 1961).

31    Cetto quoting Villagran in Max Cetto, *Arquitecural Moderna*, op. cit, (note 30), p. 26.

32    Catarinna Cetto to Ise Gropius, 25 February 1959, Gropius papers, Houghton Library, Harvard University, HOU b Ger 208.Original in German: "fuer die (halb wild gewordenen) Mexikaner von gutem Einfluss und Nutzen, ja sogar nötig."

47

33    Arthur Drexler, "Preface and Acknowledge-ments" in Henry-Russell Hitchcock, *Latin American Architecture since 1945* (New York: The Museum of Modern Art, 1955), p. 9.

34    Drexler to Hitchcock, telegraph 29 December 1955, Museum of Modern Archives, Exposition 590.

35    John McAndrew, "Good Building by Good Neighbors" in *ARTnews* 54 (January 1956).

36    Jorge Silvetti, Rodolfo Machado, Diana Agrest, Mario Gandelsonas, Rafael Viñoly, Susanna Torre, to name but a few.

48

# TOWARDS A GLOBAL ARCHITECT
## Beatriz Colomina

*"This American country is dimensioned for the plane. It seems to me that airline networks will become its efficient nervous system."*

— *Le Corbusier, Precisions, 1929.*

*"Today, after more than a century of electric technology, we have extended our central nervous system itself in a global embrace, abolishing both space and time as far as our planet is concerned." Marshall McLuhan,*

— *Understanding Media, 1964.*

Towards the end of his life, in his last retrospective book, *My Work* (1960), Le Corbusier published a full-page map of global flight paths, probably taken from Air France—the center of the world is Paris—and wrote,, "The world now has 24 solar hours at its disposal. Marco Polo took his time. Nowadays we say: 'Here are your papers, Sir, your contract and your airline ticket. Leaving at six to-night, you will be in the antipodes to-morrow. You will discuss, you will sign and, if you wish, you can start back the same evening and be home next day.'" [1]

Air travel was revolutionized in the late 1950s with the arrival of commercial jetliners. The Caravelle and the Boeing 707 introduced by Air France in 1959 cut flying time in half with the company claiming to possess "the two best jets on the world's largest

gence of a new kind of human. En route to India, in his favorite airplane seat, he notes: "January 5, 1960. I am settled in my seat by now acquired number 5, -alone, admirable one-man seat, total comfort. In fifty years we have become a new animal on the planet." [3]

This posthuman is an animal that flies, the airline network is its "efficient nervous system"-its web covering the globe. The hyper-mobile architect is a symptom of a globalized society in which humanity will be necessarily transformed. Nearing the end of a fifty-hour set of continuous flights, Le Corbusier notes: "Nov. 30, 1955 (10pm Paris time= 6am Tokyo time). We will arrive in 2 hours. 50 hours in a plane. One could write a *Condition Humaine* on the basis of discovering-revealing airplane flight." [4]

By 1923, in his most famous book, *Vers une architecture,* Le Corbusier wrote about the airplane itself as "a product of high selection." Crossing the Atlantic in 1936 in the Graf-Zeppelin, he said he had discovered "a new fauna: *the machines,*" which included the "fountain pen that you put in your pocket" as well as "the airplane that handles the overseas transports of people and letters" and which included "this Zeppelin in which I am writing this very moment. I just had a look at the enchanting interior skeleton of the air vessel. What are its laws? Precise, dramatic, rigorous: economy." [5]

The evolution of these machines stimulates an evolution in the very condition of the human. By 1960 Le Corbusier was speaking about electronics as the brain of the new posthuman: "Electronics is born, that is to say, the possibility of letting robots study and establish files, prepare discussions, propose solutions. Electronics is used to make films, to make sound recordings, television, radio, etc. Electronics will offer us a new brain of incomparable capacity." [6] The evolution of the airplane accelerates not only the speed of travel but also the speed of human transformation. The arrival of the ballistic logic of jet travel reconfigures both

49

## Le Corbusier could be said to be the first global architect. In an age in which almost every architect is global it is hard to appreciate how radical Le Corbusier's mode of operation was.

network," then covering 350,000 km. Yet, it was not just that space collapsed with the introduction of rapid air travel, but also that time expanded. Le Corbusier already foresaw the implications of this new condition for the architect. Practice is no longer local; time is continuous. Today this is almost a banality. Architectural offices with outposts in cities around the world, connected through the internet and video conferencing, work around the clock; the office in Beijing, for example, picks up a project that the New York office—by then asleep—worked on the day before. Work is not just twenty-four hours a day but Monday through Sunday. As Bernard Tschumi puts it: "Now you work around the clock, seven days a week. In Abu Dhabi, for example, Sunday is not a holiday, so you travel on Saturday and work on Sunday." [2]

Le Corbusier saw this collapse of traditional space and time as nothing less than the emer-

passenger and world: "The genius of the forms: The Super Constellation is beautiful: it is like a fish; it could have been like a bird…. etc. But since the advent of the "jets," a new threshold has been crossed: it is a *projectile*= a perforator and not a glider." [7]

### SEAT NUMBER 5
Le Corbusier could be said to be the first global architect. In an age in which almost every architect is global it is hard to appreciate how radical Le Corbusier's mode of operation was. As he wrote in one of his sketchbooks on the plane Ahmadabad-Bombay, November 13, 1955:

> Corbu is all over the world, traveling, his dirty raincoat in his arms, his leather satchel stuffed with business papers, with razor and toothbrush, brillantine

for a few hairs, and his suit from Paris, which clothes him here in Tokyo or in Ahmadabad (without the vest).[8]

Starting in 1951, when he was hired as a consulting architect by the government of Punjab for the construction of a new capital in Chandigarh, Le Corbusier went to India a total of twenty-three times, traveling twice a year, and staying over a month each time. The pace was much slower than what he suggested in 1960. Required by his contract to travel Air India, a company he loved and compared very favorably over Air France, the typical itinerary took him from Paris to Geneva or to Rome, then Cairo, Bombay and Delhi, where he traveled by car to Chandigarh and moved around by Jeep.[9]

Despite the grueling schedule, he seemed to have been deliriously happy in the air, constantly making staccato entries next to the drawings in his sketchbooks. As he wrote in 1951 on the plane to Delhi:

Plane
2½ hours Paris-Rome
4½ Rome-Cairo
9 Cairo-Bombay
3¼ Bombay-Delhi

I have been in the plane since 2 o'clock Saturday. It is Monday noon. I am arriving in Delhi. I have never been so relaxed and so alone, engrossed in the poetry of things (nature) and poetry pure and simple (Apollinaire's *Alcools* and Gide's *Anthologie*) and meditation. [10]

In monitoring every detail of the evolving mechanics of air travel (time tables, speed, cabin temperature, outside temperature, food, airports), he often becomes ecstatic and lyrical. The sketchbooks are

I refused the Boeing because it's American taste, even when run by the Indians! Constellation 550km instead of 1,100. But here I am at home, in airborne India This airplane asylum of salvation.[12]

If the airplane is the home of the new human, its details are prototypes for a new kind of house on the ground. Le Corbusier took specific inspiration from the airplanes that he is living in, paying attention to every little detail of the design. He admired the interior, the reclining chairs, the storage bins, etc. He even requested drawings from the designer.[13]

The tight economy of space in the airplane gave him ideas for his current projects, as the ocean liner and the car had once been the inspiration. In a sketch of a berth of an Air France plane he wrote: "Constellation arrived New York January 23, 1949 a couchette makes an adorable nest for 2 to chat, oriental fashion. One would not dare build it in a house."[14] Nevertheless, a few months later he used the sketch to plan the rooms of the Unité[15] And in 1961, on the Boeing to Delhi, notes that "the cream white casing above the seat" could be used in the "Ville Radieuse dwelling in Marseilles."[16] Even the dishes are of interest to him: "June 15, 1960 Paris ask Air France Boeing // where can I buy some stackable metal dishes, like those used in the New York-Paris plane on June 15th//These are very simple but very adaptable dishes//very shiny//In-flight service."[17] Fellow travelers' equipment becomes a source of interest as well. He draws a sketch with detailed measurements of a traveling bag, and around it he

50

## Publication generates travel, which generates publication; and in the middle of this cyclical engine, projects are produced.

an extraordinary diary of global movements and new perceptions generated by those movements. He writes about what he is reading on the plane, which not surprisingly often included other polemical travelers. Marco Polo and Don Quixote keep reappearing. Travel becomes an opportunity to reflect on travel. The plane is an escape from the "cacophony" and "one man upmanship" of the world:

1957. Airplane 6:15pm Paris time.

In this really atrocious, crushing life that I have been leading for so many years (these last years) these first six hours in flight have been a paradise. I am alone (with myself) free…. I read, I think, they offer me some whiskey: one, then two. I am free, no one nor anything is bugging me.[11]

Le Corbusier claims to be "at home in airborne India." He even has a seat reserved on Air India, "Number 5, called 'L-C seat.'" The airplane is his "home," an "asylum of salvation." Le Corbusier becomes one with the airplane:

Zurich, March 3, 1961//1:30pm we take off in Air India, my usual seat Number 5 = huge space in "Super Constellation"….

writes: "Air India plane//zipper//A serious Japanese man (minister perhaps), has this soft wild boar's hide courier's bag//find out about that to replace mine."[18]

Even the outside decoration of planes becomes a key source of inspiration. Observing the bright gleaming paint on the metal fuselage, he develops the concept for the enamel painted doors of Chandigarh.[19] But, ultimately, he wants to redesign the space of an airplane himself. Believing Air France to be inferior to Air India, he repeatedly proposes the French company to "outfit their planes" in a more modern way[20] The dream never materialized, which may explain his increasing diatribes against Air France. On a trip to India via Tokyo Le Corbusier writes:

October 31, 1955. Air France's "Super Constellation" plane is not "Super" … The 1st class (cabin) = a line of portholes overlooking engines the remainder 5 or 6 lines overlooking wings you don't see a thing. Sickening uproar! Air India … 1st class cabin = nice portholes, table, comfort, elegance of the woodwork."[21]

In 1957 he tries to do Air France's headquarters, writing to the head of the company: "This state of French inferiority. If L-C does Air France = international activity."[22] In fact, Le Corbusier's real ambition seems to be to design international activity itself. His fascination with jet travel and the new space of global airline networks grows out of a relentless fascination with the global communication that structured his career from the beginning.

## GLOBAL CIRCUITS

Even before transatlantic air travel became possible, Le Corbusier was dreaming of a global practice in his publications. In his journal *L'Esprit Nouveau,* no. 17 (1922), he published a map of the world with the location of subscribers to the journal; they spanned five continents, marked by dots all over Europe but also in several countries in Africa, Asia, North and South America, and even Australia. How important this outreach was for him is evident when in his last book, which included the Air France map he had requested from the company, he quotes the opening words of a

liner to Montevideo and Buenos Aires and then mostly by plane; he was accompanied by such pioneer aviators as Jean Mermoz and Antoine de Saint-Exupéry. He travelled from September to December in Buenos Aires, Sao Paulo, and Rio de Janeiro. It was in this first trip that he developed the first sketches for the plan for Rio—sixty kilometers of elevated highway with housing underneath. He returned in 1936 traveling in the Graf Zeppelin, between Frankfurt and Rio via Recife. The flight to Recife alone was sixty-eight hours long. Oscar Niemeyer describes him arriving like a god, the first to step off the Zeppelin after a rough landing worried the local architects eagerly waiting for him in the hangar.[24]

Le Corbusier published, lectured, and worked all over the world, developing urban plans—some of them unsolicited—for "Algiers, Stockholm, Moscow, Buenos Aires, Montevideo, Rio de Janeiro, Paris, Zurich, Antwerp, Barcelona, New York, Bogota, St. Dié, Marseilles, and Chandigarh,"[25] and completing buildings in such far away cities as Moscow, Rio de

51

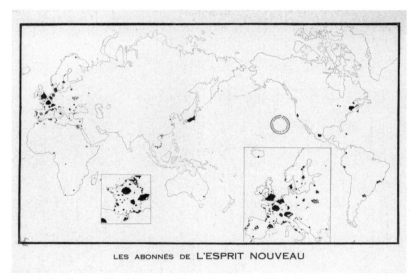

LES ABONNÉS DE L'ESPRIT NOUVEAU

Map of subscribers to L'Esprit Nouveau, L'Esprit Nouveau 17, 1922. © F.L.C. / ADAGP, Paris / Artists Rights Society (ARS), New York 2021

speech welcoming him to Sao Paulo by the State parliament in 1929: "When the first issue of *L'Esprit Nouveau* reached Brazil, we felt the impact of a great event."[23] His publications preceded him, even made the invitation to lecture possible in the first place. In reverse, his lectures while touring Latin America culminated in his book *Precisions*. Publication generates travel, which generates publication; and in the middle of this cyclical engine, projects are produced.

From the late twenties on, Le Corbusier was often in South America, lecturing and making urban proposals for Buenos Aires, Montevideo, Rio de Janeiro, Bogota, and ultimately developing projects such as the MES (Ministério da Educação e Saúde) or the Cite Universitaire of Rio, the Curruchet house in La Plata (Argentina), and the unbuilt Errazuris house in Chile.

In his first trip to South America in 1929, Le Corbusier took his time, traveling by ocean

Janeiro, La Plata, Tokyo, Baghdad, Ahmadabad, and Boston. As his global reach expanded, the space of his movements radically increased. His practice was unthinkable without jet travel. If in the 1920s he was fascinated with the global distribution of the subscribers, by 1960 he was obsessed with the architect's new kind of mobility.

Even Le Corbusier's architectural education consisted of traveling. Speaking, as he often did, in the third person, he wrote:

> At nineteen, LC sets out for Italy, 1907 Budapest, Vienna; in Paris February 1908, 1910 Munich, then Berlin. 1911, knapsack on back: Prague, Danube, Serbia, Rumania, Bulgaria, Turkey (Constantinople), Asia Minor. Twenty-one days at Mount Athos. Athens, Acropolis six weeks…. Such was L-C's

school of architecture. It had provided his education, opening doors and windows before him—into the future.[26]

Le Corbusier drew a map of his journey, publishing it several times from 1925 on, until the maps of jet travel take over. The path of the solitary student gave way to the nervous system of a new kind of human ...

## GLOBAL EDUCATION

International travel served as an architectural education for Le Corbusier (who never went to architecture school); in the 1970s, however, the Architectural Association (AA) in London under the leadership of Alvin Boyarsky became the first truly global school of architecture. Boyarsky, who went to the AA from Canada via Chicago, used to boast that the school included students and faculty from thirty countries. That he was keeping count already indicates a high level of self-awareness. Even before he was elected chairman, Boyarski, as director of the International Institute of Design (IID), which he founded, coordinated from his kitchen table in Chicago the first "Sumer Sessions" that took place in London, housed at the Bartlett School of Architecture, in 1970. This summer school program brought together architects and students from "twenty-four countries" in Boyarsky's ac-

would soon become the fetish of a whole generation of students and teachers. Student Paul Sheppard did his diploma thesis at the AA on the 747 and many faculty from Dennis Crompton to Bernard Tschumi obsessed about its modernity, speed, size, comfort, and affordability—as if describing an ideal building.

But it was not just jet travel that brought them together but, in what seems an anticipation of a more contemporary situation of electronic social networking, Boyarsky speaks of the success of the summer sessions as "cheered on particularly by the 'global village' servicing chats and by the example of the 'linking-up' forays performed by the optimists on the London scene."[28] The objective of the summer sessions, according to Boyarsky, was simply "to provide a forum and a platform in an optimum setting ... an opportunity for cross fertilization, interchange and first-hand contact."[29]

Elected chairman of the AA on the basis of the extraordinary success and allure of the summer sessions, Boyarsky extended the same formula to the school itself. What had been a very British school, well known for its publications (many of which were little magazines produced by the students) became a truly global school of architecture. The school inaugurated a new form of pedagogy in which the objective was not to

52

Graf Zeppelin near Rio de Janerio, ca 1930. © F.L.C. / ADAGP, Paris / Artists Rights Society (ARS), New York 2021

count.[27] The faculty included such figures as Arata Isozaki, Hans Hollein, Nicolaas Habraken, Adolpho Natalini, Yona Friedman, Charles Jencks, Juan Pablo Bonta, Stanislaus von Moos, Peter Cook, Andrea Branzi, Germano Celant, Cedric Price, Gordon Pask, James Stirling, Reyner Banham, etc.

As if to emphasize the internationalism of the school, the advertisement for the summer session in 1972 had a multi-exposure image of an airplane (a sleek De Haviland Comet) taking off. The logo of the school was the front elevation of an airplane, the machine that made it all possible. The new Boeing 747

educate the student architect in the profession (Boyarsky thought that this was something that could be learned in architectural offices) but to immerse the student in a global conversation. The AA had the first commuter teachers. From 1976 onwards Bernard Tschumi, for example, went to London from New York every two weeks.[30]

But it was not just the faculty of the AA which was international and mobile. In the mid-seventies the government took away the grants that British students used to receive to support their studies at the AA. Alvin traveled around the world to places like

Malaysia, Japan, and Korea to recruit students and the internationalism of the school grew exponentially.[31]

The mobility of students and faculty was part of the philosophy of the school. Boyarsky himself claimed he didn't have a base, despite the fact

Even the most ordinary local commission has become infused with extraordinary global forces. The new economy of global movement envisaged by Le Corbusier, and prototyped in his own operation, has become normalized. The new kind of human he designed for, as if

Places like China, the Emirates, and Latin America, have become the areas where new figures and ideas can be tested. Very often, a former student returning to their country builds a project connection for their teacher. These new sites of production not only become platforms for experimentation for young architects, but also sites for greater diversity from underrepresented groups. Women architects and African architects, for example, are increasingly commissioned to do major civic buildings in disparate countries. The most radical work in the field now appears continents away from the traditional sites of academic and professional power.

53

that he was chair at the AA and living in London: "I don't have a base. I move around the world and so I always think of my activities as being involved with international events."[32]

Eventually, Alvin was rarely seen outside the school. The international network that he had cultivated through his own travel now traveled to the AA. The school itself became a compact global scene, with publications streaming back out of it to the world. What Le Corbusier called the new nervous system of the airline network, becomes the nervous system of the school itself. And as with Le Corbusier, what started as exchange and diffusion of ideas eventually turn into actual projects. The AA generation that circulated ideas through teachers and books would form the core of a new generation of global practitioners. Some of the best and most mobile teachers, like Koolhaas and Tschumi, and their students, like Hadid and Holl, would lead an international avant-garde with major projects throughout the world. A generation that grew up trafficking in ideas is now trafficking in projects.

An even younger generation, like FOA (Alejandro Zaera Polo and Farshid Mousavi), Asymptote (Hani Rashid and Lise Anne Couture), Reiser + Umemoto (Jesse Reiser and Nanako Umemoto) and Carme Pinos, for example, found their first real opportunities to build outside the United States or Europe. Places like China, the Emirates, and Latin America, have become the areas where new figures and ideas can be tested. Very often, a former student returning to their country builds a project connection for their teacher. These new sites of production not only become platforms for experimentation for young architects, but also sites for greater diversity from underrepresented groups. Women architects and African architects, for example, are increasingly commissioned to do major civic buildings in disparate countries. The most radical work in the field now appears continents away from the traditional sites of academic and professional power.

designing for himself, has become the generic client. Everyone moves in countless networks. From computer to cell phone, one no longer needs to get on a plan: everyone is already in seat 5, a window seat.

1        Le Corbusier, *Le Corbusier, My Work,* trans. James Palmes (London, 1960), p. 152. Originally published in French as *L'Atelier de la recherche patiente* (Paris, 1960).

2        Bernard Tschumi, interview with the author, New York, August 25, 2009.

3        Le Corbusier sketch 501 [1960], in *Le Corbusier Sketchbooks,* vol. 4. (Cambridge, Mass., 1985).

4        Le Corbusier sketch 337 [1955], in *Le Corbusier Sketchbooks,* vol. 3 (Cambridge, Mass., 1985).

5        Le Corbusier, "Les tendances de l'architecture rationaliste en rapport avec la collaboration de la peinture et de a sculpture," written "on board the Zeppelin (Equator) 11 July 1935," presented at the Volta Congress, Rome, October 1936, FLC U3 (17) 90, p. 2. Published in *Convegno di Arti,* Fondazione Alessandro Volta, Reale Accademia d'Italia (Rome, 1937), quoted by Jean-Louis Cohen in "Sublime, Inevitably Sublime: The Appropriation of Technical Objects," in *Le Corbusier: The Art of Architecture,* ed. Alexander von Vegesack et al., exh. cat., Vitra Design Museum, Weil am Rheim et al. (London et al., 2007), p. 224.

6        Le Corbusier, "Preface to the Second French Printing," *Precisions: On the Present State of Architecture and City Planning,* trans. Edith Schreiber Aujame (Cambridge, Mass., 1991), p. x. Originally published in French in *Précisions sur un état présent de l'architecture et de l'urbanisme,* (Paris, 1960).

7        Le Corbusier sketch 637 [1956], in *Le Corbusier Sketchbooks,* vol.3.

8        Le Corbusier sketch 440 [November 13, 1955], in *Le Corbusier Sketchbooks,* vol. 3.

9        I am grateful to Vikram Prakash for his help figuring out Le Corbusier's movements in India.

10       Le Corbusier sketches 628-629 [1951], in *Le Corbusier Sketchbooks,* vol. 2 (Cambridge, Mass., 1985).

11       Le Corbusier sketch 881 [1957], in *Le Corbusier Sketchbooks,* vol. 3.

12       Le Corbusier sketches 688–90 [March 3, 1961], in *Le Corbusier Sketchbooks,* vol. 4.

13       In 1951, for example, he reminds himself in a sketchbook: "On return [to] Paris//Write to Tata= congratulate him on plane Bombay-Delhi leaving October 29, 1951 at 8:30am ask him for drawings of the plane + drawings of the reclining armchairs (remarkable)//for 226 x 226 x 226." Le Corbusier sketch 625 [1951], in *Le Corbusier Sketchbooks,* vol. 2.

14       Le Corbusier sketch 330 [1949], in *Le Corbusier Sketchbooks,* vol. 1 (Cambridge: MIT Press, 1985).

15       "June 11, 1949. Room 1//room 2//cross section inspired by Air France Constellation February 22, 1949 Paris New York" Le Corbusier sketch 331 [February 22,1949], in *Le Corbusier Sketchbooks,* vol. 1.

16       Le Corbusier sketch 791 [1961], in *Le Corbusier Sketchbooks,* vol. 4.

17       Le Corbusier sketch 575 [June 15, 1960], in *Le Corbusier Sketchbooks,* vol. 4.

18       Le Corbusier sketch 104 [1958], in *Le Corbusier Sketchbooks,* vol. 4.

19       Le Corbusier sketches 276–77, 360, in *Le Corbusier Sketchbooks,* vol. 4.

20       Le Corbusier sketch 123 [July 24, 1954], in *Le Corbusier Sketchbooks,* vol. 3.

21       Le Corbusier sketch 323 [October 31, 1955], in *Le Corbusier Sketchbooks,* vol. 3.

22       Le Corbusier sketch 817 [1957], in *Le Corbusier Sketchbooks,* vol. 4.

23       Le Corbusier, *My Work,* p. 49. Also "American Prologue," in *Precisions.*

24       Le Corbusier traveled to Rio in the Graf Zeppelin, "the magnificent 237-metre German airship that, between 1928 and 1937, made 143 impeccable transatlantic flights. 'I went to meet him.'… Le Corbusier descended from the air, 'a mighty god visiting his pygmy worshippers,' says Niemeyer." Jonathan Glancey, "I Pick Up My Pen. A Building Appears," *The Guardian,* The Arts, Wednesday August 1, 2007, p. 23. "The 13th of July of 1936, all the architects of the project of the MES were waiting for him in the hangar of the Zeppelin, 45 km from the center of Rio de Janeiro. A wretched landing had them very worried but Le Corbusier was first off the plane." "Interview with Carlos Leao," Rio de Janeiro, 1981, quoted in Elizabeth D. Harris, *Le Corbusier: Riscos Brasileiros* (Sau Paulo, 1987).

25       Le Corbusier, *My Work,* p. 50

26       Ibid., p. 21

27       Boyarsky described it as "an unusually active commuting axis embroidered by a network of lecture circuits and sundry snoops on both sides of the Atlantic" and went on to talk about the "kaleidoscopic nature" of applicants coming from "every corner of the world": "Oslo, Santiago, Zurich. Cincinnati, Stuttgart, Trondheim, Sydney, Buenos Aires, Helsinki, New Delhi, Ljubljana, Washington, DC, etc."Alvin Boyarsky, "Summer Session, 1970," *Architectural Design* 41, no. 4 (April 1971), p. 220. By the next summer session in 1971, the outreach had expanded even further to Tokyo, Lima, Ankara, Guadalajara, Brisbane, Ahmadabad, Yokohama, Stockholm, Chicago, etc.

28       Ibid.

29       Ibid.

30       Bernard Tschumi, in interview with the author, August 2009.

31       Ibid.

32       Alvin Boyarsky, interview by Bill Mount, 1980, in Alvin Boyarsky's archives in London. Cited by Irene Sunwoo in "Pedagogy's Progress: Alvin Boyarsky's International Institute of Design," *Greyroom* 34 (Winter 2009), p. 31.

54

# OTHER CRITERIA
## Sanford Kwinter

Throughout the 1980s and '90s, when bold, radical, and risqué architectures first began to peel off from the familiar formal languages of the decades-long modernist consensus, so-called 'disruptive' gestures—to use the loathsome a business-world jargon—became the standard model to which critical, theoretical, and popular attention would, perhaps for the first time ever in unison, be focused. This amounted to nothing short of a renaissance of design within public consciousness; nearly every conservative disciplinary framework that had previously established architecture's borders as a cultural and civic practice was shattered.

The fact that these developments coincided with the rise of economic liberalism, the digitization of the public sphere, and the shift from a text and numeric-based system of knowledge and communications bureaucracy to a graphic and pictorial one, meant that the integration of 'design-thinking' into both commerce and everyday life would be near seamless; its former distinctions would become almost impossible to discern. As with all 'seismic' transformations, there followed a period of great creativity and free speculation—what one could even call a 'cosmopolitanization' of architectural science in the 1990s—only to be routinized and calcified soon after through over-exposure within the artificial networks of wired attention that increasingly came to mark public life.

One of the curious hallmarks of these developments was the unprecedented spread of conventional architectural 'excellence' throughout the globe. The 2004 publication of the mammoth Phaidon Atlas of Contemporary World Architecture marked, for this writer, the astonishing democratization and globalization of a new "international style" which was typically marked by deep and pervasive sophistication, and precious little genuine innovation. It also revealed an

tion, merged into a kind of self-cancelling, undifferentiated, and for the first time, 'planetary' blur.

The apparatus of 'communications' into which architectural experience had uncomplainingly migrated—into the anxious new 'commons' represented by the aggregation and sharing social media sites—had now become the artificial, and fundamentally dissociated and immaterial 'ecology' within which design was not only being received, but also generated.

The emerging global architectural "communicon" (to invoke a term previously taken up by Foucault to describe the merging of a grid of artificial intelligibility—the Panopticon—into that of the physical world),[1] a self-reinforcing and ultimately parochial cyberspatial system that is still being celebrated in many circles as "open and universal," and which has provided now several generations access to ideas and styles as well as the knowledges and expertise required to execute them, distributed architectural culture with unprecedented efficiency but also trivialized it and sequestered it within a system of visual platitudes that continually distracted the field from architecture's broader promise in the modern world. The mandate the design profession abandoned was to assertively define design problems on the basis of 'its own sovereignty' as a field of either applied or speculative thought.

The focus on individual buildings over the last two decades has brought wondrous and beguiling performances and 'case-studies' to contemporary attention, but relatively little in the way of social, philosophical or historical ambition, and little in the way of leadership, foundational (re)thinking, or big picture vision. The field has largely occupied itself with incorporating technological innovations and delivering attention-capturing refinements and updates that delight and confirm formalist appetites and expectations. But the greatest delinquency, perhaps, is the time lost and the opportunities missed to have wrangled openly and bravely with significant provocations and developments particular to 'our' historical era, ones that pertain to the human-environment interfac-

The apparatus of 'communications' into which architectural experience had uncomplainingly migrated—into the anxious new 'commons' represented by the aggregation and sharing social media sites—had now become the artificial, and fundamentally dissociated and immaterial 'ecology' within which design was not only being received, but also generated.

extreme proliferation of technical audacity in the generated forms that was so various and unrelenting that, in its aggregate, ultimately manifested as little more than a Muzak-like background drone to a set of historical developments in politics, economics, geography, science, and culture that the design field seemed suddenly unwilling and unable to address. Specifically, 'buildings' during this period became endlessly captivating, acrobatic, affecting, surprising, even beautiful, but now, given their sheer sparkling preponderance and the stridency of their individual claims on atten-

es that operate at once at scales greater than and less than that of the individual buildings, be they at the corporate, civic, or private scale.[2]

Throughout the four decades of architectural design production that followed the events of 1968, a single and simple means for a designer to gain the upper hand to address the things 'that matter' was to inquire of a project "How does this pertain to *the city?*" The invocation of 'city' naturally implied more than simply the municipal context of a work or building. It referred rather to a project's embedment in a meshwork of social, economic, and historical conditions that were widely seen as inseparable from cultural, psychic, and subjective processes and terms. This litmus test drove most of the design discourse and even many of the popular assessments of the post-'68 era,

not to be found within the limited domain of what we still call "architecture"—the dominant point of view continues to be that the latter has to do with nothing but buildings—but the ways in which the science and art of architecture is no longer disturbing and re-'directing'

## The Mies Crown Hall Americas Prize is a notable enterprise in the contemporary scene if for no other reason than the staggering accomplishment it represents as an aggregator of contemporary architectural excellence.

and even when it did not, it continued to pose the primary challenge to architecture's higher conscience. This standard has today been largely replaced by feckless connoisseurship and endless titivations as ultimate references or keystone terms. It has also arguably been superseded by a host of complicated new conditions and bewilderingly rich emerging 'ultimate' contexts—geographical, economic, environmental, technological—that all require specialized knowledge and reconfigured boundaries in order to grasp and address.

The Mies Crown Hall Americas Prize is a notable enterprise in the contemporary scene if for no other reason than the staggering accomplishment it represents as an aggregator of contemporary architectural excellence. The website archives several hundreds of individual building projects, each brilliantly inventoried in photographs, drawings, and concise explanatory and descriptive texts. As a compendium of contemporary output and creation, it rivals any editorial project this writer has seen (the aforementioned Phaidon book of 2004 serves as a direct precursor). The parade of works and compositions is breathtaking in its variety and virtuosity and serves as an almost tacit advertisement for contemporary technical and stylistic 'mastery' across all scales of 21$^{st}$ century industrial and economic activity and life. Yet, while searching and clicking thirstily through the posted files, it begins to dawn on one that this density of textures, postures, and forms is at once unnatural and virtually pornographic in its precocity, rhythm, and teasingly deferred promise. The thrill is in the frictionless simplicity of the access and in the incongruous ratio of effort expended to the outright luxuriance that is delivered. To this degree, it represents a kind of treason of our native human sentience that is both existentially and biologically rooted in time, place, and matter. What we have here is a full on virtual reality spectacle, in effect a drastic routing of our pathways of carnate experience and of the metabolic habits through which the external world is reconstructed and organized for later—presumably creative—response within us.

The scenario at the MCHAP website described above is typical and customary today, even if the standard experience is for the most part considerably less refined and condensed. What matters, however, is to grasp the 'continuous' way in which this deceptive reworking of contexts operates today so that it is "always already" reshaping how we intuit, assess, and re-imagine architectural experience in the present. The more significant issue, and the hidden risk it entails, is

how we use our senses to interpret and reimagine the ambient world, but has rather begun to adopt an increasingly servile role with respects to the terms and resources it draws on to invent its language and moves.

When is the last time an architect invoked a non-standard insight, psycho-sensory experience, or 'body state' (as historian Daniel Smail terms it),[3] as the trigger of a project's impetus, concept, or parti? Given the increasing presence of 'virtual' or 'augmented' reality equipment in pedagogical and research-based design-profession settings (one example among others), one would naturally imagine that experiments in sensory information processing analogous to how EDM (Electronic-Dance-Music) DJs deploy sound to modulate not only listeners but the entire psycho-physical environment, would be the order of the day, but they are not.

This is not to say that today's design projects do not contribute directly, if subtly, to architecture's ongoing project of probing the possibilities of our built environment to alter and modify human experience and subjectivity. But the field neither possesses, nor has developed, speculative frameworks, either cultural, scientific, or theoretical, to direct this research to coherent and systematic ends nor to make imaginative sense of its outcomes. In fact, it leaves nearly all default concerns in place and largely puts its genius at the service of trite vested interests. There is simply no revised or updating culture to speak of, and even in the schools where speculation is traditionally encouraged and protected, most attention continues to be referred in the end to problems of method or 'style.'

The fact alone of putting these comments to paper brings to mind a small tsunami of emergent concerns that for all of their putative urgency scarcely appear in any authentic way on the architect's horizon today. Among these are the new grids and matrices provided by transformations—some would argue 'revolutions'—in the contemporary understanding of seemingly familiar terms such as: nature, knowledge, experience, society, technics, to name just the four addressed below.

Now "Of course," the profession will argue, "design addresses these centrally and saliently today. Do we not have a rich tradition of engagement with landscape, multiple new orders of sustainability measures and research, and a new set of protocols with which to address problems of contemporary climate, energy, and environment?" But this is precisely where the failing today lies and just where the architectural

56

profession is most egregiously losing ground to other fields. The posture of polite but effete assimilation simply obscures the fact that what is required is a bold and sweeping transformation of the global topology in which 'design' reckoning takes place. As the sports metaphor expresses it, only by "moving the goalposts" does one change the game.

With respects to 'nature,' the design field must come to terms with the complexities, paradoxes and counter-intuitions that are the hallmarks of thermodynamics and its truly beautiful concerns with order, information, and "transformity."[4] It must learn to think in terms of systems, metastability, boundary problems, energy and *work*, equilibrium and path independence, etc. These are not mere measurable additions for inclusion within the classical architect's quiver, but rather foundational challenges to the very ground on which design planning and understanding unfolds. At an entirely other scale, architecture must open itself to a properly 'biological' framework of understanding, and in many ways weaken its desperate and outmoded grasp on physics alone; it must, in a word, begin to operate within a truly 'ecological' mindset in which every element and gesture is understood to entail exchanges and consequences in every other. It must also adopt a richer understanding of the role

of magnitude that are as invisible as they are powerful, and the fundamental and enduring *processes* that constitute worldly 'substance' and whose dynamism must be henceforth properly engaged. As Henri Bergson asserted: "Reality makes or unmakes itself but is never something made." There is a complacency in the field with respect to the assumption that architecture concerns exclusively what is made, and it is one that needs to be vigorously upended.

The invocation of the term 'experience' continues to elicit dismissive reactions in architects who either cut their teeth in the 1960s or '70s or were educated by others who did. The wholesale rejection of experiential discourse by several post-1968 generations was a formulaic response to a preceding group of critics and practitioners who advanced a distinctly trivial version of 'phenomenology' whose hollow rhapsodies were widely rebuffed as mere 'impressionism.' But with the recent discoveries and advances across the neurosciences, and in the disclosing of how little we firmly know or how wrong we've been about our senses and the role they play in how we pick up information from the world (and how we in turn orient ourselves within it), the tables are now turned. This, compounded with the rapid development of sensory-enhancing technologies and interfaces that transport us in the blink of an

57

## The posture of polite but effete assimilation simply obscures the fact that what is required is a bold and sweeping transformation of the global topology in which 'design' reckoning takes place.

played by the structuring 'milieu' in the determination and unfolding of any object, whether living or inert. What is required in each example is of course a change in ethos and procedure and not simply of terms.

With respect to the problem of 'knowledge,' it is important to stress that no discipline stands alone today, and each contributes something that is unique to its perspective. Architecture has never been fully certain of its entitlement to the status of knowledge system—hence the persistent rhetorical use of the term 'science' in this essay—but it is a complex that must be overcome and the place to start is by extending the outcomes of its polymorphous practical experiments as speculations into other adjacent domains. To do this, architecture must have a theory of the world that is proper to itself. And architecture must also pay due attention to developments in knowledge and science all around it. Architecture must begin again to play the game of building and testing ontological 'models' and exploring on its own, and in its own terms, the nature of reality and the means through which reality can be actively directed and shaped. Can architecture have a more sophisticated understanding of form and matter than the one it passively inherited from the ancients? Decidedly yes. In nearly every domain of knowledge today we see an array of transformations taking place—the acknowledgement of the multiplicity of scales that determine the realities we take for granted, the communication between orders

eye to perceptual universes largely distinct from the ones our bodies are in, and it is clear that we need to begin again with an entirely new idea of what constitutes architectural 'substance.' Perceptual *space* has grabbed clear ascendancy over physical space. We must now confront the rich conclusion that architecture has perhaps always belonged to the same anthropological register as gustatory, literary, sport, religious, social, musical, etc. practices, as so many means of organizing and patterning the external world in order to shape and modulate our internal world in turn.

Here again, the radical development that would transform architectural practice in its foundations is the acceptance of the indissociability of interior experience and physical composition—the flow and structure—of the ambient world. Neurobiology has taught us two things preeminently in the last two decades: that our sensing apparatus is endlessly 'plastic' and hence adaptive, and that we are literally shaped and assembled of stimulus and can neither thrive nor even persist without it.[5] What this means is that we not only make the world, but we make ourselves literally through it—that we 'are' the world, just as the world endlessly becomes us. In some ways, architecture is becoming an affair of 'matter becoming conscious and sensate' both 'in' us and 'of' us. Our relationship to it takes place not within a 'subject-object' relation but as a co-relation along an endlessly excitable continuum. Once this formulation has been intellectually assimilated, contemporary problems of immersive experience become newly tractable… and urgent. Regardless of how odd or farfetched this seemingly syllogistic formulation of mutual engenderment of self and world may at first appear, the onto- and cosmogenic basis

# Architecture must begin again to play the game of building and testing ontological 'models' and exploring on its own, and in its own terms, the nature of reality and the means through which reality can be actively directed and shaped. Can architecture have a more sophisticated understanding of form and matter than the one it passively inherited from the ancients?

that underlies it is undisputed today. The attention increasingly directed to problems of *Umwelt* theory and perceptual and experiential matrices as a basis for understanding of physical reality in design theory and practice reflects this dawning intuition. What has changed today is that these problems are no longer casual speculations but are testable, graspable, figurable incidents that can and are being structured and delivered to experience in art, science, as well as in design.[6]

Last but not least, the preeminence of 'technical mediation' in our universe of physical interactions must be seen as possessing thresholds that represent not only changes in degree but also changes in kind. The simplest and most direct turn, albeit of staggering difficulty for the architect trapped in tectonic and spatialist habits, is to engage the socius as a 'transductive'[7] medium of continual modification and genesis, that is, as a continuous and sometimes insidious emergence of responsive structure pegged to every aspect and scale of our temporal life. The whole point of data management is said *to predict,* but the armature of data enlisted thereby and in which we are continuously swathed, has the effect more often to envelope, to constrain and 'to direct'. Big data, distributed ledger technologies, and Artificial Intelligence, to name just three unregulated umbrella developments perilously poorly theorized and understood are already reshaping our physical, psychic, and collective (political, social) landscape by transforming the very nature of what 'things' are made of and how they operate and behave, without perceivably changing the things themselves. We are being redesigned and forcibly re-integrated into a continuously unfolding matrix of "command-control-communications" ($C^3$) invisibilities at a fully ecological scale. There is no practical discipline other than architecture/design that bears the transdisciplinary mandate to address, engage, grasp and, if needed, 'redirect' these various forces of subsumption and to put them at the service of human sensori-psychic expansion and discovery, and no longer exclusively at the service of soft and reductivist tyranny. Architectural "excellence" must no longer be confined to the circulating object or its image but rather to the context 'its action' both fits into and inevitably conditions. What is beautiful is what augments 'life,' not what solely delights the eyes.

58

1        See Warren Neidich's "Computational Architecture and the Statisticon" for a powerfully credible variation on this same theme in Warren Neidich (ed.), *The Psychopathologies of Cognitive Capitalism: Part Two* (Berlin: Archive Books, 2014).

2        See Libby Banks, "Mind and Body Take Center Stage at This Year's London Design Biennale," (New York Times, September 3, 2018).

3        Daniel Lord Smail, *On Deep History and the Brain* (Berkeley and Los Angeles: U.C. Press, 2008).

4        This term is a central one in the late (1990s) work of the eco-physicist and systems ecologist Howard Odum. The term, which refers to the "quality" of energy and its vicissitudes, was co-coined by him and David Scienceman.

5        The best treatment of the anatomical and biological component of brain organization is Peter Huttenlocher, *Neural Plasticity: The Effects of Environment on the Development of the Cerebral Cortex* (Cambridge: Harvard U. Press, 2002). The best treatment of the environmental component is Bruce E. Wexler, *Brain and Culture: Neurobiology, Ideology, and Social Change* (Cambridge: MIT Press, 2006).

6        The gamut here is vast and is developing rapidly across multiple platforms and fields of concern: Umwelt Theory (von Uexküll and followers), the theory of Affordances (J.J. Gibson, Donald Norman), as well as in philosophical and experimental work on perception and even consciousness (such is in the work of Thomas Metzinger, Olaf Blanke, Isabella Pasqualini to mention just a few examples among dozens), art practice (Robert Irwin, Olafur Eliasson) and so on.

7        The term *transduction* was coined by Gilbert Simondon to describe the process by which an activity produces at once a form and the milieu that both supports it and provides the platform for its continued development. For a reference in English see Gilbert Simondon, "The Genesis of the Individual", trans. Mark Cohen and Sanford Kwinter, in Jonathan Crary and Sanford Kwinter (eds.), *ZONE 6: Incorporations* (New York: Zone Books, 1993), pp. 310-313.

ON EMPTY LAND
David Sisso

"Things are not as they really were, but as they are remembered," said the renowned film director Andrei Tarkovsky. Sisso's photographic work builds on this idea. The images of "On Empty Land" echo climates rather than a certain territory or time. According to the photographer, the images do not describe but evoke. He is interested in the processes by which memory cuts, edits, corrects, and signifies landscapes.

# THE CAUSAL SEQUENCE
## Enrique Ramirez

*Hey sport. You connect the dots.*
*You pick up the pieces*

— *Laurie Anderson, "Sharkey's Night"*

BERMS, VAULTS, CHAINS OF BEING
At the heart of this essay are words and images, the stories about how I encountered them, and hopefully, the many avenues for their significances. By way of a warning, I feel obligated to tell the reader that I am, by nature, an elliptical thinker, and this astronomical term really does capture my approach to writing about, say, a movie by Andrei Tarkovsky, a painting by Pieter Bruegel the Elder, or perhaps a building on an archaeological site on the Pacific Shore of Peru. And though this essay begins with a recollection from the summer of 1991, it is really just a starting off point as I take a perambulating path through my own interest in art, history, science, film, and architecture, to orient you, the reader, to a brief inventory of moments taking place since that time. These moments, I should add, are significant not only because they are ones that I associate closely with various buildings and landscapes, but also because they are just that—moments—and my duty as a writer is to make some kind of connection between them with the hope of that in the end a reader can see the resulting cloud of dots instead of the myriad connections that I was at pains to make—the forest for the trees, as is often said.

So, 1991. I was then taking summer classes at Northwestern University and living in a shared suite in one of those old Collegiate Gothic quads on the north end of campus, not far from the engineering school, which was then called the Technological Institute. It was one of those typically hot and humid summers along Lake Michigan, one where I often found myself walking along the mile-long stretch of campus to

on the life and work of Sir Isaac Newton. And whether she was lecturing on, say, epicycles and eccentric orbits and introducing students to theories of planetary motion from antiquity to the early modern period, she almost always used "vault" to describe the night skies, which at the time I imagined as a glittering expanse suspended over our heads. Nothing seemed as impossible as the notion that the sky, an infinite-seeming thing that contained the air that we breathe as well as countless flying objects, from gossamer-winged insects to impossibly large, aluminum-skinned airliners, a realm whose cerulean fringes transformed into the deepest violet at the edge of vision, only to be shattered by a splintering photon beam from a dying star some 92 million miles away, a shard breaking the air apart into a vast field of light—this, apparently, was a 'thing.' Strange, then, how my other professor, the architectural historian David Van Zanten, described both the ceiling of Chartres Cathedral and Michelangelo and Giacomo della Porta's thin-shelled dome at St. Peter's Basilica as "vaults." There is a bit of cognitive dissonance here, a logic of transformation, one where the architectural understanding of "vault" changes state and becomes more metaphorical, which is to say that a kind of engineering innovation allowing buildings to resist lateral thrust while achieving awe-inspiring heights is transfigured. One wonders, then, if the ultimate goal of architecture is just that, to transcend its physical and natural confines, to defy memory and be transmitted from generation to generation with words.

Although this was certainly on my mind that summer, I did not have the words to describe such sense of expansive wonder—at least not my own. I only had vistas and images, at first tempered through books. Of vistas and books, there is this, a memory that anchors my location to a specific time and place during that summer of 1991. It is a hot afternoon and I am on a grassy berm, rereading a book Professor Dobbs assigned for her seminar—Arthur O. Lovejoy's *The Great Chain of Being*. It was a paperback reissue, Harvard University Press, with that now-iconic cover featuring

73

One wonders, then, if the ultimate goal of architecture is just that, to transcend its physical and natural confines, to defy memory and be transmitted from generation to generation with words.

visit used bookstores, or just sitting on the beach and staring at airplanes above, ascending and descending along their mysterious, predetermined flight paths to and from O'Hare Airport. This was the time during which I began to understand something of what a university education was supposed to be, or at least wanted it to be. I took classes in the History of Science as well as Art History, which now seems fortuitous if not prescient. Specifically, it was during my first survey in architectural history that I began to see a connection between these two realms, all mediated through a single word: *vault*.

It was a term that two professors of mine would use frequently. One was the late Betty Jo Teeter Dobbs, who became one of the foremost experts

the book's title in Herb Lubalin's Avant Garde ITC typeface (although I would not recognize it as such until now, this very moment, as I am remembering these instances from a younger time.) The book was written in 1936, and yet I detected something all-too-tangible about it, as if Lovejoy's description of a universe was really a description of a building. In his own historical reckoning, so Lovejoy tells us, there is "the conception of the plan and the structure of the world which, through the Middle Ages and down to the late eighteenth century, many philosophers, most men of science, and indeed, most educated men, were to accept without question—the conception of the universe as a 'Great Chain of Being.'" Lovejoy continues with his architectural wanderings: "[T]he architecture of the Heavens was not a piece of Gothic design—which is not surprising as it was, in fact, a Grecian edifice. The world had a clear intelligibility of structure, and not only definite shape, but what was deemed at once the simplest and most perfect shape, as had all the bodies composing it. It had no loose ends, no irregularities of outline. The simplicity of its internal plan had, indeed, under the pressure of observed astronomical facts, come to be more and more recognized as less complete than one would wish."[1] It seemed a rather radical thing to me at the time, to think of architecture, so stout, so solid, so lasting, as something that was elusive, fleeting, limning the air like a slowly-moving current. Indeed, and many years later, I experienced something similar on an unusually hot Sunday afternoon in September in Brighton Beach when I watched matter cycle through its various states in the course of mere moments. The midday sun turned the Atlantic into a vast, grey sheet that dissolved into the superheated air, and I was there, transfixed, unable to keep my eyes away from this wondrous event, much less get my bearing.

As dizzying as that one experience may have been, there was another from that summer of 1991 that left me reeling somewhat. It was another of those afternoons on which I would find myself on some kind of lonely jaunt into Chicago. I wandered into one of those video stores that had—at least as it seemed at the time—ersatz and offbeat titles. There were, of course, VHS copies of independent films, promotional and industrial items, underground cinema, bootlegged trailers, and even art films. On a wall opposite the register, underneath a sign that read SCIENCE FICTION— NEW RELEASES, I spied a VHS cover showing a man in a flight suit walking in a curved hallway that seemed to be made of metal. The surfaces were not smooth, but rather burnished, even old looking. The walls contained panels, buttons, and displays. Tubes ran along the top, curving, giving the sense that all of the film's action took place inside a great circular space, and given that this was in the part of the store for science fiction films, my guess was that it was a depiction of the interior of a space station. This was, of course, the cover to the Fox Lorber Video edition of Andrei Tarkovsky's 1972 film "Solaris," which is popularly referred to as the Russian version of "2001: A Space Odyssey." It is not, and even the most intrepid cinephile would stray away from such a pronouncement: despite their similar *mises en scène*, the two films are universes apart. If Kubrick's "2001: A Space Odyssey" is a kind of purely cinematic experience, one that is really about the abstract power of images, then Tarkovsky's "Solaris" moors its science fiction story to more tangible, physical concerns, like buildings and landscapes.

## WEEDS, LANDSCAPES, MOVEMENTS, ETCHINGS

I had no idea what to expect when I took my rented copy of "Solaris" back to my room and started watching. This was, after all, a film touted as being a 'classic.' I also had a paperback copy of an English translation of Stanislaw Lem's *Solaris*, the novel that Tarkovsky

adapted for the screen. The movie begins with titles against a black screen set against a choral prelude by Johann Sebastian Bach and then cuts to close-up shot of waterweeds fluttering in a moving stream. There is no music here, only the sounds of nature, and the languorous motion of the weeds, which now appear almost hand-like, waving as the camera tightens and moves, recall the personification of twilight in the Homeric epics as "rosy-fingered dawn." Each instance is gestural, each a poetic evocation of waving hands. But whereas the rosy light of the *Iliad* signifies the passage of time, the verdant, underwater waving in "Solaris" is a reminder of how at the heart of all forms of science fiction literature there exists a pronounced inability to come to terms with the future, a conceit that anchors this far-looking genre to the interminable present.[2] This is perhaps why a science fiction film like "Solaris" begins with these ravishing shots of nature—they are visual cues reminding us that even the most spectacular leaps of imagination are tethered not just to the unavoidable now, but also to our ineluctable environment. No wonder, then, that the opening scene of "Solaris" is in essence a montage of familiar things: water, weeds, a willow tree, flowers, a horse. Here we encounter Cosmonaut-psychologist Kris Kelvin (Donatos Banionis) on his last day on Earth before departing on a mission to the planet Solaris. He collects a sample of dirt that he will take to Solaris before washing his hands in a stream of water. He stands in the middle of a grassy field as the sky begins to rain. These are all part of ritual cleansing that signals his imminent departure to another space—and time.

The house that we see in the middle of this scene belongs to Kelvin's parents, and though this will not be his last homecoming during the film, the scene is a reminder of how architecture plays an essential role in depicting this inability to rectify the future with the present. Nothing, neither the house nor the interiors, reveals to the audience that the film is set in a far off future. The family home appears rather ordinary, its sturdy wood framing and hesitant polychromy reveal an lived interior, literally—Kelvin himself peeks through a window to see all manners of vases, books, and other tchotchkes that will stand in stark contrast to the metallic and industrial interiors inside the space station orbiting around the Solaris. The lived spaces on Earth are real, and as for those aboard Solaris, they are the setting for a rumination of a completely different order.

## REPLICAS, LANDSCAPES, JUXTAPOSITIONS

As viewers of the film will know already, the conceit behind "Solaris" is that the planet itself is a kind of titanic brain that is able to project the thoughts of the cosmonauts aboard the space station and make them into a tangible reality. There is a deeply-felt irony here, however, for such manifestations of thought, like a recording of a recording on a VHS deck, suffer a bit of generation loss and become harder to read over time. That, or it is like looking through a broken mirror, as if everything is a reflection of something else, but imperfectly so. One of the memories that the planet keeps projecting into Kelvin's reality aboard the space station

74

is that of his dead wife, Hari (Natalya Bondarchuk). She appears as real as any other person. Her clothes, hair, and skin: everything points to Hari as a living, breathing person who is there talking with Kelvin. Yet she is only an image, or rather, Kelvin's memory of Hari transubstantiated into flesh and words. Yet her image becomes into a kind of imperfect reality aboard the space station. Every one of her appearances is a painful reminder of her suicide ten years before, and for every instance that Kelvin tries to repress or eliminate the memory of her by physically jettisoning her body into outer space, she is resurrected and appears back on board the space station. Yet Hari appears changed with each successive reappearance, and each of these variations reveals something about her un-reality—subtly and profoundly. One of these is that she remembers her death, and yet cannot fathom why she is still "alive." In another instance, she allows Kelvin to undo the laces on the back of her dress only to reveal that the grommets and cords have no function, an indication that her clothing is an imperfect copy of what would be found on Earth. She even understands her predicament and drinks a vial of liquid nitrogen, knowing that she will be back, albeit imperfectly so.

This is the setting for what is, at least in the eyes of this viewer, one of the most remarkable scenes in this movie. Or, to put it another way, it is

onto Tarkovsky's vision of a space-traveling future. It is, however, extraordinary because of just how different it is from the rest of the environment. The space station interior becomes a kind of temporal montage incorporating architectural and designed elements from bygone eras. It continues—next we see Kevin and Hari sitting before a series of paintings by Pieter Bruegel the Elder (1525-1569). The camera takes over their own purview, and we begin to see one of Bruegel's paintings through their own eyes: "The Hunters in the Snow (Winter)" (1565). This work is notable too for its juxtapositions. Three hunters are returning to their village with little to show for their work. They are joined by their hunting dogs, whose hung heads and winnowed bodies are not different from that of the dead fox carried by one of the hunters. Their return, as humdrum and ordinary as it may seem, is but one indication that lean times are in store for the village. Yet there is a sense that everything is continuing as before. Sparks bloom as a blacksmith hammers on a forge. In the distance, we see skaters with hockey sticks and curling rocks. It is a scene of survival amidst desperation.

We wonder, then, why exactly this is the painting that Tarkovsky chooses to depict Kelvin's and Hari's reunion. Perhaps it has something to do with what the camera is actually seeing—and hearing— as it moves over parts of the painting. Again, note the

75

Jäger im Schnee (Winter), Pieter Bruegel, 1565. Courtesy of Kunsthistorisches Museum Wien.

remarkable because it seems, well, so unremarkable. It takes place after Kelvin has "accepted" Hari and has begun a kind of transitory existence with her on board Solaris. He has just finished arguing with the pragmatic Dr. Snaut (Jüri Järvet) about "annihilating" Hari when he encounters her inside a dining room. This is a space that is unlike any other in the film, for inside this futuristic space station is this room, with wood paneling, baize coverings, as well as crystal chandeliers and brass candelabra. This interior appears as if it were an architectonic emissary from the 18th or 19th century, grafted

recursive, juxtaposed temporalities and technologies here. A man rejoins his once-dead wife, resurrected for a second time. They are in a space station orbiting a faraway planet, in a room filled with designed objects from the 18th and 19th centuries, looking at a painting from the late 16th century. This study in contrasts continues. Whereas the scenes that take place on Earth are all variations on choral and organ preludes by Bach, here, Eduard Artemyev's electronic score is mixed with sounds from nature. Chirping birds and rustling streams are mixed with the spectral polyphonies of

Artemyev's ANS Synthesizer, a machine invented in the late 1930s by the Soviet electronics pioneer Yevgeny Murzin (1914-1970).[3] As a musical instrument, the ANS Synthesizer used photo-optical techniques from cinema to create sounds, but in a different way. Recall that the so-called "optical track" of a film is in reality a method of recording and storing the sounds recorded as the film was being made. The ANS used the same process albeit in a reverse fashion: it converted hand drawn lines etched on glass plates into sounds. The effect was one in which cinematic sound was effectively divorced from its optical source, and as viewers, we too are experiencing something similar as the sounds heard at the very beginning of "Solaris" are here removed from their original context and superimposed over what is, in essence, a tracking shot of Pieter Bruegel's "The Hunters in the Snow (Winter)."

Moreover, the significance of landscape here should be considered more closely. This extended, languorous shot of "The Hunters in the Snow (Winter)" is really a way for Kelvin to revisit his home back on Earth. The houses appearing on the edges of Bruegel's painting mimic those from Kelvin's memory, causing

scape, a patch of earth, furrowed and scarred, or perhaps even an abstracted aerial view of mountains and rivers, one where idealized versions of vertical peaks are combined with a riverine system expanding horizontally in space.

## READERS, EYES, FALLING, DISTRACTION, MAPS, WRITING

There are other things to note when watching Bruegel through Tarkovsky's eye. One is how different closeups of "The Hunters in the Snow (Winter)" are either superimposed or fade into one another. The effect is similar to how one takes in the landscape in fragments, which is really a good approximation of our own apperception. A viewer in a landscape is not like the anthropomorphic, gangly-legged camera seen on the Sternberg Brothers' iconic poster for Dziga Vertov's "The Man With a Movie Camera" (1929). The viewer is not a bedeviling "kaleidoscope equipped with consciousness" as described by Charles Baudelaire (and celebrated by Walter Benjamin.)[4] Nor is the viewer the eyeball-headed museum-goer, confronted by a panoply of surfaces and planes in Herbert

A viewer in landscape pauses and blinks while taking in the vista in a piecemeal fashion. A viewer in the landscape is self-conscious, alert and responsive. This is to say that more than anything, the viewer in the landscape is a reader, scanning the surrounding expanse, contemplating, understanding.

us to pause and wonder whether this is really a scene about Kelvin reimagining his own visit home. When we first encounter Kelvin, he too is like the hunters returning home. Though we may not be sure as to 'which' version of home he is visiting, the fact that Kelvin peers inside his childhood home through a window that has basically the same dimensions as a movie projection is certainly telling. The cinematic image becomes a means for framing, or rather, experiencing the landscape. It is a vehicle that enables telepresence by allowing one person to be in two places at the same time, which is to say, in the 'space of the viewing' as well as in the 'viewed space.' For Kelvin, then, looking at the inside of the house through a window is akin to looking at a Bruegel painting hung on a wall. And in "Solaris," it amounts to translation in several senses of the word, of converting something into something else. There is, of course, temporal translation, as elements from the past, from interior decorations to Hari herself, appear as disturbances in the present. Kelvin's entrance into this room from the space station is also a kind of spatial dislocation, of translating from one space to another. Artemyev's score literally translates light into sound, cinema into music. But perhaps the most significant translation is one that takes by dint of the ANS Synthesizer itself. When looking at the actual optical plates, riven with hand drawn crags and fissures, their resemblance to a landscape is notable. Here, the etched glass bears marks of human activity much like a land-

Bayer's Extended Field of Vision diagram from 1935. In each of these, the viewer appears passive, an optical medium, channeling a deluge of visual information as it enters the eye into a memory, a recollection, or perhaps a play of light of shadow onto an emulsion on a plate or a spool rotating at 24 frames per second. These viewers may have eyes (or in some instances, eyelashes), but their mode of vision should not be equated with the actual act of seeing. This is because a viewer in landscape pauses and blinks while taking in the vista in a piecemeal fashion. A viewer in the landscape is self-conscious, alert and responsive. This is to say that more than anything, the viewer in the landscape is a reader, scanning the surrounding expanse, contemplating, understanding.

Tarkovsky's eye is a reader's eye. This much is clear in the sequence with Bruegel's "The Hunters in the Snow (Winter)." Note how much of the camera movements are horizontal pans, a necessary conceit in that it suggests Kelvin and Hari are entering the painting by just looking at it closely. For a moment, the camera allows us to substitute our own vision for theirs, and like them, we do see many details up close during these moments. There are also some instances where the panning animates the paintings, as in the case of the close up of the bird. Unlike, say, Étienne-Jules Marey's camera gun, which captures a bird on the wing and kills it in the middle of its flight by dint of the photographic image, Tarkovsky's camera does the opposite. It focuses on the bird and pans left, bringing life to a centuries-old bird through the illusion, momentary as it may seem, that it is flying forward. And is not this constant panning, this literal translation and displacing of images from right to left, also reminiscent of the ways we turn pages on a book?

In the same baize-covered chamber, next to "The Hunters in the Snow (Winter)" is another Bruegel painting, the "Landscape with the Fall of Icarus," also from 1565. The vantage point here is very similar to the one in "The Hunters in the Snow (Winter)." In the foreground, a ploughman maintains to his crop and a shepherd seems momentarily distracted, looking at something in the air above. Presumably, and as indicated by the painting's title, it is Daedalus and Icarus. The scene is lifted directly from Book VIII of Ovid's *Metamorphoses*:

> An angler with his quivering rod,
> A lonely shepherd propped upon his crook,
> A ploughman leaning on his plough, looked up
> And gazed in awe, and thought they must be gods
> That they could fly.[5]

In an image filled with distractions, theirs is only a momentary one. But you too, as viewer, are distracted. Consider, for example, the ploughman and shepherd from Ovid's verse. In Bruegel's painting, they appear in Flemish dress whereas the sun, whose transit is lost to a glaucous aura hovering in the sweltering air, gives the water an almost emerald-like hue, as if this is a scene that is occurring somewhere in the Mediterranean coast. And the understanding of this part of the world comes from Icarus himself, surveying the world below, its islands, making a map of it before he too is distracted:

> Delos and Palos lay
> Behind them now; Samos, great Juno's isle,
> Was on the left, Lebinthos on the right
> And honey-rich Calymne, when the boy
> Began to enjoy his thrilling flight and left
> His guide to roam the ranges of the heavens,
> And soared too high. The scorching sun so close
> Softened the fragrant wax that bound his wings;
> The wax melted; his waving arms were bare;
> Unfledged, they had no purchase on the air![6]

This is, of course, the definitive account of the Icarian myth, perhaps the original cautionary tale. But more must be said about this business of flying and making maps. As Thomas Pynchon wrote in *Mason & Dixon* (1996), mapmaking is more than just flight; it is its crucial prerequisite. Before flying, surveyors "had to learn about Maps, for Maps are the *Aides-mémoires* of flight."[7]

As for the fall of Icarus, it bears no witnesses and goes by unnoticed. It is, however, committed to memory, a testamentary device, as Icarus's flight has transformed from forgotten flight to cartographical 'fact:'

> And calling to his father as he fell,
> The boy was swallowed in the blue sea's swell,
> The blue sea that for ever bears his name.
> His wretched father, now no father, cried
> 'Oh Icarus, where are you? Icarus
> Where shall I look, where find you?' On the waves
> He saw the feathers. Then he cursed his skill,
> And buried the boy's body in a grave,
> And still that island keeps the name he gave.[8]

Mapmaking has become a form of historical recollection. And this means that, in a very general sense, it is a form of writing. A very recent case in point is art historian Alexander Nemerov, who makes what is perhaps the most evocative link between the two. In *Wartime Kiss* (2013), he muses on a set of photographs, moments from the American home front during World War II. He writes as an airminded, aeriformed soul, which is to say, aloft. And his own thoughts about writing about such are also buoyant and fleeting. "Gravity is usually thought to be the historian's element," writes Nemerov, "but butterfly-wing atmospherics slow-drawn in air are another form of historical recollection. [...] When it is truly carried away, historical writing is a kind of flying."[9] Flight is that most contradictory and illogical of enterprises. It requires control of a machine and complete surrender to the air. This, then, is a way to understand the very final moments from the sequence in "Solaris" when Kelvin and Hari are looking at Bruegel's "The Hunters in the Snow (Winter)." They embrace each other and begin to levitate as if they too are surrendering their own selves—and in turn, their agency—to Tarkovsky's own vision. Our two levitators, in thrall to their loving embrace, are also readers.

### FLIGHT

This is to say that reading is also a kind of flight. At least this is what Italo Calvino tells us in *If On A Winter's Night a Traveler* (1979). In one passage, he describes reading as more than just an entertainment that mollifies our agitations and *ennui* during long flights:

> How do you occupy this absence of yourself from the world and of the world from you? You read; you do not raise your eyes from the book between one airport and the other, because beyond the page there is the void, the anonymity of stopovers, of the metallic uterus that contains you and nourishes you, of the passing crowd always different and always the same. You might as well stick with this other abstraction of

travel, accomplished by the anonymous uniformity of typographical characters: here, too, it is the evocative power of the names that persuades you that you are flying over something and not nothingness. You realize that it takes considerable heedlessness to entrust yourself to unsure instruments, handled with approximation; or perhaps this demonstrates an invincible tendency to passivity, to regression, to infantile dependence. (But are you reflecting on the air journey or on reading?)[10]

Calvino's question at the end of this passage is, at first glance, coy and perhaps a bit smart-alecky. There is a whiff of the (very) capable postmodern writer writing a novel in the guise of a metanovel whose very goal is

medium that connected the two was landscape, a figurative and literal terrain that is more than a space captured by images and reworked into things. There are words, and those words are on a page, and that page is in a book.

Bruegel's *Landscape with the Fall of Icarus* makes another appearance in film. There is a scene in Nicolas Roeg's "The Man Who Fell To Earth" (1975) when Dr. Nathan Bryce (Rip Torn) senses that Thomas Jerome Newton (David Bowie) is actually an alien. In his home office, Bryce opens a book called *Masterpieces in Paint and Poetry* to a spread featuring Bruegel's "Landscape with the Fall of Icarus" and the last stanza of W.H. Auden's poem "Musée des Beaux Arts" (1938). Already is there an equivalence of image and text. The book's title is making a connection between these two forms of art, and the appearance of

78

Pachacamac Museum by Llosa Cortegana Arquitectos MCHAP 2 Finalist. Ph. Florencia Rodriguez.

to blur the distinction between reality and fiction, and perhaps reading and writing. Reading and flying are, of course, two separate endeavors, each with their own mores, customs, and equipment. However, there is something so beguiling about the passage, and it is not just because Calvino threatens to undo his very logic. Perhaps it has something to do with the fact that reading is a form of surrender, of forgetting one's self.

But when it comes to issues of landscape, Calvino's own quote can be problematic because it suggests that there is a world outside our own reading of it. It all begs the question: is there anything that attaches us to something greater than ourselves than a landscape? If this is the case, then reading takes on a special kind of importance, one with a kind of physicality that requires some attention. What is the relation between reading and landscape? Going back to Bruegel's "Landscape with the Fall of Icarus," I was implying that if the painting was, in a sense, a visual evocation of the Icarian myth as presented in *Metamorphoses*, then to 'see' Bruegel was to 'read' Ovid. The

Bruegel and Auden on the same spread is certainly apposite. To continue a bit of logic introduced earlier, if to 'see' Bruegel was to 'read' Ovid, then in Roeg's film, the opposite is true: to 'read' Bruegel is to 'see' Auden. This is established by a sequence of shots. We begin with a medium shot of the spread, which focuses on Bruegel's painting, which then hovers Auden's poem on the opposite page, before focusing on details from "Landscape with the Fall of Icarus." The camera movement here replicates those of the reader's eyes, going back from *recto* to *verso*, and then *verso* to *recto*. As it is already established that the painting is printed in a book, we nevertheless confront "Landscape with the Fall of Icarus" in its original state, as an image, as something to be 'seen.' Yet the next shot reveals only part of Auden's poem. We do not experience it as poetry as such. We know nothing about the text, but as the camera lingers, we stop reading and notice the stanza as a grouping of words, arranged somewhat orthogonally, and the implication are that these words are connected to the image. They serve a purpose other than the wall text we see in a museum, and this poem excerpt, cropped and skewed, is now understood as related to Bruegel's painting. Nothing about the text tells us this, and it is the use of montage that makes the connection between, as the book's title suggests, "paint" and "poetry:" they are both images.

### TO PACHACAMAC

It begins with a book on your table. It is night, late night, in fact, but there is a part of you that wants to pick up that book, to stay up and not go to bed. This is how you reclaim all those hours lost to your day job. To your commute. To your three cups of afternoon coffee. To finding time to recharge your phone. To an impossibly crowded subway or persistent traffic jam. So here, on this night, just as you feel the all those things that otherwise mark your day to day existence weigh your eyelids down, you do this: you open the book, crack the spine, take a dip in the ocean of words and surrender to their undertow. At some point, your head starts to nod, you come back to a momentary state of lucidity. You may find feel slightly lightheaded. You may feel like you are levitating, but maybe you are just imagining that you are levitating. The book you are trying to read is still there. In this liminal state between wakefulness and sleep, the book becomes a landscape. Vistas reveal words. Words form textures, razzle-dazzles of figure-ground silhouettes nestled in a vast terrain of white space, parts of which you can still see beyond and behind the blackletter ascenders, descenders, loops, ligatures, bowls, and finials. And if the book is still open on your lap or balancing on your stomach, you may notice how the pages bunch up the closer they get to the gutter, forming a valley of sorts. The gutter is not the middle of a valley, but a shoreline. Or a line on a map that acts as a demarcator between land and sea. The right hand part of the spread, the *recto*, is the western part of Peru. On the other side, the *verso*, there is the South Pacific Ocean. You run a finger from the top of this meridian. Lima District is there, near the top. Below it is an inventory of names—La Punta, Miraflores, Costa Verde, La Herradura, Punta Hermosa—neighborhoods and beaches, places that mark transitions from sea to land. The valley of the book on your lap, with its spine nestled between your crossed legs, has its own topography. The *recto* slopes upwards like the land itself, rippling up towards the first ridges of the Andes Mountains. Somewhere in the middle of the page is Pachacamac District, and a closer look reveals ruins. There are walls and streets, windows, stairs. There are remains of buildings with square and rectangular footprints. A city is summoned miraculously from its earthen grave.

The Argentine writer Jorge Luis Borges summoned cities from earthen graves in his 1953 short fiction "The South." He did it with mirrors. "Reality favors symmetries and slight anachronisms," he wrote.[11] It is a way of saying that everything is a reflection of something else, but imperfectly so. A mirror may have a bump or spot that distorts the reflection. Everything looks familiar, but then there is a flaring of light, a fluttering in the reflective fabric—this imperfection is like a hole in a gauzy fabric, gives you a privileged peek into another place, another time. That book on your lap: it reminds you of another book, a map, or even a map in a book. You notice that something is different. In "The South," Borges uses an architectural metaphor to describe this kind of action. Reading a book, crossing a street—each is a secret passage into "a more ancient and sterner world," and like the narrator, you too search in vain for "the new buildings, the iron grill window, the brass knocker, the arched door, the entrance way, the intimate patio"—evidence of a modernity left behind.[12] This is what it is like to be far away in time and space from a building, to see its last traces dissolving into a forgotten realm.

To summon a building, you almost have to avoid it. You avoid the walls, the foundations, the windows. You avoid the forms, the textures, the materials. Instead, you weave around the building. Stories, images, descriptions, histories: these are your threads, these are the warp and weft of building. But these are not the building, which is to say that to write about a building, you have to see it differently—maybe not see it at all. The building is not form, but is formed. Like the cyclonic winds that give a hurricane's eye its center, you write to create a defined void.

You write from above, from below, from outer space, from the Southern Cross, and finally to an underwater current that originates in the South Polar regions. This current moves upwards in a roughly counter-clockwise arc, a gyre that mixes the dense, cold waters with the warmer waters of the South Pacific Ocean as they join those whirling near the equator. It is the Humboldt Current, named after Alexander von Humboldt, who visited Peru in 1803, and it runs in a graceful arc along the coastline, traversing isotherms and merging with the prevailing western winds, churning the waters while bringing the dense, cold stream near to the surface. As the water evaporates, a movement in the upper atmosphere draws moisture away from the coast. This disturbance in the air is a mirror image of the Humboldt Current. Both move in the same direction, dual circuits of air and water in concert, gyrating towards and away from the coast. The current supplies the outlying islands with a supply of deep water fish. On its return West, it draws orphaned seed pods and sweet potato into the ocean. The upper level disturbance—a Walker circulation—sweeps the air away revealing a landscape scarred with ripples and fissures, imperfections that mark the last of these emanations, as if the waters receded and left behind a desert plain. The air is indeed dry here, and in Pachacamac, it appears to be the same air that once was here, circulated and recirculated again as it has been for centuries.

79

1    Arthur O. Lovejoy, *The Great Chain of Being: A Study of the History of an Idea* (Cambridge, Massachusetts: Harvard University Press, 1933), pp. 59, 101.

2    Frederic Jameson, *Archaeologies of the Future: The Desire Called Utopia and Other Science Fictions* (New York: Verso Books, 2005), p. 289.

3    The ANS synthesizer was named after the Russian composer Alexander Scriabin (1871-1915), who incorporated elements of synaesthesia into his orchestral works. The most well-known synaestheste is Vladimir Nabokov, who wrote about his experiences with "colored hearing" in his literary autobiography, *Speak, Memory* (1966).

4    Walter Benjamin, "On Some Motifs in Baudelaire," in Hannah Arendt, ed. *Illuminations* (New York: Schocken Books, 1968), p. 175.

5    Ovid, *Metamorphoses*, VIII 218-21, trans. E.J. Kenney (Oxford: Oxford University Press, 2008), p. 178.

6    Ibid, VIII, pp. 221-30.

7    Thomas Pynchon, *Mason & Dixon* (New York: Henry Holt, 1997), p. 504.

8    Ovid, *Metamorphoses*, VIII 232-40, trans. E.J. Kenney (Oxford: Oxford University Press, 2008), p. 178.

9    Alexander Nemerov, *Wartime Kiss: Visions of the Moment in the 1940s* (Princeton, New Jersey: Princeton University Press, 2015), pp. 3-4.

10    Italo Calvino, *If On A Winter's Night a Traveler*, William Weaver, trans. (New York: Harcourt Brace Jovanovich, 1979), p. 210.

11    Jorge Luis Borges, "The South," in *Ficciones* (New York: Grove Press, 1962 [1956]), p. 169.

12    Ibid.

# ARCHITECTURE, NATURALLY
## Mason White

Architecture has maintained an oddly consistent relationship to notions of nature throughout history. Nature is assumed to be muse and metaphor to architecture. Fast-forwarding through history, consider Vitruvius's 1st century treatise *De Architectura* that celebrated "the truth of nature" as inspiration to architecture.[1] Or, consider Laugier's 1755 allegory *Essai sur L'Architecture* on the primitive hut composed from nature as an origin story of architecture embodying simplicity and purity.[2] And more recently, consider mathematical biologist D'Arcy Wentworth Thompson's 1917 *On Growth and Form*, which served as an inspiration to early generative and computational architecture in the 1990s.[3] These are only a few examples that illustrate the envy by which architecture emulates, references, or adopts aspects of nature. However, as notions of nature have expanded to become increasingly complex and multivalent, architecture's previously singular understanding of its relationship to nature has shifted. In what way have social attitudes toward nature marked and informed architecture's complex relationship with nature today?

While notions of nature have historically provided a powerful and symbolic conceptual partner to design, recent assessments of nature consider it a threat to the stability of architecture. In fact, much of the celebrated technical progress in architecture's materials and detailing since 20th-century modernism relates to developments in environmental control protecting an arguably stable interior from an unpredictable exterior. Advancements in glazing, sealing, insulation, membranes, and material durability are among the celebrated triumphs of architecture over nature. This position articulates a perception of architecture as defending itself from nature and its environment. Be it atmospheric or biological matter, nature is a risk to building performance, destabilizing architec-

serving as metaphor, as perpetuated historically, and offering managed climatic collaboration, as introduced in modernism. How is this relationship negotiated today, and what might new understandings of nature offer to the discipline and practice? A current stocktaking of its relationship with nature reveals these complex pairings:

1. Architecture is increasingly technologically guided; Architecture mimics nature as a muse.
2. Architecture contributes to climate change; Architecture is regulated with sustainability policies.
3. Architecture creates interior climates; Architecture hopes to resist exterior ruin.
4. Architecture hosts nature in its interior; Architecture displaces nature on its exterior.

From these dichotomies, there is little evidence that the field is destined for a stable relationship with nature. It is likely to remain fluctuating, with ever-shifting positions in response to disciplinary interests and societal "matters of concern."[4] However, could a broader understanding of nature as an architectural element offer a more relevant model for contemporary design thinking? Could nature be repositioned as a design matter in architecture?

### POSTHUMANISM TURN

A defining attribute of architecture, generally, is that it is anything 'but' nature. Despite passionate metaphors, inspired imitations, and technical mimicry of nature, architecture is manufactured and assembled by humans for a specific human purpose. Similarly, some theorists and practitioners have also argued that nature itself is manufactured by and for humans, even more so today with advances in bio-engineering and genetic-modification. It is this expansion of the notion of nature has broadened the means by which architecture interacts with nature. Observing current

81

As this agenda unfolded within late modernity, the role of nature in architecture became charged in a complex balance between serving as metaphor, as perpetuated historically, and offering managed climatic collaboration, as introduced in modernism. How is this relationship negotiated today, and what might new understandings of nature offer to the discipline and practice?

ture's desire for environmental control. Architecture environmental success is often measured by the efficacy with which it controls separation from the exterior. Only in limited, managed ways is nature permitted to comingle with the building—through operable windows (with bug screens), air intakes (with filters), rainwater management (with filtration system), and indoor plants (in pots), among them. As this agenda unfolded within late modernity, the role of nature in architecture became charged in a complex balance between

positions in the field's sister discipline of landscape architecture suggests that even it no longer considers pure nature as an aspirational design muse. Instead systems ecology, resilience, and infrastructure serve as contemporary models in landscape architecture. Beyond the mantra of nature as metaphor or nature as material, some contemporary practitioners and theorists have sought out a third way: nature as architectural matter. This is not to argue that architecture is identified as a natural element, but that nature is considered as co-equal within other built matter, such as space, materials, or environment. With this third way comes the potential destabilization of architecture's human bias, which broadens the understanding of nature in architecture in two ways: the biological and the atmospheric. A consideration of recent interest in posthumanism will be relevant to these understandings.

American philosopher Cary Wolfe's 2009 book, *What is Posthumanism?* characterizes the divergent positions of posthumanism as sharing the foundational premise of the "decentering of the human."[5] His broad overview surveys theoretical as well as cultural and artistic practices, including architecture among film, poetry, and music. In the chapter titled "Lose the Building," Wolfe observes two projects that were controversial at the time: the 2000 Downsview Park competition entries, especially the winning submission "Tree City" of OMA and Bruce Mau, and the 2002 Swiss Expo installation "Blur" by Diller Scofidio + Renfro. He cites both as emblematic

highlights as representative of posthumanism in architecture represent two qualifications of nature: the climatic-atmospheric (Blur) and the biological-animal (Downsview Park) element. While it would be suspect that these two projects alone could embody architecture's turn toward posthumanism, there has been more recent substantive evidence that the field's relationship with nature is even more complex than in previous eras. The writing and theoretical positions of Keller Easterling, David Gissen, Catherine Ingraham, and the work and practice of Ants of the Prairie, cero9, R&Sie, Weathers, among others, provides a rich parallel to more conventional notions of architectural sustainability. An interest emerges in these thinkers and practices that is equal part posthumanist in terms of subjectivities, and post-sustainable in terms of technologies. Joyce Hwang, as Ants of the Prairie, courts animals as clients. Cristina Diaz Moreno and Efrén García Grinda, as cero9, use energy systems to construct "another nature."[9] The work of

82

The Blur Building, Swiss Expo 2002, Diller Scofidio + Renfro. Ph. Courtesy of Diller Scofidio + Renfro.

of understanding how to "think anew the relationship of nature and culture."[6] He identifies a radical condition within these projects, of an architecture subsumed by nature to the degree to which there was no building, just nature. For instance, Wolfe cites "Blur" as "an imitation of nature that formally renders the impossibility of an imitation of nature."[7] Instead, the formlessness of Blur realizes the possibility of nature as architectural matter. Nature, in this case as atmospheric material, is equivalent to space, rooms, or walls. While the Blur project is positioned by DS+R as a work of "media," it also calls upon a posthumanist agenda in its integration of a climate, complete with weather and atmosphere, as an inhabitable space. With a similar absence of building, Tree City offered a park with an incremental process in which "vegetal clusters rather than new building complexes will provide the sites identity."[8] Nature is architectural matter.

What might be useful to reflect on from Wolfe's observations is that the two projects he

Weathers, run by Sean Lally, is invested in the spatial potential of gradients in the design of energy and climate in architecture.[10] And, finally, the elusive practice R&Sie are interested in architecture's response to marginal and deviant natures, such as dust or mosquitos.[11] These contemporary architects identify nature in how it produces new subjectivities beyond instrumentality and beyond the human, and see atmospheres, animals, energy, and climate as raw design matter. This produces an architecture that invites nature to participate and collaborate in its making, and which celebrates the posthumanist realm within design. While the narrative of architecture and nature for this young 21st century has predominantly been oriented toward sustainability, posthumanity in architecture offers an emerging counter-narrative. Rather than seeking an ideal human-approved and human-measured 'sustainable' environment, this counter-narrative suggests that architecture and nature produces other environments.

## OTHER ENVIRONMENTS

Caught between architecture and nature are shifting notions of and attitudes toward the environment. The contemporary complexity of environment is productively situated within the purview of both architecture and nature. In nature, environment implies the nuanced immediate world to which nature responds. Theoretical biologist Jakob von Uexküll and his concept of *Umwelt*, or environment-world, illustrates this understanding.[12] Von Uexküll's concept of *Umwelt* was used to identify the perception of an animal's surroundings by filtering and highlighting only aspects that are important to it. Environment-world reveals an edited nature. In architecture, environ-

modern aesthetic with their mechanical capabilities and integrate their expression as "exposed power."[15] Banham also observes that in "freeing architecture from local climatic constraints mechanical environmental management techniques have given *carte blanche* for formal experimentation."[16] This reveals another form of power, the power of architecture to overcome local climate with a manufactured managed interior climate. Banham's revelations on modern architecture's embrace and dependence, and ultimately integration, of mechanical innovations was a visionary re-reading of modern architectural history. However, technical advances and socio-cultural positions on manufactured environments have expanded and deep-

To consider architecture's relationship to nature redirected under the influence of posthumanism and inclusive of other environments, it would benefit to consider four realms in which architecture and nature seem to come into contemporary conflict: climates, ruins, nature outside, and nature inside.

83

ment-world might refer to either a climate-controlled interior or the climate of the exterior. Architecture's *Umwelt* includes both the environment within and around a building. Design attitudes and approaches to these environments in architecture are often reflected in the social attitudes toward nature. This, in turn, establishes an environment-world. Roles and perceptions of nature and environment operate in parallel within design. For example, nature in late modernity offered architecture a validating alibi as *genius loci*.[13] As innovations in climate-control on the interior, and environmental control at the exterior envelope were developed, architecture sought out a controlled consistent atmosphere in contrast to unpredictable exterior environments. This tendency is encapsulated in the colloquial phrase "the great indoors." However, rather than accepting a singular understanding of an environmental ideal in architecture, one oriented exclusively toward human comfort, an alternate understanding of nature broadens the acceptance of 'other' environments. Other environments are inherently posthuman, in that they don't necessarily seek out an ideal conception of comfort. These other environments arise in response to the modern bias of a 'well-tempered' environment.

Reyner Banham's *Architecture of the Well-Tempered Environment* (1969) ushered in a novel and radical understanding of environment in late modernism. Banham's observations on the "well-tempered" environment exposed the intertwined history of environmental management technology and modern architecture.[14] He highlighted the role of the mechanical to achieve idealized atmospheric qualities while accepting the strict aesthetics of modern architecture. Banham recognized the heroes of this balance as Louis Kahn's Richards Memorial Laboratories in Philadelphia (1961), the Architects Division's Queen Elizabeth Hall, London (1967), and Studio Piano & Rogers's Centre Georges Pompidou in Paris (1977). These projects balance the

ened in the ensuing five decades. Maybe architecture has been too subservient to its well-tempered environment. Since Banham, architecture's relationship to environment has been able to suggest many other environments besides a single well-tempered one.

These other environments embody a contemporary unsettled understanding of environment and nature in architecture. David Gissen's *Subnature: Architecture's Other Environments* (2009) highlights a minor narrative within contemporary architecture of the suppression of select natures. If modern architecture had Banham's "well-tempered" environment, then contemporary architecture has Gissen's "subnature." As with Banham's desire to expose the unwritten history of mechanical and environmental control within modern architecture, Gissen seeks to expose the unwritten condition of minor natures within contemporary architecture. Subnature offers an opening for the acceptance of less desirable, yet inevitable, biological and atmospheric matter. Gissen's subnature seeks to recover "denigrated forms of nature" and his theory attempts to identify "a new material-aesthetic between architecture and nature."[17] This includes dust, debris, exhaust as airborne matter, dankness, puddles, mud as watery matter, as well as insects, pigeons, and crowds. Architecture should acknowledge previously considered minor natures. While typically seen as environmentally undesirable and even atmospherically unhealthy, the subnatural is inevitable. Arguably, the emergence of subnature is nature's response to architecture as an unnatural matter. Gissen elucidates that subnature "supports the notion that architecture and the environment are produced simultaneously."[18]

To consider architecture's relationship to nature redirected under the influence of posthumanism and inclusive of other environments, it would benefit to consider four realms in which architecture and nature seem to come into contemporary conflict:

climates, ruins, nature outside, and nature inside. These territorial disciplinary concepts will be expanded upon in relation to new notions of nature in architecture.

## CLIMATES / RUINS

Climate serves a primary role in the complex larger relationship between architecture and nature. Mid-20th century cultural movements in environmentalism and technological innovations celebrated a vision of architecture better integrated with climate. Architects could "solve" climate problems with design innovation and technology that embraced nature. Architectural visionary Buckminster Fuller popularized this promise through his contributions to energy efficiency in design, or "synergetics," with the belief that he wasn't "trying to imitate nature, I'm trying to find the pencil she's using."[19] Fuller's engineered architecture sought to create climates at multiple scales, and he considered architectures interior and exterior responses to climate equally. Most notable to this discussion is Fuller's sustained belief in the dome as an efficient spatial enclosure. Arguably, the dome embodies an *Umwelt* in its own right. Others at the time, such as Victor Olgyay, posited an analytical approach to "climate management" as a precondition for architectural design.[20] An important illustration in Olgyay's study was the bioclimatic chart that visualized an ideal "comfort zone." It is a playfully represented quantitative chart featuring an illustration of a recumbent person reading with labels hovering at the perimeter of this zone, indicating areas on the chart as "too dry," "too humid," "shading needed," or "sunshine needed."[21] The bioclimatic chart illustrates the factors that influence the sought-after, idealized climatic condition. Meanwhile, in terms of energy innovations, prototype solar houses, such as Eleanor Raymond's Dover Sun House, developed at MIT, or George Keck's "House of Tomorrow," imagined climate-responsive modern architecture using technology at the domestic scale.[22] These priorities, for the most part, have remained the dominant narrative of architectural climate. However, there are today those at the frontier of other notions of climate that would include a wider range of atmospherics and ecologies.

essentially a curtainwall system with regulated self-cleaning water and a few frogs.[23] Another project, Living Light, provides a dynamic pavilion in Seoul that uses data collection to visualize air quality issues in the city through light. Other contemporary architects, such as Phillipe Rahm and Sean Lally, have also found ways to integrate climate, and its expression, as a design aspect rather than as something that needs to be solved or as an assumed ideal.

In order to represent the atmospheric representations of climate, drawing has even integrated diagrammatic elements, such as flowing vectors or temperature gradients. Gissen has argued that the vector "becomes an animistic force that fuses the urban environment and architectural object."[24] The descriptive choice of animistic is notable as it positions these vectors as biomatter. This representational practice has expanded to include comprehensive ecosystems, projecting complete cycles of energy and resources. Yet, these vectorial and gradient-based modes of expression are limiting in their participatory possibilities for architecture. They perpetuate a deterministic and scientific bias in architecture's interface with climate—again, environment as a problem to solve rather than an equal realm to establish an exchange with. For example, architectural thinking about pollution, Gissen argues, could "shift further from 'curing' the city of pollution to curating pollution within architecture."[25]

It is also of interest to consider climate, like environment or nature, as a force upon architecture; something that architecture attempts to resist. An ultimate outcome of climate's strongest influence is the detrimental overpowering of architecture: the project in ruin. A ruin presents a glimpse of architecture weakened of its climatic defenses and subjected to the reclaiming force of nature. The broad fascination with architecture in ruin—think "ruin porn"—reveals an underlying wonderment of nature's ability to overcome architecture, to overwhelm and subsume it. Architecture's mortality is exposed. However, arguably, a building undergoing ruin is architecture in its most direct exchange with nature. It is an architecture consumed by the spasm of a natural event or slow incremental subnatural event. Strangely, architecture as a

The broad fascination with architecture in ruin—think "ruin porn"— reveals an underlying wonderment of nature's ability to overcome architecture, to overwhelm and subsume it. Architecture's mortality is exposed. However, arguably, a building undergoing ruin is architecture in its most direct exchange with nature. It is an architecture consumed by the spasm of a natural event or slow incremental subnatural event.

Several projects by the design practice The Living, directed by David Benjamin, embody this type of contemporary agenda. For example, The Living's prototype Amphibious Envelope "re-imagines the insulated glazing unit as a living ecosystem," which is

ruin also expresses its endurance, or lifespan, in the face of various natural forces. Historian David Leatherbarrow and architect Mohsen Mostafavi's book *On Weathering: The Life of Buildings in Time* (1993) observes that "in the mathematics of the environment weathering is a power of subtraction, a minus, under the sign of which newly finished corners, surfaces, and colours are taken away by rain, wind, and sun."[26] They posit that architecture never really is complete until it begins its natural wearing down in the face of climatic and environmental forces. For example, the patina process in several metals creates a chemical compound coating when exposed to natural elements. This process is functional but has also acquired an aesthetic interest such as in the frequent usage of corten steel as cladding to marvel at its visual rot. At a larger scale, the full-body of all the design disciplines has been tasked with resilience to climate change. With climate actions occurring

This reflected modern architecture's contradictory position of nature as elevated enough to be a muse or metaphor, but inferior enough to be used to hide mistakes. Differing approaches appear in regard to the management and design of nature at the exterior versus the interior. Nature in the exterior has produced the lawn, the courtyard, and the garden. Nature in the interior has produced the potted plant. Reconsidering nature's role in surfaces, a more contemporary integrated approach than Wright can be found in the work of Patrick Blanc, a French botanist who has created notable façades composed entirely of plants.[28] Blanc's 2004 façade work on the Quai Branly Museum, designed with Jean Nouvel, is

85

Exhibition view of Shaped Touches by Sean Lally. Venice Biennale, 2021. Ph. Courtesy of Sean Lally.

from multiple directions—above, below, and beside—the call for resilience is a call for architecture to endure and ward off ruining forces. The potential of resilient design suggests architecture that is inclusive and even collaborative with climate. Architecture that does not endure becomes a *memento mori* for architects.

Climate has alternately represented a collaborator in the heating and cooling of spaces and a force pulling architecture into ruin. However, this binary eludes other possibilities of curating climates and coordinating ruin. If architecture is accepted to always produce climates, could climate not begin to function as a spatial and atmospheric matter in design, just as structure, light, and materials are accepted in this way? And could the effects and transformation of ruin be integrated into the design process beyond resilience?

## NATURE OUTSIDE /
## NATURE INSIDE

Equally critical to shifting positions on nature in architecture is the understanding of how nature, as a landscape or ecosystem, is integrated with architecture. Wright famously advised architects who regretted design decisions to cover it in nature. He wryly stated: "The physician can bury his mistakes, but the architect can only advise his client to plant vines."[27] Wright suggested nature as a cover-up to architecture.

of particular note. It is 800 square meters of 15,000 plants from 150 species anchored to a thick felt cover. The only exposed non-natural materials are thinly-framed windows.

Architecture's legacy of associated exterior landscapes includes forays into gardens, lawns, and courtyards. Possessing and manicuring nature associated with architecture is an extension of the mindset of land ownership and property value. Much has been written about the transformation of approaches to these conditions of architecturalized nature. A range of contemporary attitudes emerges; from Aben and de Wit's *The Enclosed Garden* on the courtyard building as an architectural typology; to Teyssot's *The American Lawn*, which chronicled the importance of highly-manicured landscapes in American civic spaces; to Dixon Hunt's *Cultural History of Gardens in the Modern Age*, which documents the evolution of new materials and attitudes in garden-making.[29] The courtyard, arguably the most architectural, provides a room of quarantined nature. It offers a contained oasis of nature, in which it is invited into an interior surrounded by architecture, without entering the building envelope. The courtyard is isolated from its wider territory and has its own Darwinian ecosystem with contributions from the building and its inhabitants. The role of the garden and lawn as landscapes associated with architecture has often been used as a setting for architecture and to again reinforce nature in contrast with architecture.

Even considering the seemingly most minor element of nature in architecture, the potted plant, we find a profound understanding of nature's role. Within high modernism, potted plants have provided evidence of architecture's confidence of controlling and choreographing nature. Nature endures as a symbol (the plant) and confined to a tiny sample of land (the pot). Biology is invited to the interior in a managed way, complete with nourishing soil, as both decoration and status within the domestic. The presence of the interior plant, both as literal nature and as symbol of nature, exploits the plant's "disciplinary ambiguity between horticulture and decoration."[30] Operating in a manner similar to other mobile interior elements, such as furniture or art, nature can be moved around and placed within almost any space. This ability reinforces a sense of control and domestication of architecture over nature. Notably, the ubiquity of potted plants "create situations that defy our expectations of the roles of the interior and the exterior and, in doing so, encourage us to rethink the distinction between these two spatial categories."[31] Even in its smallest gesture, nature inside not only disturbs assumptions of interior and exterior as distinct, but even assumptions of nature and architecture as distinct.

CONCLUSION

Nature as metaphor and muse in architecture will persist as this mode is also reinforced in postmodern creative practices. And nature as quantifiable and scientific alibi toward an ideal spatial condition or design will also persist. But the notion of nature as spatial matter, both biological and atmospheric offers a turn that brings nature in an equivalent position to aspects such as light, space, structure, and material. Reconsidering architecture's relationship to nature under the influence of posthumanism and inclusive of other environments, climates, ruins, nature outside, and nature inside reveal new notions. Similarly, the introduction of subnature and posthumanism in architectural theory releases nature from the strictures of naturalness. Likewise, it offers a potential naturalness to architecture that had been hiding under modern assumptions and biases. Much as Banham offered an "unwarranted apology" with the observation that "the idea that architecture belongs in one place and technology in another" has had a crippling effect on the discipline, the same could be said of architecture and nature.[32] Architecture does not exist in distinction to nature—architecture exists naturally.

1       Vitruvius Pollio, *Ten Books on Architecture,* trans by M. H. Morgan (New York: Dover Publications, 1960).

2       Marc-Antoine Laugier, *Essai sur L'Architecture,* 2nd ed. (Paris, 1755), frontispiece.

3       D'Arcy Wentworth Thompson, *On Growth and Form* (Cambridge: Cambridge University Press, 1917).

4       Bruno Latour, "Why Has Critique Run out of Steam? From Matters of Fact to Matters of Concern," in *Critical Inquiry* (Winter 2004), p. 231.

5       Cary Wolfe, *What Is Posthumanism?* (Minneapolis: University of Minnesota Press, 2009), p. 6.

6       Ibid., p. 203.

7       Ibid., p. 224

8       Julia Czerniak (ed.), *CASE—Downsview Park Toronto* (Munich: Prestel, 2001), p. 74.

9       Sean Lally (ed.), *Architectural Design: Energies,* vol. 79, no. 3 (May/June 2009), p. 77.

10      Ibid., p. 56.

11      "R&SIE: Corrupted Biotopes," in *Design Documents* (vol 5, 2004).

12      Jakob von Uexküll, *A Foray Into the Worlds of Animals and Humans: With a Theory of Meaning,* trans by Joseph D. O'Neil (Minneapolis/London: University of Minnesota Press, 2010).

13      Christian Norberg-Schulz, *Genius Loci: Towards a Phenomenology of Architecture* (New York: Rizzoli, 1979).

14      Reyner Banham, *The Architecture of the Well-Tempered Environment* (Chicago: University of Chicago, 1969).

15      Ibid., p. 234.

16      Ibid., p. 239.

17      David Gissen, *Subnature: Architecture's Other Environments* (New York: Princeton Architectural Press, 2009), p. 21.

18      Ibid., p. 26.

19      Buckminster Fuller, *Buckminster Fuller to Children of Earth* (Garden City: Doubleday & Company, 1972).

20      Victor Olgyay, *Design with Climate: Bioclimatic Approach to Architectural Regionalism* (Princeton University Press, 1963).

21      Ibid.

22      See the excellent Daniel Barber, *A House in the Sun* (Oxford University Press, 2016) for more on solar energy experiments in architecture during the Cold War-era.

23      The Living website: http://www.thelivingnewyork.com/ (Accessed 12 Feb 2019).

24      David Gissen, "A Theory of Pollution for Architecture," in *Imperfect Health: The Medicalization of Architecture,* Giovanna Borasi and Mirko Zardini (eds.) (CCA and Lars Muller Publishers, 2012), p. 122.

25      Ibid., p. 123.

26      Leatherbarrow and Mostafavi, *On Weathering: The Life of Buildings in Time* (Cambridge: MIT Press, 1993), p. 5.

27      1931, Two Lectures on Architecture by Frank Lloyd Wright, To the Young Man in Architecture, (Start Lecture page 33), page 62, The Art institute of Chicago, The Lakeside Press, R.R. Donnelley & Sons Company, Chicago. (HathiTrust).

28      Patrick Blanc, *The Vertical Garden: From Nature to the City* (New York: WW Norton & Co., 2008).

29      Several publications would be of note on this topic, the following serve to illustrate the range of ways in which landscapes have become associated with architecture include: Rob Aben and Saskia de Wit, *The Enclosed Garden: History and Development of the Hortus Conclusus and Its Reintroduction Into the Present-day Urban Landscape* (Rotterdam: 010 Publishers, 1999); Georges Teyssot, *The American Lawn* (New York: Princeton Architectural Press, 1999); John Dixon Hunt, *Cultural History of Gardens in the Modern Age* (London: Bloomsbury Publishing, 2016).

30      Carrie Smith, "A Few Notes on Plants Indoors." Available online at https://www.cca.qc.ca/en/issues/22/ideas-of-living/39966/a-few-notes-on-plants-indoors (accessed 28 December 2018).

31      Ibid.

32      Banham, p. 9.

87

# ORANGE 'BLACK BOXES:' FROM THE TECHNOLOGICAL TO THE THEATRICAL
## Uriel Fogué

### THE TECHNOLOGICAL 'BLACK BOX'

The 'black box' is a device installed to operate imperceptibly in planes, trains, boats and other means of transportation throughout the entire voyage. Indeed, this ingenious little contrivance only becomes visible in the event of a breakdown. When something fails to work as planned—in an accident—the 'black box' is opened to retrieve the information stored in it (such as recordings of conversations in the cockpit or the activity of navigational instruments) for use in reconstructing the scene of the causes leading up to the accident.

The term 'black box' is used in a number of different fields of knowledge. In behavioral psychology, it was used as a metaphor for the unobservable dynamics in stimulus-response relationships. In the field of Science and Technology Studies (STS),[1] 'black box' is a key concept to understanding technological processes that take place invisibly within successful socio-technical transactions, i.e. in contexts in which the technology does its job so efficiently that it actually goes undetected in the background. In the glossary included in his celebrated *Pandora's Hope* (1999), Bruno Latour defines the term "'to blackbox' or to enclose in a 'black box'" as follows:

> an expression derived from the sociology of science that refers to the way scientific and technical work is made

We lead our lives surrounded by technological 'black boxes' that silently operate alongside us. Most of our day-to-day situations are mediated by 'black boxes' that act on different scales, from the space of microphysics[4] to the city or landscape. And yet, they go unseen. 'Black boxes' operate on what some authors have called the "sub-political plane,"[5] a plane intangible for the ordinary world because it sits beyond the realm of formal politics. 'Black boxes' are designed and monitored by experts and, hence, outside the grasp of common citizens. In one way or another, societies delegate to those with expert knowledge the responsibility of conceiving and governing the 'black boxes' on which most of our everyday actions depend.

The very term 'black box' is, in a way, 'blackboxed' in our collective imaginary (which only proves the point on the efficiency and omnipresence of its economy of visibility): airplane 'black boxes' are in fact not black at all, but bright orange.[6]

### OPENING THE BLACK BOX

The very invisibility of these impenetrable forms of technology has given them an aura of mystery, an enigmatic quality that has aroused suspicion and admiration in critics and advocates, respectively.[7]

On one hand, critics from the Foucauldian school see 'black boxes' as tacit forms of distributed power. Power inscribes (or 'blackboxes') forms of domination on materials, things, spaces, places, bodies, and architectures for the purpose of meticulously regulating every aspect of our daily life, from behavior to ergonomics. From this perspective, the everyday world forms a disciplinary constellation, a normative architecture grounded in a 'sub-political' circuit of 'black boxes' through which power's precepts

88

'Black boxes' operate according to normalized processes of input/output: we know what goes into the 'black box' as well as the results and effects of its performance, but we do not know its inner workings because they are hidden from us. 'Black boxes' take shape in a particular way in the "economy of visibility." They are like "hermetic hideouts" that hold particular forms of intelligence and information, which—as we shall see—is a bone of contention for the main critics.

invisible by its own success. When a machine runs efficiently, when a matter of fact is settled, one need focus only on its inputs and outputs and not on its internal complexity.[2]

'Black boxes' operate according to normalized processes of input/output: we know what goes into the 'black box' as well as the results and effects of its performance, but we do not know its inner workings because they are hidden from us. 'Black boxes' take shape in a particular way in the "economy of visibility."[3] They are like "hermetic hideouts" that hold particular forms of intelligence and information, which—as we shall see—is a bone of contention for the main critics.

and logics flow. Daily life is therefore considered highly suspect: the material and symbolic universes all around us are liable to form part of a network charged with the task of disseminating 'enfolded' ('blackboxed') norms of control[8] on everything around us.[9] These critics, then, set out to 'open the black boxes' in order to condemn these implicit forms of power and reveal the architecture of 'microtechnologies' on which the "microphysics of power" is organized.

On the other hand, we have the apologists' position, heirs to Latourian philosophy, who see the 'black box' as the condition that enables social articulation. In this case, the materials, things, spaces, places, bodies, and architectures are construed as constructions, socio-material crystallizations capable of settling the conflicting interests of different actors. From this perspective, the alignment of different agents and the articulated products from the inputs and outputs of the 'black boxes' end up creating durable contexts of coexistence that, in turn, enable us to delegate specific relational skills to bodies. True to Latour's statement "technology is society made durable,"[10] apologists do not see 'black boxes' as a threat; the efficiency of the 'sub-political' plane is exploited to pragmatic ends. Everyday technologies—they argue—are not disciplinary devices, but surfaces of consensus on which specific forms of coexistence are 'enfolded' ('blackboxed') in a sort of material politics based on the delegation of competencies over matter.[11]

Both positions question architectural practice, inviting it to open its 'black boxes' and to rethink itself as a discipline. The first position not only denounces the invisible way that architectural devices

mative illusion" that makes them assume it is imperative to do what 'black boxes' "make (us) do" as.[14]

### 'UNBLACKBOXING' ARCHITECTURE

While these philosophical discussions were taking place, architecture and urban planning took up the notion of the 'black box' as well; adding it to design vocabularies in different ways.

For Buckminster Fuller, the 'black box' was an opportunity to reformulate the principles of settling in a particular environment. Fuller envisioned the 'black box' as an "individual package" that would transform inhabitation in the 20th century. A sort of astronaut's backpack "not much bigger than a good-sized suitcase," his 'black box' would contain everything needed to set up at any "beautiful spot" with the "most advanced standard of living." On the basis of cost and profitability forecasts, he declared that it was ridiculous

89

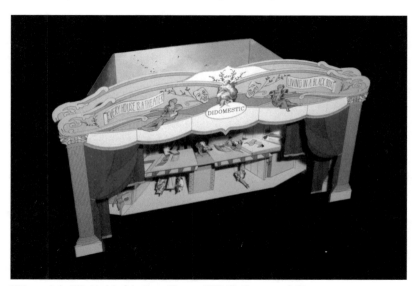

Didomestic by Elii. Model of the Paper Theatre, 2013. Ph. Courtesy of elii.

are designed to steer their users' behavior, but also insists on enforcing policies of transparency to 'unblackbox' spaces. This position criticizes the naiveté, even the connivance, of some of architecture and urban planning, demanding greater commitment in praxis. In contrast, the second position sees architectural design as an opportunity to come up with "a good common world,"[12] to envision frameworks of civility from a socio-material perspective. From this second point of view, architecture, making use of 'black boxes" high standards of performance, is an ideal sphere in which to try out and 'prototype' different forms of social articulation.[13] Both perspectives understand the need to look to the ordinary world as a crucial space for political action, calling for architecture to reexamine the political ecology of its construction processes. This is because architectural design's political battleground is both micro and macro in scale. Both perspectives also take for granted that 'black boxes' actually operate effectively. In other words, there is a degree of "perfor-

to live in urban centers or to rent, often at exorbitant cost, a conventional home. With "your little 'black box,'" "your geodesic dome," and "a beautiful space umbrella," you could live a nomad's life.[15]

At the city scale, geography and urban planning find the image of the technological 'black box' useful to describing the invisible stratum of infrastructures on which the urban metabolism depends. For authors such as Stephen Graham, Simon Marvin,[16] and Maria Kaika[17] modern cities planned along the Haussmannian lines of large-scale urban renewal in the nineteenth and twentieth centuries made use of a dichotomous political ecology based on the 'sub-political' plane of the 'black box'.[18] A 'blackboxed' city lies invisible beneath our feet; side by side with the city where we carry out our everyday activities, it is designed and governed by experts. That city is peopled by what might be called technological inhabitants (infrastructure networks and other city-wide devices) that tirelessly and silently toil to make sure everything is working on "this side."

Steve Hinchliffe[19] takes the idea of the 'black box' to explain the "image of permanence" and "invulnerability" of the infrastructure networks that make modern urban life possible. The phrase "opening in the black box" is used to illustrate "destabilization" of large-scale urban systems.[20] The 1970's witnessed an intensive 'opening' of the urban 'black box' in different settings due to a number of factors, among them the oil crisis; thereby

Architect Andrés Jaque and the Office for Public Innovation describe their project *Cosmo* as "a device to 'unblackbox' water management." A "transmaterial"[24] design developed for MoMA PS1 in 2015, *Cosmo* 'spatialized the black box' in a purifying landscape of plants and pipes suspended in light-weight structures. An app[25] provided information on the process, thereby expanding its scope and turning the 'black box' into

## 'Unblackboxing' is an opportunity to scrutinize 'sub-political' processes, to reexamine the ontological status of agents in the ecosystem, to make way for 'other' ways of interacting with the environment, and to protest against the politics of the body, demanding what urban political ecology calls the "right to metabolism."

altering the 'economy of visibility' of modern cities. What had until then been invisible was now visible—and even became an object of design. New urban renewal programs were thus developed based on the notion of 'spatializing' the processes of 'opening the black box.'

Along these lines, György Kepes, working at the Center for Advanced Visual Studies (CAVS),[21] developed an infrastructure program for the Boston Harbor in 1971 designed not only to make visible some of the processes normally 'blackboxed' in cities (water treatment, for instance), but to turn them into "art and music events."[22] Creators such as Keiko Prince, Mauricio Bueno, and Juan Navarro Baldeweg, among others, developed projects that made the urban ecosystem legible: 'black boxes' shed their invisibility to take on a pedagogical role, thereby ushering in a framework for interaction between the city and its inhabitants that expanded the architectural imaginary.

A number of these ideas would be reformulated years later in projects such as *Parque de la Avenida Diagonal* in Barcelona, developed by Herzog & De Meuron in collaboration with Marceli Meili and Markus Peter (1989); *Parque de La Gavia* in Madrid by Toyo Ito (2003); and the *Whitney Water Purification Facility and Park* by Steven Holl (2005). These projects brought water-purification infrastructures into the public domain, turning the 'black box' into a livable space and giving some of the infrastructural competences back to the commons. Toronto's *Elevated Wetlands* by Noel Garding (1996) furthers the 'unblackboxing' of water treatment, as does the *+Pool* project (in progress). Developed by an interdisciplinary team, *+Pool* consists of floating pools that clean the water in the Hudson River.[23] *One Guy, One Bulldog, One Vegetable Garden And The Home They Share*, a project designed by Plataforma Husos (2018), does something similar on domestic scale: graywater is collected and recycled to water a vertical garden. This project evidences the importance of the body as political space to 'unblackbox' ecosystemic processes and to channel other proximities, challenging the hackneyed dichotomy of public vs. private.

Other practices have taken 'unblackboxing' as an opportunity to question some of the conditions of co-habitation that are usually 'blackboxed.'

something both celebratory and controversial. In her research, architect Nerea Calvillo looks to the concept of the "hybrid black box" to describe infrastructural 'spatialization' on another stratum, one that is usually invisible in modern cities: the air.[26] In projects such as *In the Air*—a mapping tool produced in Madrid in 2008—and *Yellow Dust*—an open-code infrastructure project produced in Seoul in 2017—Calvillo, and her C+ platform, developed spatial interfaces that 'opened the black box' that is the air.[27] That not only made it possible to critically assess environmental policies and discourses, but also enabled citizens to interact with that information to make decisions about their daily lives. In these cases, 'unblackboxing' is an opportunity to scrutinize 'sub-political' processes, to reexamine the ontological status of agents in the ecosystem, to make way for 'other' ways of interacting with the environment, and to protest against the politics of the body, demanding what urban political ecology calls the "right to metabolism."[28]

In the transition from the industrial city to the city based on the cultural industry that took place in the last thirty years of the 20th century, a number of constructions that formed part of cities' large-scale technological networks and, as such, of their 'black boxes' underwent ambitious restoration projects. Some former 'black boxes' were repurposed into modern 'white cubes:' the Zeche Zollverein[29] coal mine, was reopened in 1986 as a cultural space; the celebrated Bankside power station in London, built by Giles Gilbert in 1955, was turned into the Tate Modern in 2000 in a project by Herzog & de Meuron. Like fetishes,[30] these buildings embody the memory of their modern and industrial heritage as infrastructure.

One final use of the term 'black box' is in the sphere of architecture criticism and history. "'Black Box:' The Secrecy Profession of Architecture," written by architecture critic Reyner Banham and published posthumously in *New Statesman and Society* in 1990, uses the 'black box' concept to refer to a type of architecture-specific knowledge that is hidden even to architects. Guarded in the 'black box,' he argues, is a form of knowledge that bestows principles of legitimacy on the discipline to draw the line between what architecture is and what it is not. Accordingly, architects use those principles to put into practice a set of shared—and yet "unnamable"—assumptions underlying concepts. In short, this "secret value system," upheld and validated by the vast majority of architects, becomes in itself a particular form of power, namely, power over the historical narrative, power to decide who belongs to the tribe of architects. A tribe that could well close ranks and resist *opening the black box,* operating like "a conspiracy of secrecy, immune from scrutiny, but perpetually open to suspicion, among the general public, that there may be nothing at all inside the *black box* except a mystery for its own sake."[31]

### THE THEATRICAL 'BLACK BOX'

I would like now to point out another use of the term 'black box.' In the performing arts, the 'black box' refers to the place that constitutes the stage, whether in a theater or in any other venue. It is, then, an area designated for performance. In this case, the name does, in fact, reflect the color: the theatrical box is usually black to make it easier to control shadows and other lighting and visual effects that work together with other spatial, acoustic, and staging tools to compose the different sets. It is an architectural structure designed for performing and experimenting with different types of action. The one thing that characterizes stage is its flexibility: it can be adapted to fit any kind

Fuller, but North American artist Loïe Fuller.[33] In the view of artist La Ribot, "engaging the vastness of the 'black box' [is] one of her greatest—most abstract and far-reaching—contributions. Loïe Fuller overrode the concrete in the scene. She proposed a theatrical space of sheer experimentation."[34] For La Ribot, the 'black box' as conceived by Fuller is, fundamentally, a space for experimentation.

Fuller's design was groundbreaking not only because it could handle a wide range of technical requirements and was so original in typological terms. It was pioneering chiefly because it actually turned the stage into a laboratory, a space fully outfitted with then state-of-the-art technology to make radical experimentation possible: "Loïe Fuller brought to the stage the major inventions of the day: electricity, fluorescence, chemistry, and printed colors. In some subtle way, the black background engaged in a dialogue with the symbolism of its times while also looking to the future."[35] Fuller challenged the idea of a static space "where nothing changes to make everything change." The 'black box' was not only a support in which to undertake theatrical experiments, but itself became an object of research: the architecture was (also) the experiment.

After questioning the theatrical 'black box' and the conventions of performance, a number of artists, performers, choreographers, and directors went on to question the 'black box's' very architecture, ad-

91

The theater's 'black box' is an experimental space, a laboratory where inventions and prototypes are tested out. It is a place for understanding not only what has happened (the past)—which is what the 'black boxes' in airplanes are for—but also to interpret what is happening (the present) and what is about to happen (the future). It is a framework in which to question the very space in question.

of performance (a play, dance, performance art, etc.). Consequently, it is a support where nothing changes, so that everything can change; the stage is a stable yet mutating architecture that enables a particular sort of experience: the viewer's collective individuality.

The typology of performance spaces, and of the 'black-box' device in particular, has changed in the modern era. Since the time Bayreuth's "magic box" opened in 1876—Richard Wagner, with the counsel of Gottfried Semper and Otto Bruckwald,[32] was directly involved in its construction—stages have undergone astonishing transformations. The theatrical 'black box' has evolved in parallel to the arts, in types of audiences, and in the sociological contexts. While for a long time the stage structure remained basically unchanged, today there are as many types of performance spaces as there are theatrical formats. Many contemporary practices break through the limits of the 'black box,' to explore other spatial settings for their experiments.

One of the key moments in the development of the 'black box' stage came about with the innovations carried out by Fuller—not Buckminster

vocating a more direct experience in other spaces, such as the visual arts' 'white cube.' Ribot herself works with the idea of the "black cube" to suggest an intermediate space between the theatrical apparatus and the museum's regime of the white cube.[36] Artist Philipp Gehmacher suggests moving into "gray space" (*Grauraum*[37]) as a third option, one that goes beyond both the 'black box' and the 'white cube.' Claire Bishop even referred to the matter sarcastically as "fifty shades of gray."[38] The paradox is that the theater's 'black box,' insofar as space of experimentation, might actually end up invalidating its own architectonic configuration as a 'black box.'

But what interests us here is to note this other conception of 'black box,' a 'black box' different from the one described above. The theater's 'black box' not only acts as a performance device that joins planes of the visible and the invisible, but is also—from this other perspective—a space technologically outfitted[39] to house experiments of diverse natures (architectural, spatial, technical, theatrical, live arts, set design, material, performance, choreographic, experiential, narrative, fictional, discursive, political, aesthetic, scientific), experiments bound to forms of public participation, to imaginaries, to time, to the body, to technology, and even to intellectual property.[40] From this point of view, the theater's 'black box' is an experimental space, a laboratory where inventions and pro-

nor the convention of the viewer would exist were it not for the invisible technology of 'black boxes.' Furthermore, both one and the other deploy tacit forms of power, prescriptive frameworks that determine certain planes of authority, politics of the body, hierarchies and axes of vision, norms for articulating

In The Air by Nerea Calvillo and collaborators. Ph. Courtesy Nerea Calvillo.

totypes are tested out. It is a place for understanding not only what has happened (the past)—which is what the 'black boxes' in airplanes are for—but also to interpret what is happening (the present) and what is about to happen (the future). It is a framework in which to question the very space in question.

### THE TECHNOLOGICAL 'BLACK BOX' VERSUS THE THEATRICAL 'BLACK BOX'

There are clear parallels between the stage 'black box' and the technological 'black box.' To start with, the former depends on the latter: the stage 'black box' relies on the support of an array of technological 'black boxes,' such as the backstage, the gridiron and other technologies that imperceptibly toil to ensure the performativity of the staged action and to maintain the illusion of the representation. Likewise, as elements that articulate spheres of visibility and invisibility, technological 'black boxes' also partake of a theatricality: the relationship between what is hidden and what is shown to the public involves a kind of stagecraft. Moreover, they also have a choreographic dimension, since their performance depends on the coordination of the actors' agencies that are involved. There is also a parallel between the urban 'black box' and the theatrical 'black box:' both render invisible a series of technological processes for the sake of a bourgeois experience of space based on a structure of representation, whether in the public realm—a sort of stage supported by a backstage of infrastructure—or in the realm of the theater, including the audience, "protected" in the dark. Neither the figure of the *flâneur*[41]

the common, definitions of what is possible, etc. More or less explicitly, both 'black boxes' spatialize power relations, reaffirming conventions of the performance, the distribution of roles and skills, social inertias, behavioral biases, mandates on what is supposed to be experienced, the decisive role of experts, etc. At the same time, they both act as devices of socialization on different levels and as spaces of individual and community experiences of perception. In the case of Loïe Fuller, the 'black box' also acted as a space of mediation that enabled her not only to share a number of her innovations with a broader public,[42] but also to come into contact with some of the most outstanding scientists of the time, like Thomas Alva Edison,[43] Marie and Pierre Curie, Camille Flammarion, and Charles Henry.[44] Finally, there is a degree of similarity between their respective 'unblackboxing' processes: just as technological 'black boxes' were beginning to be opened, theatrical 'black boxes' were likewise being questioned as devices of representation and support for performance in artistic praxis.[45]

However, the technological 'black box' and the theatrical 'black box' also differ greatly in a number of ways. For example, in relation to risk management, while both are based on logics and languages of assurance and precaution aimed at minimizing contingency and accident, the theater's 'black box' (at least in Fuller's terms) is also a means to modulate and experiment with risk. Whereas the technological 'black box' is articulated in a vocabulary of experts, of positive knowledge, and of controlling the facts, the theatrical 'black box' affords experimentation with other vocabularies and other registers, such as artistic language, and therefore with other formulations that are not restricted to forensic evidence or proof, but that can evoke fictions, ghosts, and other spectral ontological entities. While it is true that the theatrical 'black box' allows for rigorous control over the actions, it can also be used, as we have seen, as a small testing ground, open to vast uncertainty. "Control" here is at the service of the performance and of experimentation. A number of scientists of the period recognized the sense of risk and innovation in Fuller's "electric" and "kaleidoscopic" 'black box.'[46] She even used her own

tecture, Cedric Price designed a project with an entirely different way of addressing the problem of the theatrical 'black box' and the city: the Fun Palace for London (1960); a sort of architectural infrastructure designed to activate scenes of enjoyment and pleasure and to encourage interactions between citizens, the Fun Palace[53] was more programmatic and less symbolic in its approach. Here, the architecture itself was a large-scale scenery-rigging system—not because it included spaces equipped for theatrical or audiovisual performances, but because the "palace" was configured

Domestic spaces are part of a network of spaces that condition and guide the construction of personal subjectivity and identity. This domestic 'black box' (which is not devoid of technological 'black boxes') designs conditions for experimentation with that subjectivity and identity. In this domestic support, the users can experiment on themselves, 'fictionalize' their life, characterize themselves in different ways, try out ways of living, and challenge social norms.

93

body in her theatrical laboratory, risking her health by testing out different technologies and radioactive substances.[47] Another difference between the technological 'black box' and the theatrical 'black box' has to do with time. If the output of the technological 'black box' is based on the logic of chronological time,[48] the output of the theatrical 'black box' is beyond measure, open to the time of events as they unfold, to the mysterious and the unfathomable.

These two meanings of the 'black box' concept may be seen as a merely casual coincidence in terminology. However, they may also be construed instead as an opportunity to broaden the technological notion of 'black box' that is normally used in architecture.

### 'BLACK BOXES' FOR URBAN EXPERIMENTS

When we think about the relationship between architecture and theater, what inevitably comes to mind are some of the most paradigmatic images of postmodern culture from the second half of the twentieth century. We think of Teatro del Mondo, the "floating" and "borderline" structure Aldo Rossi designed for the 1979-80 Venice Biennale, or the scale model of the Teatrino Scientifico[49] he nicknamed the "theater of memory."[50] We recall Denise Scott Brown and Robert Venturi's neo-mannerist[51] reflections on the theatricality of architecture and the city,[52] whether in their attempt to reconcile history or in their fascination with commercial vernacular iconography. Either way, both architects' approach to the problem of the theater was symbolic and figurative at core. Insofar as experimental, the notion of the theatrical 'black box' provides a means to rethink the architectural space beyond the paradigm of re-presentation.

A few years before Venturi published his famous Complexity and Contradiction in Archi-

like an enormous 'black box' with moveable walls, flooring, ceiling, and passageways, as well as fly systems and cranes to move parts of sets. It even had an "artificial cloud to keep you cool or make rainbows for you." The Fun Palace would never close and would urge users to actively participate in designing its physical layout. "It's up to you how to use it,"[54] explains the British architect in the project description. It should come as no surprise that the original idea for The Fun Palace actually came from Joan Littlewood, a theater producer in those days with whom Price often collaborated. One of the aims of their projects was to try to move the performing arts out of their formal and normed venues in the bourgeois tradition and into daily life. For Littlewood, the Fun Palace should be a sort of "laboratory of fun." And it had an expiration date. "It must last no longer than we need it"[55] (according to Price, ten years), because experimental 'black boxes' must be updated and adapted to each era.

For Rem Koolhaas, Venturi/Scott Brown and Price[56] are connected by a fascination with the ordinary. In its way, Fun Palace also participates in that attraction to everyday things, both in its engagement with popular street culture (Littlewood called Fun Palace the "university of the streets") as well as in its use of conventional industrial technology solutions. As Arata Isozaki affirms,[57] Fun Palace is a sort of architectural hardware that can be programmed and re-programmed for each use to intensify citizens' 'performative' experience. This hardware-in-building-form provides the conditions for an experimental living; its aim is to "provoke events," not to anticipate them. Though many of the activities that were envisaged to take place there were urban or metropolitan, Price stated at the time that "it will also create new activities, at present without name."[58] It thus becomes a great theatrical 'black box' that open up to the public to perform the (as yet) unnamed.[59]

The Fun Palace is not, however, without contradiction. Just as, through its drawings, it materialized an inhabitable version of the theatrical 'black box' on an urban scale, it can be argued that it also deployed a 'black-boxed' political technology for use by the society of the spectacle and of working-class entertainment. On the other hand, it can equally be claimed to represent a very specific way of understanding experimentation analogically by appealing to a particular type of active citizenry. Either way, the Fun Palace's influence has been vast.

## INHABITING THE 'BLACK BOX'

In their exhibition "Spaces without Drama, or Surface is Illusion, but So Is Depth,"[60] Ruth Estévez and Wonne Ickx investigated the range of affinities between a number of contemporary architectural practices and the stage, from their systems of representation to their conception of space. This is no coincidence: the theatrical conception of space has been a key issue in modern architecture, as Beatriz Colomina explains in her analyses of domestic interiors by Adolf Loos. "The inhabitants of Loos's homes are both actors and spectators in the theatre of the family". This is not only true of the Josephine Baker House (1928), which had been thought of as a performance space. Indeed, in other cases, "Loos eliminates the box seat of public theatre to place it in the 'private theatre' of the home". Thus, at the Müller House (1930) or the Moller House

Madrid, is conceived as a transformable stage that enables its user, a young woman who recently moved out of her family home, to test out a new life, to experiment with this new phase. *Didomestic* incorporates a number of elements to make the space easy to transform: walls, ceilings, and floors are equipped with a set of devices that enable multiple domestic configurations in order to intensify the performative and choreographic dimension[63] of home, thereby enriching the experience of its inhabitant. Sliding panels, secret hatches, foldable contraptions, adaptable compartments, and furniture that dangles from the ceiling with pulleys and cranks are some of the elements that can deploy different domestic scenes and choreographies. The devices make up the rigging system of a "domestic theater" and enable the props and equipment of daily life to appear and disappear as needed. The project not only encourages the space's functional versatility, it also enables—without requiring—experimenting with daily life.

Domestic spaces are part of a network of spaces that condition and guide the construction of personal subjectivity and identity. This domestic 'black box' (which is not devoid of technological 'black boxes') designs conditions for experimentation with that subjectivity and identity. In this domestic support, the users can experiment on themselves, 'fictionalize' their life, characterize themselves in different ways, try out ways of living, and challenge social norms. It is not so

94

It is impossible to envision the world without 'black boxes.' They form part of the 'economy of visibility' that gives shape to reality: whenever one thing is shown, another is invariably hidden (and vice versa). How to articulate the spheres of the visible and the invisible is one of the challenges of our time and one of architecture's collective projects.

(1929), the furniture, curtains, mirrors, openings, visual connections, etc. comprise stage-like interiors that trap and control the viewer's gaze in this type of "home box seats." This is an observational mechanism that "produces the subject" because it "precedes and frames its occupant." In each case, the dwelling is projected as a machine that enables a certain 'economy of visibility,' for performing the "domestic melodrama."[61]

Apropos this point, I would like, if I may, to mention a project designed at Elii, our architecture firm, to explain a slightly different theatrical conception of domestic living from the one described above. The *Didomestic*[62] project (2013) was likewise conceived as "domestic theatre," but not so much on the visual plane (to draw one's gaze) as on the experiential plane, in its 'performative' dimension. Thus, rather than explore the relationship between the box seat and the stage, it explores the fly space high above the stage for hanging set pieces and its relationship with the stage. *Didomestic* is an "inhabitable 'black box'" that in this case carries the experimental dimension of the theatre's 'black box' over to the domestic space. Here, a small attic space located in downtown

much about acting out "domestic melodramas" as it is about re-writing and experiencing them. Of course, the theatrical 'black box' is not the only experimental or flexible space possible. Other sorts of experiments require other architectures, some of them without rigging systems or moveable elements. But in this domestic 'black box,' however, the inhabitant also ends up being both the audience and the actor, viewer and performer, choreographer and dancer,[64] though not so much at the moment of the performance, the re-presention of a social script, as happens with Loos's interiors, but at the time of the process of creation itself.

It should come as no surprise that, in its relation to the space, this work draws on other stagings used in fiction, contemporary with Loos's houses, such as the house in Buster Keaton's *The Scarecrow* (1920),[65] a transformable dwelling full of things that appear and disappear, where technology is at the service of the unexpected in a domestic space, where things are not literal, where—at the slightest physical provocation—anything can turn into something else. After all, theatrical 'black boxes' are, ultimately, the architectures of fiction. And, though they are not the only spaces where fiction can ensue or experiments can be performed, they do facilitate and accelerate both of those processes.

In one final version of the 'black box,' the flexibility of the space is due not to the use of certain theatrical technologies that users activate, but to a set of conditions that, together, heighten the space's potential, inviting (and inciting) users to appropriate the space in different choreographies of bodies and objects. For Jun Aoki, projects that "allow people to imagine a more positive way to use a building and to

they undertook a careful geometric study of the space and devised a felicitous systematic distribution of the different areas. That allowed them to expand points of interaction and to reduce server spaces, thus enabling things to happen, that is, heightening the potential of the spaces in a sort of "playground." The publication you are reading right now features a number of projects that operate according to this logic. Alongside this article there is an account of Tower 41 (2012-14) in Mexico City, designed by Alberto Kalach.[68] The building takes the shape of a set of seemingly undefined

Tower 41 by Alberto Kalach. Ph. Florencia Rodriguez.

live"[66] constitute a "different [form of] flexibility," one that is being tested out in some works by Kazuyo Sejima, such as the Stadstheater in Almere (1998-2006).[67] In that facility dedicated to stage productions, flexibility does not reside in the fact that "everything changes so that the use can change," but rather in the notion that "nothing changes so that everything can change." Rather than design a state-of-the-art device to alter the spaces literally, the SANAA firm came up with a spatial strategy based on indetermination. First,

spaces ready to be defined through use. The dimension of each floor and the generous height of the various spaces resting on reinforced concrete walls and steel façade entails superimposing ambiguous environments that accommodate different uses. The design is thus in keeping with Aoki's maxim, "flexibility is another word for adaptability."[69]

In these projects, the private also enters into the domestic, not to reaffirm it, but to question it and turn it into an experimental 'matter.'

## CONCLUSION: 'UNBLACKBOX' OR 'REBLACKBOX'?

It is impossible to envision the world without 'black boxes.' They form part of the 'economy of visibility' that gives shape to reality: whenever one thing is shown, another is invariably hidden (and vice versa). How to articulate the spheres of the visible and the invisible is one of the challenges of our time and one of architecture's collective projects.

This text has aimed to underscore the importance of the multifaceted concept of the 'black box' for architecture. It has shown how the technological 'black box' and processes of 'unblackboxing' have influenced the imaginary of architecture and urbanism in recent years, revamping the agenda of the "tribe of architects." The performing arts, meanwhile, have provided us with a different understanding of the 'black box,' one based on experimentation with the space. Both conceptions provide an array of interesting opportunities to act on reality. The challenge may well be to imagine spaces constructed on the basis of a twofold movement: 'unblackboxing' (that is, opening up 'black boxes' of one sort or another to show the processes they 'invisibilize,' to re-assemble 'sub-political' planes, to question modes of representation passed down from modernity, and to reformulate the role of experts) and 'reblackboxing' (that is, inhabiting 'black boxes' of one sort or another to recover the value of fiction, to rearticulate the theatrical relationship between the visible and the invisible, to manage risk, and to lead lives that are experimental in different ways).

'Reblackboxing' means "cheating typology." It means putting fiction's tools into practice. It is not for naught that architecture is—among other things—a science of fiction.[70] If it is true that, as Latour states, "technology is society made durable," it is no less true that fiction is also "society made durable."

96

1        Woolgar, S., *Ciencia: Abriendo la Caja Negra* (Barcelona,: Ed. Anthropos, Editorial del Hombre, 1991), p. 59.

2        Latour, B., *La esperanza de Pandora* (Barcelona: Ed. Gedisa, 2001), p. 362.

3        Michel Foucault used this concept to refer to ways of articulating the planes of the visible and of the invisible in the context of specific power configurations. Foucault, M., *Vigilar y castigar. Nacimiento de la prisión* (Madrid: Ed, Siglo XXI, 1978), p. 192.

4        Ibid.

5        "Sub" here does not mean a lesser category of politics, but rather a position at the margins of formal politics. Marres, N. y Lezaun, J., "Materials and devices of the public: an introduction," in *Economy and Society* 40.4. (2011), p. 491.

6        To make it easier to locate after an accident.

7        Domínguez Rubio, F. y Fogué, U., "Unfolding the political capacities of design," in Yaneva & Zaera-Polo (Eds.), *What is Cosmopolitical Design?* (Farnham: Ashgate, 2015).

8        Ibid.

9        Foucault viewed school desks, for example, as forms of 'enfolded' power that build bodies. Ibid.

10       Latour, B., "La tecnología es la sociedad hecha para que dure" in VV. AA., *Sociología Simétrica. Ensayos sobre ciencia, tecnología y sociedad*, Domènech, M. and Tirado, Fco. J. (eds.) (Barcelona, Ed. Gedisa, 1998), pp. 109-142.

11       Though that consensus often brings other sorts of controversies. Hence, the pacified image of the social as stable or "durable" is limited to the symbolic regime, Latour, 2001.

12       Cf. Stengers, I., "The Cosmopolitical Proposal," in VV. AA. *Making Things Public*, Bruno Latour and Peter Weibel (Eds.), (Cambridge MA: MIT Press, 2005), pp. 994-1003.

13       This is how Latour understands, for example, speed bumps on roads, that is, as a socio-material articulation that works out a collective controversy. Latour, 2001.

14       It is important to bear in mind the scale of "delegation"-based solutions: what works on a small scale may well not work on a larger scale. To what extent skill delegation is scalable must be explored.

15       "The World of Buckminster Fuller" (1971), directed by Baylis Glascock and Robert Snyder, United States, Robert Snyder Films.

16       Graham, S. y Marvin, S., *Splingtering Urbanism. Networked Infrastructures, Technological Mobilities and the Urban Condition,* (London and New York: Routledge, 2001), pp. 178-216.

17       Kaika, M., *City of Flows: Modernity, Nature, and the City* (New York, Routledge Taylor & Francis Grou., 2005).

18       Domínguez and Fogué, 2013.

19       Hinchcliffe, S., "Technology, power and space–the means and ends of geographies of technology," *Environment and Planning D_ Society and Space*, 14, (1996), pp. 659-82.

20       Graham and Marvin, 2001; Kaika, 2005.

21       CAVS was founded by György Kepes at the Massachusetts Institute of Technology (MIT) in 1967. Kepes, G., *Arts of The Environment (Vision + Value Series)* (New York, Braziller, 1972).

22       Wechsler, J., *György Kepes the MIT years, 1947-1977* (Cambridge, Massachusets: MIT Press, 1978), p. 15.

23       See https://www.pluspool.org/pool/

24       Jaque, A., *Politicas transmateriales/ Transmaterial politics* (Madrid, Ministerio Educación y Cultura 2017).

25       See http://cosmomomaps1.com/

26       Calvillo, N., *Sensing+Aeropolis*. Doctoral thesis. Madrid, Departamento de Ideación Gráfica de Arquitectura, Escuela Técnica Superior de Arquitectura de Madrid, Universidad Politécnica de Madrid, 2014.

27       Ibid.

28       VV. AA., *Escenarios del cuerpo. La metamorfosis de Loïe Fuller,* Herrera, Aurora, Ribot, María José y Buitrago, Ana (Ed.), (Madrid: Gecesa-La Casa Encendida, 2014), p. 12.

29       Ivancic, A., *Energyscapes* (Barcelona: Ed. Gustavo Gili. Land & Scape Series, 2010), p. 119.

30       Kaika, M. y Swyngedow, E., "Fetishizing the modern city: the phantasmagoria of urban technological networks" in *International Journal of Urban and Regional Research,* 24 (1) 2000, pp. 122-148.

31       Banham, R.,"A black box. The secret profession of architecture" in *A Critic Writes. Essays by Reyner Banham* (Londres: University of California Press, 1991).

32       Wagner, R., *Art Life Theories of Richard Wagner* (Nueva York, ed. H. Holt., 1889); Quesada, F., *La caja mágica. Cuerpo y escena.* (Barcelona: Arquia/Tesis n. 17, Arte y Arquitectura, 2005).

33       Lista, G., *Loïe Fuller: danseuse de la Belle Époque* (Paris, Stock/Editions d'Art Somogy, 1994) http://www.danceheritage.org/fuller.html

34       VV. AA., 2014, p. 35.

35       Ibid.

36       See http://www.laribot.com/work/56

37       See https://www.kaaitheater.be/en/agenda/my-shapes-your-words-their-grey; http://www.philippgehmacher.net

38       Bishop, C. "Black Box, White Cube. Fifty Shades of Grey?" In: *RA3 Cultural Transformation and Performativity Studies*, (International Graduate Center of the Study of Culture, Universitat Giessen, 5 June 2017).

39       Her work is an indivisible mix of dance, theater, and technology. The technological elements Fuller tested out in the box included phosphorescent materials, salt printing, X-rays, backlit floors, kaleidoscope-like structures of nails with faceted heads placed on the edge of the stage to reflect and decompose projected light, specular devices that multiplied images to produce an effect of irreality, etc. Ibid and Sperling, J. (2012) "Loïe Fuller" in *Dance Heritage Coalition*. Available online: http://www.danceheritage.org/treasures/fuller_essay_sperling.pdf

40       Fuller patented a number of devices for costumes, staging, etc., as reported in *Scientific American*. Ibid, p. 13.41 A number of writers have pointed out women's 'blackboxed' role in making up the modern public space. Wolff, J., "The invisible Flâneuse. Woman and the Literature of Modernity" in *Theory, Culture & Society*, vol. 2, no. 3 (November 1985), p. 41.

42       The 1900 Paris Exposition had a pavilion on Fuller's work designed by Henri Sauvage. VV. AA., 2014.

43       Fuller worked with a number of Edison's companies in New Jersey before she opened her own laboratory in Paris in. Ibid., pp. 10-14.

44       And some figures in high society, like Queen Marie of Rumania. Ibid.

45       Alan Kaprow demanded the use of the 'white cube' for his 'happenings' in New York in 1959. Kaprow, A., *Assemblage, Environments and Happenings* (New York: Abrams, 1966); Quesada, 2014, pp. 160-181.

46       This earned her the nickname "the electric fairy".

47       VV. AA., 2014.

48       Although, from a Latourian perspective, time is considered to be a result of the networks, which would imply a notion of time associated with the technological 'black boxes' closer to the time of the event rather than linear time.

49       Estévez, R. e Ickx, W., *Spaces Without Drama, or Surface is Illusion, but so is depth* (Chicago: Graham Foundation, Feb-May 2017).

50       Rossi, A., *Autobiografía científica* (Barcelona, Gustavo Gili, 1998), pp. 79-85.

51       Venturi, R. y Scott Brown, D., *Architecture as Signs and Systems for a Mannerist Time* (Cambridge, Massachusetts and London, The Belknap Press of Harvard University Press, 2004).

52       Ibid.

53       Price, C., *The Square Book*.(West Sussex: Wiley Academy 2003), pp. 60-61.

54       Ibid., p. 30.

55       Ibid., p. 31.

56       Koolhaas also mentions the Smithsons, Ibid., p. 6.

57       Ibid., p. 35.

58      Ibid., p. 56.

59      The *Fun Palace* is featured in the chapter of *Square Book* entitled "Uncertainty and delight in the unknown."

60      Estévez and Ickx, 2017.

61      Colomina, B., *Privacy and Publicity. Modern architecture as Mass Media* (Cambridge: Massachusetts Institute of Technology, 1994), p. 158.

62      See http://elii.es/portfolio/didomestic/; https://youtu.be/lVEi86-3850; https://youtu.be/TJ52-pkAKao.

63      On the choreographic dimension of the space, see Spanberg, M., "Post-dance, an Advocacy." Available online: https://spangbergianism.wordpress.com/2017/04/

64      A number of Elii's projects engage the idea of the technological 'black box,' among them Árboles Urbanos,

Insider, and P.N.S. General Vara del Rey). This project, however, explores the theatrical 'black box.' www.elii.es

65      Fogué, U., Gil, E. y Palacios, C., (*What is Home Without A Mother (Living in a Black Box)* (Madrid: HIAP, Matadero, Madrid, 2015).

66      Aoki, J. "La Flexibilidad de Kazuyo Sejima" in *Pasajes de Arquitectura y Crítica nº 29 Especial Japón* (Septiembre 2001), pp. 50-51.

67      The design is authored by SANAA (Kazujo Sejima + Ryue Nishizawa).

68      See https://www.kalach.com/torres-1#/tax/

69      Aoki, 2001.

70      Fogué, Gil, and Palacios, 2015.

# POROUS DESIGN: THE VALUE OF VOIDS, PASSAGEWAYS, AND OTHER NON-FUNCTIONAL SPACES IN CITIES AND BUILDINGS[1]
## Sol Camacho

An early application of the concept of "porosity" to buildings and cities can be found in Walter Benjamin and Asja Lacis's 1925 description of Naples.[2] The pair described the city as being as porous as the stone upon which it was built, understanding porosity not only as a set of material qualities, resulting from the building of courtyards, little passages, and small alleys, but also as an architectural ethos, a measurement of the reach and vivacity of social life. In a porous city, every place is available for inhabitance, be it for intermittent or short amounts of time.

For Benjamin and Lacis, porosity is based on a "passion for improvisation, which demands that space and opportunity be at any price preserved."[3] A porous city—or building, if one extrapolates—is, therefore, less defined by a temporal simultaneity of activities, although these might very well be present, and more by its ability to provide space for a multiplicity of activities, in qualitative sorts. The forms corre-

or triple-height corridor with glass skylights.[4] While most of their European counterparts were fitted into the modern plans and urban designs of the 19th century, the São Paulo's *galerias* occurred mostly in a moment of late modernity and dealt with modernism as a well-established architectural rhetoric.

As a product of their time and place, *galerias* are also shaped by the constructive technologies more widely available at the time of their design. Throughout the 20th century, concrete consolidated its ubiquitous position as the choice material for any large-scale construction in Brazil, and it holds that title until this day. Both *galerias* and other less commercially-oriented contemporaries share constructive techniques and overall material and structural expression, shaped by the tectonics of reinforced concrete. The material's ascendance as the standard option is such that it even obstructs the sustainable development of other technologies in a free market panorama. It does hold particular merits: it demands less specialized knowledge in construction while still providing for a tectonic structural system and the entailing solutions, including the possibility of openness and formal experimentation.

Fontenele notes how the porous *galerias* contrast against the Corbusian *Ville Radieuse* convention of fully-opened ground floors interrupted only by the quasi-virtual volumes of the *pilotis* that hold the towers above. A departure from those expec-

99

> A porous city—or building, if one may extrapolate—is, therefore, less defined by a temporal simultaneity of activities, although that might very well be present, and more by its ability to provide space for a multiplicity of activities, in qualitative sorts.

sponding to such respect for improvisation are also multiple, a coexistence of scales and levels of open and closed-ness. Conceptual refinement, or reduction to an all-encompassing drawing gesture are out of the question. Porous architecture is not one of simplicity or easy apprehension.

Furthermore, porosity is interconnected with a city's urban dimension and collective subjectivity. It is a design mechanism that allows built form to operate with a degree of freedom and adaptability that cannot be reproduced in a completely mechanical way. One way to translate Benjamin's reading on urban porosity in the Americas is to illustrate the experience of improvisation and connectivity through/within the galerias of downtown São Paulo.

São Paulo's *galerias* are situated at the intersection of architecture and urban design. Most were built between the 1940s and 1960s and are connected to an office or mixed-use tower; they are comprised of inner walkways that join two or more streets, and sometimes extend across multiple levels. Architect Sabrina Fontenele, who researched modern buildings in downtown São Paulo, states that, unlike the original French arcade, the Brazilian *galerias* usually connect two or more streets and do not have a central double

tations, *galerias* are "areas of passage and coexistence,"[5] still intrinsically modern in the sense that they reflect aspirations of a modern society, public life, of consumption both of goods and culture. The occupation of the ground floor by material structures does not configure an obstruction to urban life and access to the city. On the contrary, it becomes enhanced through multiplication. Ways of moving through the downtown area become manifold, as do the activities offered, as many of the galerias containing cinemas, cafés, bookstores, clothing shops, and semi-public areas for rest and contemplation.

*Galerias*, therefore, are instruments of porosity on a territorial scale. Stravros Stavrides advocates for the relational dimension of urban life that porosity "activates," as in opposition to "separation."[6] The surpassing of thresholds, generating juxtapositions, happens not only in single spatial terms, but has also a spatio-temporal quality: "[i]n urban porosity, different spaces as well as different times become related, and thus compared."[7] This established relation is present in the galerias that are geographically close to the modern avenues designed for automobiles in plans like Prestes Maia's Plano de Avenidas. The entrances and borders of galerias became transitional spaces between two different "times/speeds:" the first, the unapproachable speed of the cars; the second, the modern flaneur that strolls and observes the shops' displays.

However, there are strong antagonizing forces against porosity and the more socialist desires of architects such as João Batista Vilanova Artigas (1915-1985) or Paulo Mendes da Rocha (1928-2021); among them, a widespread fear of poverty and violence that has turned Brazilian cities, with São Paulo as their main exponent, into lands of gates and walls. Teresa Caldeira attributes the (literal) growth of walls and gates to a reconfiguration of spatial patterns of occupation by the poorest and richest in the city, identifiable mostly in the last few decades.[8] As both groups

ing. Porosity remains, at all scales, a description that refers to a material relationship. It is a ratio between that which is open—to the city, or to people, or the elements—and that which is closed. That means it is not the same as sheer openness, a concept that would better suit the civic ground floor of Lina Bo Bardi's MASP, even at an urban scale. Instead, it means accounting for complexity in a way that is also embodied in the architectural form.

This complexity can be found in the SESC 24 de Maio, a former department store and a small adjacent building in São Paulo's city center that has been transformed into a multi-program diverse community center stacking theatre, gym, cafeteria,

> Porosity remains, at all scales, a description that refers to a material relationship. It is a ratio between that which is open—to the city, or to people, or the elements—and that which is closed. That means it is not the same as sheer openness, a concept that would better suit the civic ground floor of Lina Bo Bardi's MASP, even at an urban scale. Instead, it means accounting for complexity in a way that is also embodied in the architectural form.

100

marched concurrently towards the outskirts of the city—one out of option and the other out of necessity—they began co-exist in greater proximity than before. The result was the establishment of spatial barriers by the wealthiest, in an attempt to isolate themselves from the surrounding poverty.

Placing spatial barriers is an oversimplification of the complexity and constant transformation of urban life. Marcos Rosa praises a "ground level" experience of the city. Everyday life, that which "unfolds in public space," happens in "unexpected ways, (...) brimming over, blurring and re-defining the preset walls, borders and limits."[9] A return to life "on the ground" and its idiosyncrasies might be central to an answer to an over-fragmented city.

In the last decade, after years of a deteriorating downtown, the porous fabric of the *galerias* has been complemented by a couple of—now iconic—institutional buildings that respond to the ground floor in the same fashion as their commercial neighbors. Praça das Artes (the Municipal Theatre School) inaugurated in 2013 and designed by architects Brasil Arquitetura and the community center of SESC 24 de Maio opened in 2017 by renowned Paulo Mendes da Rocha + MMBB have the same blurred border as the COPAN Building where the city pierces through. In these more contemporary cases the passerby encounters new programs related to art, sports, music, community building.

Praça das Artes intersects new buildings with existing older constructions, it subtly transforms the urban scale to the scale of the building by consciously connecting public plazas to ground floor entrances. Although it adds porosity in the urban scale the building itself does not qualify as a porous build-

restaurants, courts, mediatheque, exhibition, spaces for education and children's activities, a climbing wall, and a swimming pool. Located on Rua 24 de Maio, the home of *Galeria do Rock* and *Galeria do Reggae*, the SESC construction consolidated the street's already well-established reputation for culture and entertainment. In this urban setting, the architects proposed an unobstructed continuity from the street on all levels, a vertical development of the main street that invited life to inhabit the internal spaces. Ramps construct paths between levels generating voids between programs that create spatial continuity inside the building with visual openings to the city, matching the floor levels with neighboring *Galeria do Reggae*, making one feel almost like they are floating over the street as they stroll along the *galeria's* higher levels.

The SESC allows users to enter and access spaces in the building through different points, and not only in a practical function, but also as a visual integration with internal space and urban dimension. This principle is generated through an internal and conscious relationship between material and void. It concerns access and flows and how far an individual, or nature—the external environment—can reach into the building and its different sectors. It becomes a characteristic achieved through design: the void of material can be also devoid of direct function, a space for improvisation and the unexpected dimension of life.

Mendes da Rocha's contemporary take on the city is directly related to earlier projects and his career, which has long contemplated opportunities in which a city can overtake architecture; these ideas also relate to the works of João Batista Villanova Artigas. Not only were Mendes da Rocha and Vilanova Artigas personal friends and both professors of Architecture and Urbanism at the University of São Paulo, but Mendes da Rocha's architecture also constructs certain formal continuities with Vilanova Artigas' works. Beyond the relation of void and material, the design of ramps, skylights or reinforced concrete structures on buildings such as Sesc 24 de Maio (2017), Museu Nacional dos Coches (2015) and Pavilhão de Osaka (1970) can be related directly to a single and striking example of Villanova Artigas' major works: the building for the Faculty of Architecture and Urbanism at the University of São Paulo (FAUUSP), designed by Vilanova Artigas along with Carlos Cascaldi, starting in 1961. Construction lasted from 1966 until 1969. Artigas was one of the leading figures in the curriculum reform of the Faculty of Architecture and Urbanism in 1962, which departed from a Beaux-Arts based curriculum to an approach closer to Bauhaus in an effort towards modernization. His leadership in the reform was one of the key factors that led to his being charged with the task of designing the building, a project that would embody the concepts of the new pedagogical program. The project was conceived not as a single commission, but as part of a larger design that would encompass all of the humanities, with modern buildings distributed across the central avenue of the university campus and connected through a system of free spaces. The idea's further development was soon hindered by the military dictatorship that came into power in 1964. Of the six

ern architecture, perfected and improved upon so it could become more connected to local determinants. Examples of cities that received projects include: Rio de Janeiro and São Paulo (Brazil), Concepción (Chile), Tucumán (Argentina), Caracas (Venezuela), Mexico City (Mexico), Bogotá (Colombia) and Quito (Ecuador).[10] Barry Bergdoll, like Segawa, points to two designs as the earliest experiments: UNAM (Universidad Autónoma de México) and UCV (Universidad Central de Venezuela) were both highly innovative projects at a global scale. Both designs also began in the 1940s.[11]

What the designers for the Latin American campuses seemed to elaborate was that universities were places of aspiration towards modernity in a deep sense, where more ideal and advanced ways of sociability could be put into practice through experimentation. They constituted elevated territories where architectural forms related to advanced forms could finally be constructed, resulting in bolder solutions of shape and space, program and prescriptive use.

FAUUSP condenses this frame of thought perfectly as a complex arrangement of simple geometric forms constructed in concrete, most of which remains bare. From the outside it is a clear-cut concrete box, raised by sculptural columns—the lack of doors erases any clear division between inside and outside, a feat once again afforded by the subtropical weather.[12] As one gets closer, volumes at different

101

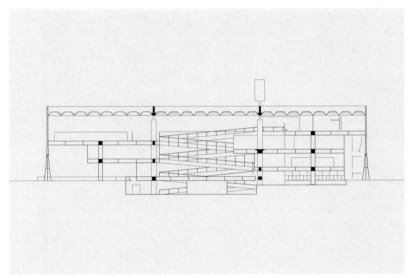

FAUUSP Section Drawing. Redrawn by Santiago Bogani.

buildings originally designed, only two were constructed: Vilanova Artigas' Architecture and Urbanism and Eduardo Corona's History and Geography.

The FAUUSP building is a later example among several initiatives to modernize university campuses in Latin America. Hugo Segawa recounts how the establishment of modern campi from the 1940s onwards was seen as expressive of social modernization. Locally generated knowledge and science obtained a space and structure for cultivation, and this cultural leap found its material and visual expression in mod-

heights project themselves over the central void that spans all the way from the sky-lit ceiling into the wide-open floor at its core. The ensemble is both physically and visually connected. As the multiple cantilevered volumes are never fully closed—they share the same roof—sound also travels unimpeded through space. Half-levels increase the original four floor height two-fold and wide ramps connect all of them, providing the user with a promenade that, composed of slightly varying vistas at every level, functions as a facilitator of social encounter.

The São Paulo building holds important similarities to slightly earlier contemporary designs further north in the Americas, representatives of a larger wave of projects for higher education schools liberally defined as Brutalist. At this moment, the focus will be detained on two of the main exponents of this group: Le Corbusier's design for the Carpenter Center, at Harvard University, and Paul Rudolph's Yale Art and Architecture Building, later renamed Rudolph Hall, for its architect.

Le Corbusier was approached in 1959 by José Luis Sert, a former apprentice of his and then Dean of the Graduate School of Design, with a proposition to design a building for the visual arts in Harvard. While studying the plot assigned for the school, Le Corbusier was impressed by the pedestrian flow, noticing how students would cross the lot using it as a short-cut between classes. He paid close attention to circulation, adopting it as the "generating force"[13] in

quence, outside space is brought inside. Curtis moves on to say that "the ambiguities of outside space passed inside, and inside, outside (...) reflect Le Corbusier's *urbanistic* intentions".[15] Such intentions are very similar to Vilanova Artigas' in the design for his school, where the indeterminate thresholds of the space are supposed to equate more democratic architectural forms—not necessarily more urbanistic, in the sense of pertaining to urban design, but certainly more urban, with the understanding of urban space as one of democracy in practice.

The use of bare concrete, as in the Carpenter Center, appeared for the first time in the architect's work at the Unité d'Habitation in Marseille, completed in 1952. *Béton Brut*, as the material was named by Corbusier, is the term that would later inspire Reyner Banham in coining the term Brutalism.[16] The circumstances of the construction of the housing

102

The Carpenter Center at Harvard University, Cambridge. Ph. Pablo Gerson.

the project. Porosity resulted from a clear intention to relate the building to a context of previous use of the space,[14] and the ramps through the building were designed to maintain the pre-existing connections.

A central feature of the Carpenter Center is an 'S' shaped concrete ramp that ascends in a curve from the street level and crosses the center of the building before descending towards the street across the block. At its summit, the ramp connects the adjacent open floor plans, exposing their interiors behind large glass panes, and revealing the activities and spaces within the building. Although belonging to a very distinct architectural form, Curtis's written description of the cantilevered levels placed along the ramp within the building could be transplanted to a description of FAUUSP without losing much: "The layers and levels swing out and back from the grid of concrete *pilotis* within, making the most of cantilevering to create interpenetrations of exterior and interior, as well as a sequence of spatial events linked by the *promenade architecturale* of the ramp." Through this se-

block in France, realized by different groups of contractors and therefore with no perspective of a refined, precise finish, prompted the architect's decision to expose the stark, bare concrete structure in all its roughness. Curtis emphasizes Le Corbusier's intention "to make roughness an aesthetic virtue, to exploit the imprint and grain of the formwork planks as if they were the chisel marks of one of Savina's sculptures."[17] This raw expression of material, remarkably bold and yet "superbly sensitive to light and shade,"[18] would spread over the formal language of modern architecture into the 1960s and 1970s, also manifesting in a number of Le Corbusier's subsequent designs.

The architect's timeline of works parallels that of modern architecture through the 20th century, in which the broader philosophy of modernism remained, but many formal and material aspects departed from the earlier production. The Carpenter Center is one of Le Corbusier's last works, and at the same time, his first and only in the United States.[19] As much as it recaptures and redistributes the Five Points of

Architecture through a more organic form, it also belongs with the other Brutalist schools built at the same period, with a complex and fragmented façade and multi-volume interior, exposed concrete throughout its floors and a central concern for providing access to inner spaces and a permanent relationship between outside and inside, not through absolute openness, but through porosity, an equation between open and closed surfaces.

Also belonging to the group of earlier higher education buildings is the Yale Art and Architecture (A&A) building, which Helene Sroat defines a milestone in the development and acceptance of Brutalism as a defined architectural style in the United States. Nevertheless, the building has long suffered from swings in its general reputation, as did the architect. Paul Rudolph was awarded the commission for the A&A building, finished in 1963, during his years as chairman of the University's Architecture Department (from 1958 to 1965). The massive project, renamed Rudolph Hall after its renovation in 2008, comprises 37 floor levels along seven stories in a dramatic composition of extending and receding volumes around a core of open collective spaces anchored by concrete towers. Both the exterior and interior of the sculptural, monumental structure expose the bush-hammered corrugated concrete, whose topography is enhanced by the interplay of light and shadow.[20]

The unusual configuration of the spaces imputes a "initially confusing and overwhelming"[21] complexity to the A&A building. In her lecture at the Paul Rudolph Symposium at University of Massachusetts-Dartmouth, Helene Sroat argues that the sense of disorientation and discontinuity is intentional, as Rudolph's brutalism "set forth a modernist

the monotonous uniform floor plans of a contemporary International Style.

The bridges and overlapping levels around the free section create a variety of vistas in a composition where visual communication is established with the intention to promote a sense of community and a shared culture based on the building. The relationship between floors allows activities to overflow from one to the other. Shallow steps create smaller spaces that afford spontaneous uses. The free section is a less-stern, older sibling to FAUUSP, with multiple levels organized around all four sides of a central core.

All three buildings share a restricted temporal window of conception and construction. The Harvard School for Visual Arts was commissioned to Le Corbusier slightly before FAUUSP. The first sketch for the Carpenter Center was done in 1960; in 1961, he finished the presentation drawings. By 1963, the building was finished, as was Yale's A&A. Vilanova Artigas's work took longer to finish—the inauguration took place in 1969—but the initial commission and sketches began at the same time as the other two buildings.

The Carpenter Center and FAUUSP share qualities and characteristics in balancing not only voids and volumes, but also entrances and openings, exploring the relationship between buildings and street. This architecture still expresses porosity as an urban attribute in the sense that the inner multiplicity of spaces is necessarily related to the multiple ways of entering the building, and therefore also the ways in which interior and exterior interact. Rudolph's design does not present such permeable boundaries. The narrowing staircase at the entrance, interjected by a column, lacks the seamlessness of Corbusier's sinuous

103

The Carpenter Center at Harvard University, Cambridge. Ph. Pablo Gerson.

spatial alternative whose fixed spatial sequences imply states of anticipation, challenge, tension and culmination."[22] In this manner, the building offers an experience that both demands effort and fosters a more *human* response from the users, a critical contrast to

ramps and pilotis or Artigas' open temple-like main entrance. The porosity at the A&A, however, may be closest to Benjamin and Lacis's original definition, in that it provides, through an infinite multiplication of its inner space, seemingly infinite possibilities of use.

There was a widespread rise of Brutalist structures in universities and colleges across the United States. A growing national economy, coupled with new appreciation for research and higher education, propelled the creation and expansion of universities across the country; Brutalism thrived. As Curtis states, when detailing the history of Le Corbusier's North American project, "it was a period in which many elite American universities were building art centers and adorning their campuses with works by internationally famous designers."[23] Praised by the media and perceived as architectural artworks, "brutalist buildings were associated with creativity, individualism, and high intellectual and cultural achievement,"[24] in accordance with universities' ambitions. Sroat ascribes the appeal of Brutalism in university campuses to its ability to aesthetically relate to the "strength, permanence and importance of past architectural monuments"[25] while expressing modern aspirations with its new, bold sculptural forms, resonating with the traditional while

stance, while also working within rigid institutional frameworks of higher education, and sometimes in direct partnership with anti-democratic regimes. Paulo Mendes da Rocha, who designed the never-built Philosophy School that would share the university axis with FAUUSP, gave an interview on the project, affirming that "regardless of aesthetic values or related notions, the plan for the university city was a libertarian movement and was fought against bitterly."[27]

Paul Rudolph himself emphasized how the relationships between conversing spaces in the A&A should allow the users to be constantly made aware of all the activities that were happening around them, in a way that young students could potentially learn from observing the presentations of older colleagues, for instance.[28] A similar effect happens in FAUUSP as a result of the affordances of vision and especially flow (be it of people, objects, sound or air) between not only studio spaces but all floors. In this instance, the protagonist is the articulation of voids

Porosity can be understood as a valid quality through which the school buildings may be specifically valued. Analyzing whether a structure provides its users with multiple possibilities for use, movement, and access, is a departure from a simple pleasant-unpleasant binary; it provides a basis for understanding through its stance on society, politics, and life.

communicating with modernity and bearing a sense of grandiosity. Located in the well-established campuses of Harvard and Yale, the Carpenter Center and A&A were pivotal in endowing the style with an image of institutional prominence and prestige.

In the Brazilian case, the stylistic traits of Brutalism, beyond the result of pure aesthetics and climate conditions, were also fit to fulfill programmatic needs of a political stance. The fortress-like appearance of FAUUSP, along with its large atrium, were in part a response to the social tension and escalation that would culminate in the military dictatorship, in an effort to provide, within the plethora of possible uses it affords, a safe space for the student congregations of the resistance, all the while embodying the monumentality aspired by the government officials.

The São Paulo projects diverge from a narrow and uninformed definition of Brutalism based on observations works in the UK and, later North America. The projects engage in more anti-establishment intentions and are inserted within a wider framework of late modernism in Brazil, all of which took place amid military dictatorship. They were thus framed as a generally progressive architectural expression conceptually opposite to the political regime.

Segawa, when concluding his detailed history of university cities in Latin America, states that they "should be understood as supports for complex political and ideological stances."[26] That is, a deep specificity: an architecture tasked with embodying the most progressive forms of sociability as a political

created by the balance between the presence and absence of material. Verde Zein explains how the most relevant architectural innovation present at FAUUSP is not "the functional program, but precisely the exponential addition of non-functional spaces (...) especially the volumetric voids."[29]

Porosity can be understood as a valid quality through which university buildings may be specifically valued. Analyzing whether a structure provides its users with multiple possibilities for use, movement, and access, is a departure from a simple pleasant-unpleasant binary; it provides a basis for understanding through its stance on society, politics, and life.

In architecture literature, permeability serves as a recurring term to define spaces in which realms are interpenetrated and the blurring of thresholds. The definitions of porosity and permeability intersect and both derive from definitions of physical and natural processes. Permeability, however, refers in large part to the fruition of the building by the user, within the larger understanding that such experience is directly related to a building's urban character. Porosity, as it pertains to architecture in material terms, is the relationship between material structures and open spaces that may provide a building with permeability.

The achievement of porosity is accompanied by prevailing forms: cantilevered volumes of different sizes, varying heights and proportions for different spaces within the building, ramps and elevated walkways that connect the different volumes, multiplication of levels within the structure aided by the application of said ramps and walkways, allowing different intensities of natural light and air throughout the building, and a particular concern with flows, fruition, and the experience of architecture.

When Robert Venturi argues against oversimplification in early modern projects in *Complexity and Contradiction in Architecture*, he equates the conceptual procedure to a conscious exclusion of aspects of life that will inhabit the building, as life itself is always complex and contradictory: "in an inclusive rather than an exclusive kind of architecture

the outside, the wall—the point of change—becomes an architectural event," he says. "Architecture occurs at the meeting of interior and exterior forces of use and space."[31] Not necessarily the wall, but the threshold of the building as its horizon, its reach, concerns the idea of porosity directly, as it is a process of interpenetration between the reach of the user and the reach of the construction. As porous architecture is one that aims to provide a diversity of possibilities, it is also one that allows for use and access through its scales and partitions. A porous threshold is one that allows things to pass

Student demonstration in the central hall of FAUUSP, São Paulo. Ph. Raul Garcez.

there is room for the fragment, for contradiction, for improvisation, and for the tensions these produce."[30]

Venturi would perhaps describe the meeting of scales and types of use and access that usually accompany a more porous architecture as *contradictory*. This contradiction is the expression of a tension, generally between what could be described as outside and inside. The point at which they meet is the threshold, the wall serves as a conceptual division and the façade of the building. "Since the inside is different from

through, from the elements, exclusively, to actual urban flow in the scale of the city. The porous architectural element can, therefore, be infinitely thick or thin.

In recent years, the UTEC building in Lima, Peru, presents itself as one of the most complete and complex examples to provide a diversity of possibilities, both in relation to its urban dimension and as interior spatial distribution. A contemporary example that formally, programmatically is comparable to Rudolph's of Artigas' educational buildings.

Designed by Grafton Architects, the building is located at the edge of a suburban area on a highway, in between two speeds—the car on the highway and the life of the suburbs. It is not in a campus nor in the middle of the city, but manages to weave the city in and through its construction.

The vertical campus distributes classrooms and laboratories over multiple stories; the resulting massive concrete geometry articulates its

recognized, (...) that from which something *begins its presenting*." Space in porosity means a possibility that is allowed for, also recognized in contrast to when it is not. It "(...) is in essence that for which room has been made, that which is let into its bounds."[33]

A porous architecture accommodates life and invites it into the building by accounting for complexity and possibility in its very form. The embrace of vitality, movement, and variation is taken,

New Campus for the UTEC by Grafton Architects. Ph. Florencia Rodriguez.

pierced façade to the highway while at the suburban scale the small volumetric cubes appear to be beside a hill or mountain.

The building strives to create a continuity with the double nature of its urban dimension, perceived through its spaces and even more clearly in its sectional representation. The section of the UTEC building illustrates the vertical campus organization in a sponge-like scheme of solids and voids. Multiple voids are constructed from the addition of classroom volumes and the in-between non-functional spaces. Residual spaces create inconstant continuity inside of the building, where improvisation and casual encounters between students and professors may happen. An undiluted fluidity of human relations occurrs beyond the functional program of the institution, in Grafton's own words "... fostering the research life of the individual student and the professor. Interaction and overlap are encouraged. Students, professors and administrative staff mingle, within view of one another. The section encourages chance and possibility."

There is chance and curiosity in porosity: it is also a relationship between what is seen and what is not. Complexity and porosity are, therefore, relational concepts, with the presence of a physical boundary being as essential to a building's multiplicity of scales of use and access as its absence. As first referred to by Kenneth Frampton in *Studies in Tectonic Culture*,[32] Martin Heidegger defines the boundary as "not that at which something stops but, as the Greeks

therefore, not as a merely conceptual choice, but as an architectural and ultimately social stance, representative of the desire for a more human built environment that is as accessible as it is sheltering.

1 Acknowledgments to researchers Alina Paias, Flora Milanez and Gabriel Iguchi Gomes.

2 Benjamin, Walter; and Lacis, Asja, "Naples," in Benjamin, Walter, *Reflections: Essays, Aphorisms, Autobiographical Writings* (New York: Harcourt Brace Jovanovich, 1978), pp. 163-173.

3 Ibid., p. 167.

4 Fontenele, Sabrina, *Relações entre o traçado urbano e os edifícios modernos no Centro de São Paulo: Arquitetura e Cidade (1938/1960)*, PhD Dissertation (São Paulo: Universidade de São Paulo, 2010).

5 Ibid., p. 82.

6 Stavrides, Stavros, "Urban Porosity and the Right to a Shared City," in Wolfrum, Sophie (org), Porous City (Basel: Birkhäuser, 2018), p. 32.

7 Ibid.

8 Caldeira, *Teresa, City of Walls: Crime, Segregation, and Citizenship in São Paulo* (Berkeley: University of California Press, 2000).

9 Rosa, Marcos, "Contesting urban borders: cultural practices, design and the construction of urban situations", in Camacho, Sol, et. al., *Walls of Air: Brazilian Pavilion 2018* (São Paulo: Bienal de São Paulo, 2018), p. 325.

10 From the original "São exemplos desses conjuntos na América Latina as cidades universitárias no Rio de Janeiro e São Paulo (Brasil), Concepción (Chile), Tucumán (Argentina), Caracas (Venezuela), Cidade do México (México), Bogotá (Colômbia) e Quito (Equador)," Segawa, Hugo, "México, Caracas: Cidades Universitárias e Modernidades 1936 - 1962," *Revista Rua - Revista de Urbanismo e Arquitetura*, v. 5, 1999, p. 39.

11 Bergdoll, Barry, "Learning from Latin America: Public Space, Housing, and Landscape", in Bergdoll, Barry, et. al., Latin America in Construction: Architecture 1955-1980 (New York: The Museum of Modern Art, 2015), p. 23.

12 The absence of a threshold between inside and outside is remarkable in the scale of the FAUUSP building, accounting for unusual scenarios; the lamps up to illuminate the central hall during the night are stadium lights and pigeons wander freely through all faculty floors.

13 Curtis, William, Le Corbusier: Ideas and Forms (London: Phaidon, 2003), p. 168.

14 Which is vastly different than understanding the context as a set of material and formal determinants present around the plot. In contrast to the red brick buildings that surround it, Carpenter Center's piloti raised, lung shaped volumes float above 'Harvard Yard', "an arcadian precinct of formal buildings on axes" (Curtis, p. 217).

15 Curtis, William, *Le Corbusier: Ideas and Forms* (London: Phaidon, 2003), p. 216.

16 Another pioneer in the use of bare concrete was French architect Auguste Perret, in whose office Le Corbusier worked as an apprentice, between 1908 and 1909.

17 Curtis, William, *Le Corbusier: Ideas and Forms* (London: Phaidon, 2003), p. 170.

18 Ibid.

19 Sroat, Helene. "Brutalism: An Architecture of Exhilariation", lecture at Paul Rudolph Symposium UMass

Dartmouth April 13, 2005 (Transcript), p. 6. Available at: https://prudolph.lib.umassd.edu/files/pr/Sroat%20Transcription,%20041305.pdf, accessed, January 21, 2018.

20 Although Rudolph notably draws inspiration from Corbusier, Timothy Rohan interestingly suggests that the textured finish of the surfaces lays closer to Sullivan's raised reliefs rather than to Corbusier's beton brût. See Rohan, Timothy, "Rendering the Surface: Paul Rudolph's Art and Architecture Building at Yale," in *Grey Room*, No. 1 (Autumn, 2000) (Cambridge: The MIT Press), pp. 84-107.

21 Sroat, Helene. "Brutalism: An Architecture of Exhilariation", lecture at Paul Rudolph Symposium UMass Dartmouth April 13, 2005 (Transcript), p. 9. Available at: https://prudolph.lib.umassd.edu/files/pr/Sroat%20Transcription,%20041305.pdf, accessed January 21, 2018.

22 Ibid.

23 Curtis, William, *Le Corbusier: Ideas and Forms*, London: Phaidon, 2003, p. 216.

24 Sroat, Helene. "Brutalism: An Architecture of Exhilariation", lecture at Paul Rudolph Symposium UMass Dartmouth April 13, 2005 (Transcript), p. 12. Available at: https://prudolph.lib.umassd.edu/files/pr/Sroat%20Transcription,%20041305.pdf, last accessed in 21 January 2018.

25 Ibid.

26 Segawa, Hugo, "México, Caracas: Cidades Universitárias e Modernidades 1936 - 1962," *Revista Rua - Revista de Urbanismo e Arquitetura*, v. 5, 1999, p. 47.

27 Mendes da Rocha, Paulo, "O que é uma cidade? What is a city?", in *The Modern Memory of São Paulo - Corredor das Humanas* (São Paulo: Contravento), p. 35.

28 In response to Michael J. Crosbie's question "What were your thoughts about how the building would serve as a model, pedagogically?" Paul Rudolph stated: "I thought it was important that first-year architecture students be very aware of what their elders, the older students, were thinking and doing. To that end, the drafting rooms were a multileveled affair, so you couldn't help but see and be quite aware of what other people were doing. You looked down," Crosbie, Michael, "Paul Rudolph on Yale's A&A: his first interview on his most famous work", *Architecture: the AIA journal*, November 1988, p. 102.

29 From the original "O que se altera profundamente não é o programa funcional, mas justamente a adição exponencial de espaços não funcionais que o projeto do novo edifício provê, e em especial os vazios volumétricos", Verde Zein, Ruth, *A Arquitetura da Escola Paulista Brutalista: 1953-1973*, PhD Dissertation, (São Paulo and Porto Alegre: Faculdade de Arquitetura da Universidade Federal do Rio Grande do Sul, 2005), p. 135.

30 Venturi, Robert, Complexity and Contradiction in Architecture (New York: The Museum of Modern Art, 1992), p. 17.

31 Idem, p. 86.

32 Frampton quotes the phrase that comes immediately prior to the ones in this text.

33 Heidegger, Martin, "Building Dwelling Thinking", in Poetry, Language, Thought, (New York: Harper & Row, 2001), p. 152.

107

WATER GOLD SOIL
Susannah Sayler & Edward Morris / The Canary Project

This is part of the story of a single flow of water in present-day California from origin point to end-use. As with other water flows in the American West, the "American River" is no longer a river, but rather a site of water capture and distribution, with a definite beginning but diffuse end. It is part of a larger collection of original photographs, archival images, and writing that also tell a parallel history of extractivism.

# WATER GOLD SOIL: WHAT IS A RIVER IN CALIFORNIA?

## Susannah Sayler & Edward Morris / The Canary Project

What is a river? This is not a question we ask every day because it seems superfluous. Certainly, a river must be a flowing body of water of a certain size. Call it a river or a creek, but one way or another, flowing is the essential thing. Yet, what if a given river does not flow *per se* but is pushed and pulled mechanically? Or what if the flowing that defines a river is arrested and controlled through dams, canals, and machine technology? What if the river no longer moves with inextricable desire towards a specific place like an ocean or a lake, but rather is widely dispersed into various uses? What if a river is wholly owned and apportioned the moment it comes out of the ground? Does all this change the essence of a river? Is it even still a river?

These speculative questions, for which the arts are particularly well suited, assume real significance in a state like present-day California that depends entirely on technological control of rivers for its prosperity and very survival. Seeing a river in California for what it is now—namely water-put-to-work—can abet a number of other vital inquiries, such as: if water in the state is essentially a resource or even a commodity, who owns it and how are these owners positioning themselves for the water shortages of the future due to climate change and population growth? How is the current regard for water connected to California's murderous, colonial past,[1] and what can we gain from such an understanding? And/or how can California avoid its seemingly inevitable fate of privatized water markets, unreliable access to clean water for the poor and profound income inequality? Such questioning "prepares a free relationship" towards the issue, to quote Martin Heidegger. It reveals and opens. It renders something that appears universal, absolute, and given—in this case our extractive attitude toward water and farming—as contingent and therefore mutable through political activism and civic engagement.

We make this particular connection to Heidegger despite all his baggage because he provides a number of indispensable analytic tools for perceiving what is really at stake with environmental issues, not to mention his inventive and evocative vocabulary. Further, an encounter with Heidegger's investigation into the nature of rivers proved transformative to our own art-activist project "Water Gold Soil." As artists working with the medium of landscape photography, we first looked towards what is visible in the land in order to represent the drought issue in California. A reading of Heidegger and other research then provoked us to consider what lies behind what can be seen. A key thought sits in Heidegger's before-and-after comparison of the Rhine River found in "The Question Concerning Technology:"

> The hydroelectric plant is set into the current of the Rhine. It sets the Rhine to supplying its hydraulic pressure, which then sets the turbines turning. This turning sets those machines in motion whose thrust sets going the electric current for which the long-distance power station and its network of cables are set up to dispatch electricity. In the context of the interlocking processes pertaining to the orderly disposition of electrical energy, even the Rhine itself appears to be something at our command. The hydroelectric plant is not built into the Rhine River as was the old wooden bridge that joined bank with bank for hundreds of years. Rather the river is dammed up into the power plant…. What the river is now, namely, a water-power supplier, derives from the essence of the power station…. But, it will be replied, the Rhine is still a river in the landscape, is it not? Perhaps. But how? In no other way than as an object on call for inspection by a tour group ordered there by the vacation industry.[2]

Seeing the way "a river in the landscape" can actually be more fundamentally defined by its economic uses (power supplier, tourism and recreation site, irrigator) became the presiding impulse of our own project. Accordingly, we photographed the transition from the wilderness incarnation of this water flow in the Sierra Nevada to its first damming, and then on to its increasing subjection to rationalization and canalization, and finally to its dispersal in various end-uses, primarily agricultural. The most basic goal of the photography and the video we took was simply to reveal the "river" as economic rather than scenic—and by "river" here, we mean both our particular water flow and by extension all such "rivers" in California.

This may seem obvious, but the productiveness of this enterprise became evident when an environmental organization giving us an award requested that we put more images of "beauty" and "wildness" into an exhibition of our work. Indeed, the typical maneuver of photographers working on environmental issues is to show a particular landscape as pure and beautiful and therefore worthy of protecting, or else to show "damage" to the land caused by the impurities of pollution and industrialization. However, such obsession with purity, which has historically motivated the environmental movement in the United States, deadens an adequate response to issues like climate change or water rights in California. In both cases, sufficiently powerful animus and solidarity must derive from a heightened sense of both the dangers and opportunities. Urgency comes from care for and protection of life, social justice, empathy, economic opportunity and restoration of the sacred. Each of these themes came together in Standing Rock.

121

The purity paradigm continues to grip the environmental community, but so long as it does it will jeopardize its efficacy. For such an interest in conservation, preservation, and beauty, tremendously understates the danger of our current ecological crisis and renders the ecological crisis the sole province of a privileged class. Here too Heidegger can be of some assistance, albeit with significant caveats. Heidegger's description of the hydro-electric plant in the Rhine comes amid a larger discussion of what he identified as "the supreme danger" to mankind. This supreme danger presents itself to Heidegger first in the guise of "modern technology." Modern technology for Heidegger differs from what precedes it in that "it puts to nature the unrea-

may be on call for a furthering ordering. Whatever is ordered about in this way has its own standing. We call it the standing reserve.[4]

Another way of saying this is that within the challenging forth of modern technology everything becomes a resource, or as Heidegger writes elsewhere "something is only through what it performs."[5] Heidegger gives a couple of other examples besides the transformation of the river. He contrasts a windmill with coal power. Whereas with the windmill things "are left entirely to the wind's blowing," with coal "a tract of land is challenged in the hauling out" with the result that the "earth now reveals itself as a coal mining district, the

Seeing the way "a river in the landscape" can actually be more fundamentally defined by its economic uses (power supplier, tourism and recreation site, irrigator) became the presiding impulse of our own project. Accordingly, we photographed the transition from the wilderness incarnation of this water flow in the Sierra Nevada to its first damming, and then on to its increasing subjection to rationalization and canalization, and finally to its dispersal in various end-uses, primarily agricultural. The most basic goal of the photography and the video we took was simply to reveal the "river" as economic rather than scenic—and by "river" here, we mean both our particular water flow and by extension all such "rivers" in California.

sonable demand that it supply energy which can be extracted and stored." Heidegger terms this essential aspect of modern technology a "challenging forth," which he contrasts with the gentler "bringing forth" (poiesis) of older technology. Poeisis, of course, is also the mode of the arts (i.e., poetry), the significance of which we explore below. In this connection, Heidegger contrasts the impact of a wooden bridge over the Rhine to that of the hydro-electric dam per the above quotation. The wooden bridge brings forth place, dwelling, cultivation of the land; whereas the dam challenges forth the river to yield energy that might in turn be used for industrial processes.[3]

To understand how this is not merely a nostalgic, wistful call for a return to a past primitivism, we must understand exactly what is so unreasonable about the demand Heidegger identifies that modern technology puts to nature. The danger here is not the loss of an attribute of the river we might call beautiful or the imposition of a stain on its purity that can ultimately be restored through effective advocacy; rather, the danger lies in the complete transformation in the nature of the river within a means-ends order. It has become, in Heidegger's terminology, a "standing reserve." The river is not alone. In a world dominated by modern technology, Heidegger writes:

Everywhere everything is ordered to stand by, to be immediately on hand, indeed to stand there just so that it

soil as mineral deposit."[6] He also contrasts older farming techniques with industrial agriculture, emphasizing the lost values of care and maintenance, words which together we might call by a different name—sustainability.[7]

By this logic, in order to answer the question, "What is a river in California?," we must first answer the question of specifically what that river is used for, of what it performs. It is not enough simply to observe that it is technological in some generic sense. Of course, a given river in California might have various uses. (It is illuminating in this regard to examine Bureau of Reclamation spreadsheets showing just who owns each acre foot of water in each river.) Notice, however, how Heidegger articulates the usage of the river in terms of a system: the water moves the turbines, which moves machines that create the electrical current, which in turn moves along cables to be stored and distributed. The underlying logic of the challenging forth is that it is extracting and storing energy with the purpose to further something else, namely some industry.

We chose to follow a water flow toward its end use specifically in the industry of large-scale agriculture because this is the dominant industry governing much of California's water infrastructure. Jay Lund, one of the leading experts on water in California and editor of the California Water Blog, describes the system of water management in California, as follows:

By 1980, a vast network of reservoirs, canals and exploited aquifers transformed California. This system was largely designed to support an agricultural economy envisioned in the latter 1800s, which greatly exceeded the gold mining economy it replaced.[8]

In this single concise quotation, you have all the elements of our project: Water, Gold, Soil. The "agricultural economy" (i.e. soil) is the descendant of the gold mining economy, and both were entirely dependent on water—agriculture for obvious reasons, and gold because not only was gold first found in the rivers, but water in the form of sluices and later water cannons was essential to mining operations. As Norris Hundley writes of the gold mining industry in California: "they built hydraulic empires of dams, reservoirs, flumes, ditches, pipes and hoses. All this in turn required knowledge of advanced engineering principles, now introduced for the first time on a large scale in the West and later used to build other great public and private projects."[9] In addition to the technological confidence and infrastructure, perhaps a more important legacy of the gold mining industry on the agriculture industry that supplanted it was the legal framework for how to regard ownership of a river in the first place.[10] In particular, the notion that one could claim a right to some water simply being the first to put it to some vaguely defined "beneficial use" originated in California with the Gold Rush. The havoc wrecked by the mixing of this "prior appropriation" right with other sorts of rights (namely riparian) has been well documented.

However, Lund leaves out half of the equation. The other major driver of water infrastructure development in California was, and continues to be, real estate development and speculation. This story has been comprehensively told in Norris Hundley's *The Great Thirst* and elsewhere. In fact, a strong argument can be made that agriculture in California is itself simply real estate investment in disguise. With a Heideggerian flourish we might say: "Water spread over land by wind and rain transforms ground to nutrient. Water spread over land by pipes transforms ground to real estate." Many in addition to Hundley have recited this history,[11] which in broad brush strokes looks like this: the government wrests away land populated by Native Americans and grants it outright to large corporations, including railroads and oil companies; the companies market the land to settlers who begin to farm it and increase its value under lease agreements; the same large landowners then successfully lobby the government for massive, multi-billion-dollar water infrastructure projects, cynically invoking the Jeffersonian image of the small farmer (this includes the San Luis reservoir, which is the hub of the water flow in our Water Gold Soil project); the construction of these projects is granted under the agreement that the large landowners will sell off their land into smaller parcels to support small business and families; this sell-off is never done and the military-scale federal investment in infrastructure is thereby translated into direct real estate gains by the large owners. Studies have shown the deleterious effects of corporate farming on communities, as the owners of these lands get rich while the people working on them are mired in some of the country's most dire poverty.[12] In the ultimate irony, many communities within these farming districts (known perversely as water districts) completely lack access to any water at all, or else are subjected to poisonous levels of pollution.[13]

Here we approach the crux of the argument and an identification both of what is valuable and vexing about Heidegger. For Heidegger, if the reduction of the natural world to a standing reserve is the danger, then the "supreme danger" is the reduction of humans themselves to the status of this standing reserve, as with the laborers of the Central Valley most obviously, but, in fact, as with all of us living within a world defined by modern technology. This reduction of nature, labor and all people to a standing reserve is a function not of technology itself but what Heidegger calls the essence of modern technology: enframing (Gestell). What sort of thing is enframing? One is tempted to call it a worldview, an orientation, a theory, a way of representing the world, or even an ideology, but Heidegger scrupulously avoids these sorts of epistemological terms—a fact that accounts for much of the difficulty of his text. For him, enframing is not simply a way of seeing things. It is itself generative as a mode of revealing the world, a mode of existence. Enframing reveals by ordering, framing, putting things into boxes. Enframing alters what is actual, not just how we see the actual. Under the sway of enframing, objects, and ultimately human beings themselves, turn into a mere function of their instrumentality.

However, while enframing is not itself a way of seeing, it is, paradoxically, both the by-product of and the necessary condition of a way of seeing, which Heidegger calls out as "modern mathematical science."[14] Perhaps a helpful way of understanding the enframing concept is to see it as that force within "modern mathematical science's" way of seeing that is productive of being—the binding force between epistemology and ontology. "Modern science's way of representing pursues and entraps nature as a calculable coherence of forces," Heidegger writes, and this "theory of nature prepares the way not just for modern technology but for the essence of modern technology [i.e., enframing]." Heidegger emphasizes that this occurs at a particular time in history—that is to say, something else came before. With an ecological dynamic, culture, in all its myriad modes of representation (scientific, artistic, conversational, etc.) is produced by, and in turn, propagates this ontological enframing force. Heidegger lays down the marker between the Renaissance and the Middle Ages: "What actuality is in Durer's picture 'The Columbine' is determined differently from what is actual in a medieval fresco."[15] Indeed, there is something crucial about this transition. The creeping ooze of enframing spread over the entire world as we moved through the epochs labeled the Renaissance, the Enlightenment, Modernity and indeed Post-Modernity (which, we understand as neo-liberalism by another

123

name). The story of enframing's creep is the story of colonialism, and it is also the story of our project in which documentation of a given "river" is both real and allegorical. Our assembly of images and words is representational of an actual water flow at a given point in time, but also of the broader historical trajectory of the Age of Extraction. California is an interesting case study in the epistemo-ontological creep of enframing because it is so compressed and so stark.

Yet, in the final analysis we make quite different hay than Heidegger out of this recognition of enframing's historicity. Heidegger's primary concern throughout his work is Being, by which he means the essence of human existence. We will not follow him into these considerations, which are dense with thorns, except to say this overarching concern of Heidegger's leads him to consider the "supreme danger" of enframing as bearing most importantly on man's ability to continue to live as he essentially is—in all his aloneness and glory. This preoccupation of Heidegger's, seeped in a brew of human exceptionalism and a pursuit of pure origins along with some other rather dubious notions, creates what seems to us like two blindingly obvious aporia in his questioning concerning technology, namely a consideration of agency in the development of enframing's challenging forth, and relatedly a con-

tivities alone that he ascribed any real power. The world had to be re-created through a heroic exertion of complicated thought, embodied best in poetry. Heidegger was silent about how this deep thought might be conveyed to the citizenry and how in turn it might lead to concrete changes in policy or political systems. Not surprisingly, this giant lacuna in Heidegger's thought resulted in personal exhaustion and disillusionment, such that he ultimately declared in an interview with *Der Spiegel*: "philosophy will be unable to effect any immediate change in the current state of the world. This is true not only of philosophy but of all purely human reflection and endeavor" because "the greatness of what is to be thought is [all] too great." Heidegger broodingly concluded that only "God can save us."[17]

Taken as disillusionment on Heidegger's part, this spirit all too commonly results from detaching the abstract work of world creating (via worldview changing) from the concrete work of political activism aimed specifically at agents of the danger. For there are indeed agents. Could not the mysterious ecological relation that Heidegger describes between the scientific mode of representation, enframing, the challenging forth of nature (and labor), and finally the transformation of the world into a standing reserve be more reductively described as the

124

Our assembly of images and words is representational of an actual water flow at a given point in time, but also of the broader historical trajectory of the Age of Extraction. California is an interesting case study in the epistemo-ontological creep of enframing because it is so compressed and so stark.

siforderation of class and regional distinctions among the humans of this world. Who pushed forward the challenging forth of nature and labor that fell out of enframing like destiny? And who can stop it? In several places, Heidegger's questioning brushes tantalizing close to Marx—for example in his observation that the challenging forth of technology is invested in "driving on to the maximum yield and the minimum expense"; or in his description of humans becoming a standing reserve, which seems to harken to Marx's analysis of alienation. However, Heidegger does not pursue a material, economic understanding of what is threatening about the enframing phenomenon. This leads to a very nebulous conception of its origins and import, as well as to a misunderstanding of the ways in which we can engage in overcoming it.

Heidegger never forged an explicit political philosophy but expressed that a revolution in thinking was needed to avoid the tragic subjection of humans themselves to the status of a standing reserve. We do not normally think of Heidegger as an activist, but in the *Introduction to Metaphysics* he states: "we dare to take up the great and lengthy task of tearing down a world that has grown old and of building it truly anew."[16] He had an exalted view of both philosophy and art in this process. In fact, it was to these ac-

application of modern science towards making money? Does he not overlook the crucial ingredient of greed as the dominant driver of certain (though not all) humans and the force that adds the unreasonable challenging forth of nature (and labor) to enframing? The development of exploitative economic systems arose out of an ability to systematically demarcate and make predictions (about how to build a ship and navigate, about how to build a dam, about how much water is needed to get a certain size crop, about where gold might be, about how to make an equivalent exchange, etc.). Heidegger shows how the self-perpetuating logic of this system alters our worldview, cuts off pathways to the sacred and defeats humility. Yet, by failing to ascribe agency in the process, he concludes that "Human activity can never directly counter the danger." This flies in the face of actual gains that social movements can and do make all the time, even as this more fundamental work of culture changing happens in the background. Shout out to: Cesar Chavez, to 350. org, to anti-fracking movements in New York, to dam-removal movements and their successes on the Yakima and other rivers, etc.

To state it simply, there are two fronts to changing the world: changing ideology (i.e., ways of seeing and representing); and changing material conditions. As such, the work of poets, artists and thinkers is symbiotic with the work of activists, not isolated a la Heidegger; it is on this level that we think of our work as art-activist. A poetic way of seeing the world—defined here as an investment in non-rational consciousness and empathic understanding—is absolutely required for an effective activism, not only because it opens up a new relation to the world, but also because

a Spanish fiction writer named Montalvo in the early 16th Century. Montalvo gave the name "California" to a fantastic land of desire and gold in his novel Las Sergas de Esplandián (published in 1510).[19] In this book, the inhabitants of California were all-powerful women who ate men after laying with them in order to bear children. There was gold everywhere. The women wore gold harnesses and hunted with gold weapons.

We believe in the role of the artist as historian, specifically in this sense of the art-activist who contributes to a transformation of worldview. To represent a river in California, our job is to show not only what it is now, but to represent its now-ness as a form of (avoidable) destiny—here again Heidegger is instructive, for he speaks of enframing and also poiesis not just as modes of revealing, but as modes of destining. History arrives, and it is always arriving. It is not unearthed intact.

it restores enchantment and inherently combats the challenging forth of enframing with the alternative form of revealing articulated by Heidegger as the bringing forth of poiesis. However, poetry/art do not happen in a vacuum and no real change can be achieved there without changes in material conditions, which is what Heidegger fundamentally missed. Once again, the phenomenon is an ecological cycle, a dialectic.

We believe in the role of the artist as historian, specifically in this sense of the art-activist who contributes to a transformation of worldview. To represent a river in California, our job is to show not only what it is now, but to represent its now-ness as a form of (avoidable) destiny—here again Heidegger is instructive, for he speaks of enframing and also poiesis not just as modes of revealing, but as modes of destining. History arrives, and it is always arriving. It is not unearthed intact. The image is the tool by which we convey this. As Benjamin said, "It is not that what is past casts its light on what is present, or what is present its light on what is past; rather, image is that wherein what has been comes together in a flash with the now to form a constellation."[18] This is the mode of the artist as historian.

With respect to California, we have found it illuminating to stare at a blank outline of the now-iconic shape that forms the boundaries of the state. That shape, which owes its Eastern contour to the desire to capture as much gold-harboring land as possible, has become one of the primary images of our project. It reflects all the capriciousness and violence, even absurdity, of political borders. These lines were drawn in 1849, the year after gold was discovered in the state. How was this same land understood before the lines were drawn? What was a river then? Is there a clue there to what it could be now?

The creation of that shape we now know as the borders of California was an arrival, not an inception. The destining started with the Spanish lust for gold, which animated their colonial adventures. Some believe the very word California was invented by

Montalvo called it California because it was a caliphate, a land of infidels. Yet, he also placed the territory "very near to a side of Earthly paradise."[20]

This was fantasy, but fantasy transforms fact. Ten years after Montalvo's book was published, the colonist Hernan Cortes wrote a letter to the King of Spain from present-day Baja California, in which he purported to confirm the nearby existence of just such a place as Montalvo described (earthly paradise, lots of gold, only women who ate men, etc.).[21] Cortes was likely angling for continued investment in his colonizing enterprise, but it is telling that he thought his report would be both enticing and sufficiently credible to his benefactor. Not long after Cortes' letter, maps begin appearing with Montalvo's word "California" labeling some of the lands Cortes colonized[22] and after a while this became the accepted name of the region. Montalvo's fantasy reified.

However, when the first Spanish mission entered into the territory of California more than two hundred years later in 1769, it was not the word "oro" (gold) that appeared obsessively in the diaries of its leaders, but the word "aqua." Nearly every day that was their primary concern. They hunted down rivers.[23] They had to hold water before they could hold gold. On 24 January 1848, everything came together when some other colonists found gold laying around in the American River. The mass hysteria that followed produced the near extermination of the Native people and rapid industrialization.

Of course, this gold had been sitting in the rivers all along but the Native Americans did not value it. Seeing value in gold is a purely imaginative exercise and dependent on a given worldview (enframing). John Sutter, the owner of the land on which gold was found on California, remarked without apparent irony that:

> It is very singular that the Indians never found a piece of gold and brought it to me, as they very often did other specimens found in the ravines.

125

I requested them continually to bring me some curiosities from the mountains, for which I always recompensed them. I have received animals, birds, plants, young trees, wild fruits, pipe clay, stones, red ochre, etc., etc., but never a piece of gold.[24]

One is reminded of Marx's paradigmatic, if racially tinged, account of the commodity fetish and the absurdity of a materialist theory of value: "The savages of Cuba regarded gold as a fetish of the Spaniards. They celebrated a feast in its honour, sang in a circle around it, and then threw it into the sea."[25]

There is a paradox at the core of history: how do we see the present as a destining, as the seemingly inevitable outcome of past events with all the gravity that implies, and at the same time see that very destining as contingent and therefore as mutable? This sort of maneuver requires a negative capability that is not the province of science, including history performed as science, but is the province of art and myth. When we ask, "What is a river?," we would do well to attend the poet, as Heidegger recommends. Paraphrasing Hölderlin, Heidegger gave this answer to the question before us:

"As a vanishing, the river is underway into what has been. As full of intimation, it proceeds into what is coming."[26]

The Nisenan Maidu name for the American River was Kum Sayo, meaning Roundhouse River, referring to a structure that the Nisenan Maidu used for dances and other ceremonies. This building was the center of a Maidu community. A particularly large and important roundhouse was located at the mouth of the American River near its confluence with the Sacramento River, in the vicinity of this highway bridge. Other roundhouses could be found all along the American River. The domesticity implied in the Maidu name for the river contrasts with later names applied by European colonists: The River of Sorrows; Wild River (so named because of the ostensibly "wild" nature of the Maidu living there); the River Ojotska (a phonetic rendering of the Russian word for hunter); Rio de los Americanos (named for the American trappers that had begun to use the river).

1        See Benjamin Madley, *American Genocide: The United States and the California Indian Catastrophe 1846-1873* (New Haven: Yale University Press, 2017) and Brendan C. Lindsay, *Murder State: California's Native American Genocide 1846-1873* (Lincoln: University of Nebraska Press, 2015).

2        Martin Heidegger, "The Question Concerning Technology," in *Martin Heidegger: Basic Writings*, trans. David Farrell Krell (San Francisco: Harper SanFrancisco, 1977), p. 297.

3        These ideas are developed more fully in other Heidegger writing on rivers, most notably in *Hölderlin's Hymn 'The Ister,'* trans. William McNeil and Julia Davis (Bloomington, IN: Indiana University Press, 1996) and "Build Dwelling Thinking" in *Martin Heidegger: Basic Writings*, trans. David Farrell Krell (San Francisco: HarperSanFrancisco, 1977), pp. 330-339.

4        Heidegger, "The Question Concerning Technology," p. 296.

5        Heidegger, *Hölderlin's Hymn 'The Ister'*, p. 40 [emphasis in original].

6        Heidegger, "The Question Concerning Technology," p. 296.

7        Ibid, p. 297.

8        Jay Lund, "What's Next for California Water?," Available online at: https://californiawaterblog.com/2011/02/23/whats-next-for-california-water/, (23 February 2011). This history is obviously told in far greater detail in many other places, notably Norris Hundley Jr.'s definitive *The Great Thirst: Californians and Water-A History*, Revised Edition (Berkeley: University of California Press, 2001).

9        Hundley, *The Great Thirst*, p. 77.

10        See Hundley, *The Great Thirst*, p. 86, but there is also an extensive literature on this crucial question. To cite just two important examples: Donald J. Pisani, *Water, Land, and Law in the West: The Limits of Public Policy, 1850-1920* (Lawrence: University Press of Kansas, 1996), and more recently, Mark Kanazawa, *Golden Rules: The Origins of California Water Law in the Gold Rush* (Chicago: University of Chicago Press, 2015).

11        General accounts can be found in Hundley; see also Stephanie S. Pincetl, *Transforming California: A Political History of Land Use and Development* (Baltimore: Johns Hopkins University Press, 2003); Walter Goldschmidt, *As You Sow: Three Studies in the Social Consequences of Agribusiness* (Monclair: Allanheld, Osmun & Co., 1978); Mark Arax and Rick Wartzman, *The King of California: J.G. Boswell and the Making of a Secret American Empire* (New York: PublicAffairs, 2005). In our project we focused particularly on Westlands, an understanding of which we owe to in part to: Lloyd G. Carter, "Reaping Riches in a Wretched Region: Subsidized Industrial Farming and Its Link to Perpetual Poverty," in *Golden Gate University Environmental Law Journal* 3 (2009), pp. 5-42. Available online at: http://digitalcommons.law.ggu.edu/gguelj/vol3/iss1/3; and Ed Simmons, "Westlands Water District: The First 25 Years," published by Westland Water District itself in 1983.

12        See Goldschmidt, *As You Sow*, and see also the work of Dean McCannell, which updated the legendary Goldschmidt study, and also the work of Paul Taylor (Dorothea Lange's collaborator). An unpublished but excellent dissertation by Daniel J. O'Connell brings much of this work together: *In the Struggle: Pedagogies of Politically Engaged Scholarship in the San Joaquin Valley of California*, unpublished doctoral dissertation (Cornell University, 2011).

13        For example, see http://pacinst.org/publication/human-costs-of-nitrate-contaminated-drinking-water-in-the-san-joaquin-valley/

14        It is hard to overcome thinking about causality in linear terms (which is itself a by-product of enframing). However, as ecological thinking is a thinking of relationships, it is also a thinking that dissolves linear causality in favor of cycles and dialectical relationships. Heidegger was perhaps more ecological than even he realized as his style of writing is cyclical.

15        Heidegger, *Hölderlin's Hymn 'The Ister,'* p. 25.

16        Martin Heidegger, *Introduction to Metaphysics*, trans. Gregory Fried and Richard Polt (New Haven: Yale University Press, 2000), p. 133.

17        Martin Heidegger, "Nur noch ein Gott kann uns retten," *Der Spiegel* 30 (Mai 1976): 193-219, trans. W. Richardson as "Only a God Can Save Us," in *Heidegger: The Man and the Thinker*, Thomas Sheehan (ed.) (n.p.: Precedent, 1981), pp. 45-67.

18        Walter Benjamin, *The Arcades Project* (Cambridge, MA: Harvard University Press, 2002), p. 462.

19        Kevin Starr, *California: A History* (New York: Modern Library, 2007), p. 5; and Charles E. Chapman, *A History of California: The Spanish Period* (New York: The Macmillan Company, 1921), pp. 59-65.

20        "Sabed que a la diestra mano de las Indias existe una isla llamada California muy cerca de un costado del Paraíso Terrenal" from García Ordóñez de Montalvo, Las Sergas de Esplandián, Seville, 1510, as found http://www.aaregistry.org/historic_events/view/california-its-naming-heritage, 7 July 2016. See also the argument for the Persian origin of the term from Kari-i-farn ("the mountain of Paradise"), suggested earlier by Carey McWilliams, in Josef Chytry, *Mountain of Paradise: Reflections of the Emergence of Greater California as a World Civilization* (New York: Peter Lang, 2013), pp. 13-15.

21        Chapman, *A History of California*, p. 64.

22        Ibid., pp. 65-66.

23        Hundley, *The Great Thirst*, p. 32.

24        John A. Sutter, "The Discovery of Gold in California," in *Hutchings' California Magazine*, (November 1857). Available online at: http://www.sfmuseum.org/hist2/gold.html (accessed 24 May 2017)

25        Karl Marx, "Debates on the Law on Thefts of Wood' [1842], in Karl Marx and Frederick Engels, *Collected Works*, Vol. 1 (London: Lawrence and Wishart, 1975), pp. 262-263.

26        Heidegger, Hölderlin's Hymn 'The Ister," p. 29.

127

# TOWARDS A SUPRARURAL ARCHITECTURE
## Ciro Najle & Lluís Ortega

Suprarural claims a new domain for the practice of architecture. By turning the discipline's dysfunctions *vis-à-vis* the urban and its systematic oversights regarding the countryside into a new set of opportunities, Suprarural issues an urgent call for a theory that can overcome both of these in the name of extending the spectrum of capabilities, and by engulfing the ordering systems of the territory. The project is carried out via a program of investigation that takes the know-how embedded in the rural—its organizational protocols, its synchronicity with the natural, and its often disregarded technification—as the raw material for a new form of architectural expertise.

The opportunity provided by the investigation is not to be confused with simple convenience at a practical level. Nor is it meant to develop a new rhetoric of punchlines and improbable statements that are merely ironic or amusing in nature. Instead it involves an earnest plea, mobilized by playing, in virtual terms, with the territory itself. The seemingly ordinary scenario of this game—that is, the fundamental operative failure of the rural domain in the face of the ubiquitous forces of urbanization, and what appears in principle as a thematic outmodedness—is reversed here into a panorama of unprecedented potential, embedded with straightforward techniques and vibrant new organizations and figures.

Suprarural's call for the rural—that marginal, enigmatic, and apparently minor territory of discussion—is directed to challenge and problematize the condition of the suburban by turning its ubiquitous model inside out and threatening it with the dark side of the commodification of the territory. The Suprarural is the underside of the myth of endless urban expansion. It involves the intensification of the rural into architectural singularities, rather than its annihilation by the urban, and calls for extreme exposure rather than refuge, engagement rather than retirement, radical technification rather than primitive form, and for the sophisticated wilderness of post-urban uncertainty rather than the domesticated mildness of pre-urban nostalgia.

In past decades the discipline has gone through a triple displacement. First, it has moved from satellite representation to the simulation of systems that manage the complex fluidity of territories beyond political, social, and cultural boundaries.

The ethics and tone of this development have also gradually shifted from different versions of landscape urbanism to various ways of appropriating ecological models for a wiser understanding of the urban. It has thereby established an array of roles for the ecological condition as part of a wider geopolitical project—one directed at integrating contemporary processes of urbanization in a single inevitable trend by using the metaphysics of survival and the myth of sustainability as its perfect vehicle.

Second, the discipline has displaced its focus from the object to the ground by engaging geographic positioning systems, renewing its forms of mapping, and refining its procedures through the popularization of field and systems theory. This shift has recently flipped back into the vertical, with the ground itself becoming the new condition of the architectural object: monumental, geomorphological, post-utopian, and figural. It also converts the organizational potential of the dynamic complexity of the territory—multi-scalarity, multi-temporality, trans-specificity, and pre-urbanity—into cartoon-like figurations that now promise to provide architecture with a solution to the conundrum of its orientation towards service through a renovated palette of persuasion.

Third, a cultural shift has taken place from the general idea of practice as a meta-domain that integrates different disciplines to a polarization between the inter-disciplinary ideology of climatic change and the regressive ethics of the old notion of autonomy, clear expressions of the rapid consumption of ideas and cultural constructs at work in contemporary culture. It seems that the expansive role of the architect as a mediator operating within the systems—an agent installed half-outside of them and an artist working through them—has declined into a model in which the modern notion of the architect as a former ideologue, now expatriated to a post-postmodern, retro-ideological, pseudo-political scenario, has taken over design research, turning it into an enemy to be obliterated from the firmament of serious architectural thought.

In this context, Suprarural aligns itself with systemic thinking and its persuasive promise of empowering the architectural project with robust structures. But this alignment is performed amorally, and with an important dose of lightness. Its protocolar machine is not conceived as an ideal means to something else, like a manual of instruments waiting to be used for the right purposes, but as a constitutional state of the in-between, which, like it or not, does not close the perfect circle of the traditional typological manual. Thus, the work is not a body of research that operates within the scientific tradition without friction. Even though characterized by identifying territorial conditions and configuring the distinguishable organizational models through which they can be competently directed, on a more basic level it endeavors to open up new spaces of imagination.

The Suprarural is, in this context, regarded as a medium of design operating through a standard that develops a focus through and by the means of production, allowing external inputs to constantly force the re-description of its models. Its methodology is thus directed at progressively constructing relevance in iterative loops, not through sense but through reverberation. The Suprarural is a platform that constitutes meanings of a kind, singularities through consistency, order through resonance. It seeks to deploy power by formulating new questions, without necessarily answering them. Similarly, the notion and the figure of the rural protocol is not to be seen as

128

an instrument for arriving at a Suprarural status, nor is it assumed to be good *per se*. Instead, the rural is the device through which the Suprarural—that blurry vision—can perhaps be instilled into our worldview and enticed into the real.

### DIAGRAM AS RECURSIVE MODEL

Suprarural consists of a set of informational regimes that index the existing formal organization of the rural. This set involves diagrams that collect intelligence from rural systems and integrates their

ferent figures; it evolves through perpetual refinement in lending as much attention to the progressively emerging target as to the gaps lying or arising in between. The gaps between protocols have, so to speak, a life of their own, and they themselves become the engine of potential constructs, thus blurring the boundaries between sources and meanings, and revealing a deeper passion for the leaps embedded in continuities than a loyalty to conserving them as they are. The ideal within the Suprarural operates as a sort of shadow or, better yet, as a fog of indistinguishable grays, enigmat-

The Suprarural is, in this context, regarded as a medium of design operating through a standard that develops a focus through and by the means of production, allowing external inputs to constantly force the re-description of its models.

rules into abstract models. The construction works as a design platform through the actualization of territorial latencies. Constituted by protocols made up of different ranges and scopes of performance, the Suprarural allows them to be redefined by various forms of feedback with each other, displaying them and making them perform against one another. In that sense the "Atlas of Rural Protocols" is not so much a set of components whose instrumentality is external to their form as a fluid medium that establishes continuities between potentials latent in the material world. Traditional representational logics, in which drawings refer to external forms of meaning that engage existing cultural narratives, achieve a status that takes the post-representational nature of the diagram to the level of an abstract register in a territorial model. The systemic condition of this diagrammatic form conducts the rural material to a plane where action and representation are one, operating together by making their relational structures explicit and constantly refining their protocols of description. The Suprarural diagram is a recursive model amongst rural protocols.

Normally, organizational protocols operate through the definition of constraints and the recognition of performances with various levels of redundancy. There is no requirement, in principle, to model them in the direction of the construction of ideals, nor is there a will to design idealizations, but rather an immanent desire to mobilize reverberations through design by intensifying them as instances in larger processes of differentiation, magnifying attributes of the organizations to a point where they are no longer efficient in their original terms, and launching a wider range and higher level of performance, now charged with a broader agenda. This lack of idealization of the rural does not mean that there is a similar loss in the legibility of its character.

Only that it is forced, here, to become operational and forward-looking, referring more to a form of imagination grounded in stimulation and a sense of opportunity than to a figural resemblance to past references. The opportunity for these actions is guided by the proximity of usage and contiguity of dif-

ic in-between states, slippery nuances, and smooth edges. Ideas flicker within this fog, sparkle and become sharper at times, and proliferate in an endless game of readjusting targets and alliances.

### TECHNIFICATION AS DIFFERENTIATION PROCESS

Apparently bare and devoid of architecture, the American Midwest and the Argentine Pampas are highly technified territories that constitute, virtually or actually, consistent forms of extraordinarily large architecture. While in the industrial era the local was merely a by-product of a larger production system at work invisibly across regions, its post-industrial technification operates as the condition of possibility of a global dynamic. The mechanical process was, in modern times, transversally isolated, functionally specialized, technically optimized, and driven by single-minded forms of efficiency that were, for the most part, alien to the multivalent potential of material systems. Currently, it is the material systems themselves that are becoming machinized and made time-efficient, multi-purpose, distributed, and therefore highly volatile, configuring a ubiquitous architectural project that resets, each time and by means of local protocols, the normative conventions by which generic structures operate.

This peculiar coexistence of bottom-up self-organizing processes and top-down territorial design strategies implies both a threat to, and a challenge for, architecture: either it is swiftly left out of any influence at a geopolitical level, or it is compelled to function as the *sine qua non* mode of control of territorial form as transformative device. The shared know-how and ownership system that is embedded in local processes commands the globalized dynamics of technification without even noticing it. And, in this context, the discipline is confronted by the possibility of constructing new and expansive forms of knowledge by simply articulating local organizations and nurturing their outcomes from within, and yet exceeding the rationality of their production frameworks. The particular and the generic are enabled to perform not merely as

129

polarities in a process of mutual feedback between local events and global conditions, out of reach for the architect and exclusive of other forms of expertise—geopolitical, geological, ecological—but also to become the matter of an architectural project themselves. Architecture now has the opportunity to unleash singularities that can become generic systems of a second order: the territory as the ultimate form of architecture.

Furthermore, rural organizational techniques working at a local level exhibit the capacity to not only articulate global processes at a territorial level but, more importantly, to change them from within and transform vast territories along the lines of increasingly convoluted and yet extremely simple patterns. Architecture can take on board this expansive capability, not just by contributing to the organization of the local performance of these patterns but by intensifying them in a symphony of redundancy at various scales, allowing generic territorial structures to be differentiated on the basis of manifold local, regional, and

## ASSEMBLAGE AS FORMAL TECHNIQUE

How do we work in a context where systems have an open logic and are robust enough to adapt to contingency yet still operate within a narrow range of performance and a very limited world view? How do we expand the narrow-minded, inward-looking scope of performance of rural systems into broad-minded, generalist ones, and do this from within, rather than from without? In other words, how do we move from the local-global dichotomy based on the opposition of rural vs. urban to the ubiquitous-singular multiplicity-based level of the Suprarural Cosmopolis?

The convention of constructing hybrid or counter-intuitive figurations by articulating fragments through montage has been the customary formal technique to decontextualize typologies in patchwork-like or field-like landscape proposals since the 1990s. However linguistically curious, formally poignant, or conceptually innovative, these techniques

Apparently bare and devoid of architecture, the American Midwest and the Argentine Pampas are highly technified territories that constitute, virtually or actually, consistent forms of extraordinarily large architecture.

global inputs, rather than operating within the range of encapsulated forms of material efficiency alone. If we read the globe as a single yet multiple informational model, productive in nature, neither urban nor natural as such, the redundant structure that this model embodies allows any form of know-how to be integrated and creatively synchronized, rather than disappearing as mere background noise in the sea of global-local efficiencies. Rural patterns can thus be said to operate as the basic organizational matter in a broader scheme of redundancy management, absorbing, with material directionality, information coming from a wide range of inputs—from the hyper-local, accidental and contingent situations of the farmer to the homogenizing tendencies that are linked to large-scale corporation logics. As a consequence, these patterns should not be understood as averages or as mere negotiations of existing conditions but as incomplete collective constructions that deal with various modalities and intensities. Catalysts of a functioning world of simultaneous processes of differentiation, rural protocols are the ultimate triggers for the constitution of global orders, megalomaniac and yet inherently architectural, self-alienating and self-transforming at base. Architecture is the ultimate and most appropriate means for the world to problematize its comfort zones of territorial efficiency through an artistic model. Inputs of extremely different kinds and degrees can be integrated within such ultra-large fluent structures, where systems provide feedback for one another in loops of proliferating or balancing patterns.

proved to be limited to the rarifying capabilities of formal disruptions or the collision of opposites. By and large they operated within the boundaries of the architectural object, no matter how expanded in scale. And by solely referring to the traditional representational conventions of architecture, frequently based on dichotomies like natural-artificial, inside-outside, rural-urban, full-void, ground-object, soft-hard, open-closed, among others, these techniques lack the organizational effectiveness that they promise and the formal fluency that give them significance. They are there to help evoke a world project by imitating ecologies through static representations of complexity, often metaphorically, but failing to respond to the challenge of constructing the material means of a geopolitical model that might integrate dynamic attributes in forward-looking simulations. By working with static assemblages of objects, these lineages fail to root themselves in the more abstract register of the protocolar and are therefore unable to technically lead a rigorous design process and a greater capacity for establishing supple and adjustable relationships. By being focused on immediate figurations and on the mediatic impact of the rhetoric of form rather than on dynamic organizational capabilities and on the potential of form to have an actual influence over the processes, they fail to recognize the very basic transformational capabilities of architecture that lay not only in persuasion but also in maneuvering performance. The notion of dynamic assemblage, based on the organizational latency of protocols, relational and relative in nature, is conducive, instead, to the integration of subsystems and to the creation of expansive trans-scalar figures, legible within the global continuum at many scales. The local becomes, in this context, not just a figure operating at a discrete scale, but an index of larger systems, whose organization it contributes to at a deep structural level.

This second order of assemblage is constructed by means of two levels of operation: one that recognizes systems, breaks them down into the smallest protocolar relationships, and constructs a manual of variations of those broken-down attributes, and another one that puts these attributes and relationships together and builds up progressively robust assemblages. However, the logic is not linear, as if moving from unit to set, but rather circular: as the resulting assemblages feed back, the systems break down, altering the original protocols and endowing them with renewed potential. In a way this circular process works like an endless dice game which constructs ever-higher forms of chance. Far from being consecutive steps in a traditional deterministic process, these iterative throws of the dice operate as forcefully deterministic actions, where everything is necessary and actually wished for, retroactively. The process is not just a way to justify the outcome but rather the opposite: it is the outcome itself that constructs legitimacy in reverse, or better still, both process and outcome keep the feedback loop they partake of in motion, as a motor of determinacy. Global design thus becomes relevant and persuasive not through the artificial magnification of localities through fields or patchworks that extrapolate and generalize effects, but rather as the intentionality in-built in a feedback process that transforms itself *en route*, setting constantly new agendas and altering the directionality of the forthcoming ones. Such a process works as a sort of vibrating machine, overcoming the segregated condition of protocols by escalating and looping back their abstract regimes.

## PROTOCOLS AS ABSTRACT REGIMES

For this dynamic assembly loop to be possible, there must be a set of inner regulations that can both build the coherence of the particular subsystems and trigger their self-transformation. Rural protocols are not just formal rules that determine relations in an absolute, permanent manner in the direction of the making of closed, descriptive procedures, but are instead relational logics of performance that connect with others and are capable of setting a generative engine in motion. This is one of the main purposes of the iterative use of protocols: to develop a successive mediation directed towards an increasing and progressively expansive form of abstraction. Once the embedded efficiency of systems is released from its restrictiveness to other systems, often assumed to be necessary, protocols become a potential part of a larger synthetic machine, in which the evaluation of performance is set free from its single-mindedness, unfolding and multiplying effects in their context. Designers become complex-system-designers and construct conditions for architectural inventiveness through the abstraction of protocols that, in turn, start operating in directions which diverge from the original instructions. The inner mate-

rial logics of protocols are therefore not simply removed in a process of abstraction but rather the opposite: they become intensified and freed of the consecutiveness of the linear processes they take part in. Material logics transform differentiation processes in convoluted patterns that contain a manifold of potential actualizations that circulate in constant feedback, oscillating between an inherent abstraction and a progressive charging of meaning and sense. This oscillatory loop promotes the engagement of the unknown as if it were known in advance, encouraging invention and operating as a rigorous but open-ended game of managing potentials.

There is a form of vitalism embedded in such a circular design process, but it is a circular form that embraces chance, intense counter-intuitiveness, and radical arbitrariness as a condition of existence, performing through the mutual adjustment of the outcomes and the protocols that set up the game structure. There is no such thing as an idealized form of efficiency, nor is there a vector of progress which can be claimed in advance or demonstrated as being necessary, not even in a nonlinear version. Instead it is the ongoing convolution of expertise in the systems of rules and the precision of the outcomes which go on continuously nurturing the game, taking its intelligence and playfulness to a higher plane. Far from operating as rules of the sedimentation of know-how, and farther still from defining a coherent model of increasingly refined efficiency, protocols assume the role of being the dischargers and the receivers of a design machine that works by ceaselessly shuttling back and forth between the constituency of rules and the organization of by-products. The Suprarural is a source of protocolar intelligence in that respect, and rural protocols the transitory sediments of an unending game. A protocol-based system of rules is therefore not just a system of nonlinear control but a system of interferences that, depending on the moment, may behave as a driving force, a source of restriction, a resource of conceptual construction, a vehicle of disciplinary problematization, a device of performance evaluation, or a reserve of cultural value. Here, techniques, figures, norms, references, and forms meet in a medium that changes register when necessary. The Atlas embodies just this multivalent medium.

## ATLAS AS POLITICAL ENGINE

The Atlas is traditionally an instrument of territorial design. The very rationale of its format consists in being able to hold and navigate across the most diverse types of information in a systematic way, the ambition being to create the conditions of a comprehensive totality. However, the Atlas not only works as an all-inclusive mechanism that serves as a passive instrument for fixing and arranging different points of view, but also as a biased platform that redefines perspectives, facilitates novel worldviews, and activates the configuration of new questions and the transfiguration of what is taken to be a given. The Atlas is a plural, multidirectional diagram, a multiplicity of blueprints that forces the user to formulate questions;

it is a transformative tool, not just a compilation of inert conditions systematically displayed and made available for the increasing knowledge of an impersonal reader located at an abstract infinite point, fully detached from the real and rendered ever-conscious. Through its systematic structure, it traces the preliminary conditions for new organizations to take place through an active interaction with the reader, an interaction conditioned in turn by its content and techniques. Its drawings create a nature of their own, its techniques construct an operative language, and its chapters structure new frames of mind.

The Atlas is an aggregation of voices that expand a spectrum of interest, a multiplicity of images and autonomous documents that proliferate in an open-ended series of collections, a set of captions that multiply the links between artifact and potential. Its objecthood coalesces the disparity and incompatibility of things in a multitude of provisionally coherent systems of relationships. This simultaneous ability for endlessly incorporating, possessing, and sustaining the world in a limited space is accompanied by an equally fluent capacity for spinning this material around itself to create new worlds. Its diagrammatic nature is there to catalyze otherwise disconnected and senseless information, and purely out of reverberation works as a tabula for the development of consistent design strategies.

Far from wishing, then, to provide a fixed portrait of a territory, made transparent through a precise system of coordinates and a coherent set of instructions to understand and use it judiciously, this Atlas defines the conditions for a series of active relationships that oblige readers to take alternative positions within the territories under question. In other words, it is not a means to safely locate the reader in an otherwise unknown territory—that is, an apparatus of knowledge that preserves the subject's prudent detachment from the real—but a weapon to empower action on the real and engage with the potency of the unknown. The Atlas is a political engine. It requires of the reader an equally earnest will to become an agent of information management. It is a means of unscrupulous resourcefulness, not just a means of disengagement and comprehensiveness. Manifold actualizations that are imprudent, blunt, forceful, and unnatural are embedded in its pages. And yet these actualizations are neither infinite nor gratuitous. They demand projective reading. An Atlas is not a means of indifference but a vehicle for differentiation. Its pages are not flat screens that make knowledge available, but unforgiving sheets that only open themselves to the playful reader who can work transversally in relation to their sequences, submitting to their rules of thumb in order to play a game with them.

## THE RURAL AS PRE-ARCHITECTURAL CONDITION

The organization of the rural in an Atlas is regarded as a pre-architectural condition whose pattern is embedded with dynamic intelligence and can foster different urbanization processes. The rural is not presented nostalgically as an inert or obsolete organizational condition waiting to be transformed by urbanization, but rather as a particular structure within which latent architectural systems are ready and willing to be intensified and equipped with prospective properties. The rural works as a set of subsystems operating simultaneously, partly in consonance, partly in parallel. Its substructure is grounded on natural systems dynamics: seasonal to daily weather variations, various conditions of topography and water flows, animal behavior, a limited array of ecologies supported by different technological regimes, artificial drainage systems, infrastructural systems, land division systems, animal management systems, sow and harvest systems, storage systems, which are activated and determined by a range of economic forces, mostly concentrated around agricultural production and cattle, and permeated by habits, rituals, routines, and various cultural traditions, historically characteristic of the prairie and the flatlands. The formalization of those systems and their performance gives a clear identity to the landscape of the Midwest, and the Pampas, and builds up conditions of possibility for urban organizations to happen. In other words, the Rural Atlas is not simply the result of stabilizing rural culture by capturing it in poignant images but also the raw organization of a prospective capability to create unprecedented urban-territorial cultures. If the rural is a matrix of preliminary inputs in a potentially evolving system rather than a given state of things, and if the transformative propensities that develop within these inputs is forced to configure questions which can surpass their status quo rather than be assumed as self-explanatory frameworks, the logics of rural production can be said to already contain logics of urbanization, as if on hold.

The substructure of the rural is differentiated through a series of evaluations that drive the feedback of its current situation with new principles, thus intensifying or modulating its embedded architectural attributes. The outcome of this process is an in-between condition, neither rural nor urban, or both, performing simultaneously at different registers that evolve over time and are fueled by architecture. In other words, the Suprarural does not bring any stabilization or consolidation into the rural, nor does it bring an imposed kind of change to it; rather, it recognizes and upgrades its in-between condition and takes it to another level of complexity, a higher cultural standing. Some of these actualizations work as material sets in evolution, in the sense that they nurture material organizations that already have their constraints and regulations inscribed within regimes of equilibrium or diversification. They can be regarded as entire cultural mindsets in their own right, in the sense that they operate at an abstract linguistic level, in reframing systemic correlations by re-conceptualizing their territory of pertinence. The dual material-mental condition of the rural is integrated within the two simultaneously multifarious and dialectic layers of the Suprarural, where the design of material organizations requires a new conceptual apparatus that can channel its potential, and vice versa—a whole series of material-based routines that can implement

132

such forms of knowledge. The complex loop established between the two layers, each of them inherently multiple and convoluting, is seldom smooth and linear. Instead it is able to generate manifold tensions and disruptions, which oblige the notion of the Suprarural to be permanently provisional and subject to definition.

### SUPRA AS META-AUTHORSHIP

Supra, as in Suprarural, is the default condition of meta-authorship. The Suprarural constructs an abstract machine for overcoming the dichotomy between subject and system by means of the internal differentiation of regulatory norms into creative guidelines; that is, of norms that are capable of challenging their own range and mode of variation, paradoxically unfolding their expansive power by accumulating and integrating specifications and various forms of know-how. The Suprarural configures a pre-architectonic ground, from which many, albeit not infinite, architectures are possible. It abstracts, organizes, coordinates, and integrates the latent architectonic potential contained in the rural and, through

ti-authorial critique or bypass them by means of an ethics of systemic integration. It involves the blunt differentiation of existing orders—and orders of orders—without falsifying them. The rural, a virtual datum within which this differentiation is developed, is not a tabula rasa and it does not allow creative narratives to be projected or instilled without grounding themselves in its normativity. Rather than discouraging creativity, this void-like inertia encourages authors to engage with extremely slow and at times dumb and pointless processes, with particular design operations that, in the midst of the more intense homogeneity and indifference, differentiate the nuances and hidden striations of this apparent nothingness towards a new status of organization. The subtle legibility of the systems of the rural does not merely call for a subjective projection on the part of the author onto what is regarded as sheer emptiness, it is also the most fertile medium for the construction of meta-authorial practices that nurture systems, inherently banal and often insipid, and cause them to collide with each other. The Suprarural is, so to speak, the odd state of the art of the rural, both constraining it anew and upgrading its operations into

133

The rural is not presented nostalgically as an inert or obsolete organizational condition waiting to be transformed by urbanization, but rather as a particular structure within which latent architectural systems are ready and willing to be intensified and equipped with prospective properties.

iterative processes of intensification, actualizes their urban power. If the systemic non-author, fully embedded within systems, was capable of transcending systemic logics by managing their potentials from within, the Suprarural meta-author designs systems of systems, operating from both within and without, making sure not to patronize the outcome as a superior, seemingly natural state that follows on from the threshold of nonlinearity. Instead, the meta-author assumes this extra-threshold state as something entirely artificial, and regards its construct as nothing other than his artistic duty, going beyond the intra-systemic notion of the in-between and overcoming the natural-urban opposition implicit in its ethics. This movement that actualizes the intra-systemic fable of self-organization into the supra-systemic artifice of localizing architecture both inside and outside of systems makes use of the circular loop of feedbacks between rural normative intelligence and urban restrictions as the basic definitions of a ubiquitous urban/territorial model. The practice of architecture overcomes the inter-disciplinary myth and ceases to be a mode of transferring knowledge between fields in order to become a mode of unfolding consistencies across fields, precisely through architectural expertise.

Meta-authorship overtakes both the representational traditions of authorship based on ideas, concepts, narratives, or commentaries, and those that either refuse them by recourse to a politics of an-

unforeseen design actions. The figure of the author is not repressed here by superficially heroic but deeply authoritarian single-statement propositions, which arbitrarily and suddenly change the conditions of the land for a more efficient urban usage, nor does it celebrate the multi-statement or the anti-statement-type proposition of the post-authorial. Instead, the Suprarural opens up a whole new set of authorial forms. It calls for a collective form of authorship, not in the sense of an interdisciplinary or participatory ethics that dissolves design expertise via politically correct committees, technocratic think-tanks, and paternalistic systems of participation, but by putting authorship under a high level of stress, and by consciously misusing the deceptively indifferent organizational forms of the rural.

### MIDWEST-PAMPAS AS
### GEOPOLITICAL PROJECT

The Midwest-Pampas is a dual geopolitical arena that articulates cultural, economic, historic, and technological determinations in a plane of consistency running along a north-south axis, parallel to that described by the two American metropolises, New York and Buenos Aires, major trading gates between Europe and America, through which the mainstream flows of immigration of peoples, goods, and civilizing drives has taken place during the 20th century. Ingeniously synthetized by the bifocal map of

Le Corbusier in Precisions (1930), this axis of the continent's unavoidable destiny grew weaker as the metropolitan model of huge capital cities and hinterlands was replaced by the distributed model of regional networks, installing a new form of geopolitical life. The north-south Midwest-Pampas axis runs today in a precise longitudinal parallel to its metropolitan predecessor and articulates not a model oriented by the inward-outward relationships between the continent and the ocean but one where interior and exterior coincide and pulsate from the two largest agricultural plains. By means of this displaced centrality, the suburban model, dominant expression of the decaying megalopolitan stage of those two major urban centers,

both the support of a highly-rationalized mechanism of capitalist production and the nurturing nature of a machinic sublime.

Three attributes are the expression of this splendor. The first is the non-horizontal property of flatness; it unfolds as the natural manifestation of how an opulent field reacts to simple actions of colonization, namely, sowing and harvesting, which trigger convoluted design loops and spinning formal patterns that literally cause the ground to revolve. The second attribute is the historical evidence of the fact that the vertical elevation of anything working anti-gravitationally against the dominance of flatness becomes a figure of praise and glory, no matter how banal. Sources of

The Suprarural configures a pre-architectonic ground, from which many, albeit not infinite, architectures are possible. It abstracts, organizes, coordinates, and integrates the latent architectonic potential contained in the rural and, through iterative processes of intensification, actualizes their urban power.

134

encounters now its antithetical reversal, the Suprarural, expression of an upcoming urban territory, alternative to the regional network model in which it allegedly takes part. With the fundamental capacity to carry the production of a concealed quantity of reserves at the verge of an age of acute lack of resources, this post-sustainability model promises to articulate the potentials of a production map that transforms the outdated model of the rural into an over-technified form, overwhelming the urban as we know it.

It is in this context that the massive monotony and ruthless insipidness of the Midwest and the Pampas build up a new form of cultural prosperity based on the economics of the countryside. If observed with low-resolution lenses, its principal attributes have the aspect of a brutal, crudely homogenous and straightforward territorial archetype, almost dull in its formal frankness and aesthetic earnestness. The prairie is a childlike territory, immature in its form, and candid in its organization. And yet its flatness, figural manifestation of an uncompromising mindset, unveils a landscape of nuanced differences. As its vastness cannot conceal its richness, lying a meter down, far from cancelling differences, it makes them all the more evident and auspicious. The Midwest and the Pampas are fine-resolution fields capable of responding to almost any action, no matter how tiny, casual, or irrelevant. The prairie is a field where any action gets effortlessly escalated to extremes, and immediately projected onto a firmament of hope, imagination, myth, and vision. Laid-back investment, prolific production, and fast development are all proof of the simple theorem of this magnifying plane. Notwithstanding its calm, tranquil appearance, its responsiveness to stimuli is unexpectedly excessive, engendering uniqueness and otherness through sheer quantity and density. The Suprarural becoming of the continent calls for a refocusing on the ground, now in a paradoxical role: to be

landscape legibility, rhythm, depth, and orientation, such emergences in elevation—machines, trucks and vehicles, abandoned tools and objects, giant trees, medium-size forests, raw constructions and industrial naves, infrastructural ruins, silos and windmills, animals, and even human figures—distinguish themselves as the sudden heroes of the expansiveness. A final attribute is spherical flatness, fashioned by the extreme proportions of the plane, resulting from merging the 360-degree horizon with impossible swelling curvatures. This traveling horizon is invisible in other types of fields, except perhaps in oceans. Curved horizons, rasterized soils that curl-in-flatness, spherical skies that surround the space with explicit, often poetic, meteorological and astronomic processes bring the earthy constitution of the rural to an oceanic perspective. The ruggedness of the populated horizon and the mirage of the atmosphere give the flatland a dense character.

Horizontal, passive, homogenous, endless, universal from one perspective; vertical, revolving, unique, counter-intuitive, singular from another; curved, surrounding, encompassing, exposing, from a third point of view; the flatland portrays an active three-dimensional field that builds up design actions as if naturally, from the tiniest stimuli and constraints, becoming a territory of clever navigation and expansive differentiation. Le Corbusier's map, that megalomaniac enterprise across the unexplored edges between oceans and continents, operating within the two-dimensional framework of the modern universalizing ground, is now flipped by its parallel counterpart, the intensive consistency of the Suprarural, that ubiquitous biological machine of the impossible escalation of minor actions through the revolution, verticalization, and curving of the flat by means of rural protocols.

The art of territorial activation grounded on the nuanced uniformity of the flatlands and nurtured by its inexhaustible plane of consistency, the

Suprarural defines the territory of an ubiquitous practice. It adopts the formal norms and informal routines of the rural, reframes them in an Atlas, and sets up the rules of a game of feedback loops that integrate manifold capabilities in a collective development that largely exceeds the communitarian. Without softening the powers embedded in the real, but instead furthering their subtleties, it boosts the sensibility of the rural with an open-ended spectrum of architectural imagination. The techniques of this Atlas are organized according to a series of rural systems: transport and infrastructure, land subdivision, soil management, water management, irrigation, socialization, storage, human inhabitation, animal management. These systems are described as protocols, that is, as rules of engagement with other systems. These rules are defined as simple variations of a series of variables, which, responsive to the variation of other variables, connect systems with one another. Variables synthesize the behavioral regime of systems, often obscured under the guise of habits, routines, and rituals, and only in particularly industrialized cases considered as intelligent, determinable, and predictable. However, these variables,

the original framework of efficiency of rural protocols than it is made present through the nurturing and strengthening of their embedded architectural potentials. The intensified actualization of rural systems—isolated, intertwined, and mutually-activated—the Suprarural works as a dynamic assemblage that reduces the responsibility of the comprehensiveness of models in order to articulate and magnify particular iterations of the architectural structures latent within systems. Such intensified actualization is a diagram in itself, fed by new sets of protocols that get continually indexed and integrated in the framework. New frames of evaluation are constructed, investing the rawness of the rural with a progressive directionality. The loop slowly constitutes a complex set and keeps incorporating determinations as it evolves as a vision. The Suprarural project thus remains an open question and retains its in-between nature as an essential part of the further development of its procedures. Narratives are left open, ideals are made relative, universals are subsumed to their own vacuum, and permanence remains unspoken. The generality of Suprarural models consists of the becoming singular of recurrent games between regula-

135

## The Midwest and the Pampas are fine-resolution fields capable of responding to almost any action, no matter how tiny, casual, or irrelevant. The prairie is a field where any action gets effortlessly escalated to extremes, and immediately projected onto a firmament of hope, imagination, myth, and vision.

mechanized or not, constitute one of the clearest procedural bodies in the world, consisting not only of mechanisms and instruments of territorial determination, but also of devices, tricks, and trickeries to adapt to the manifold contingencies and accidents that such prolific territory can bring about. Sensible, sensitive, practical, down-to-earth, sequential, astute, prudent, tactile, simple, economical, these rules construct the machine of sensibility of the flat plain. They regulate processes of high efficiency and adaptability with low cost and energy. They are transmitted through the generations without ambiguity, or better yet, with exactly the necessary ambiguity to enable change under unusual circumstances. If anything, rural protocols show that sustainable architecture lies in the methods more than in the artifacts or the materials, and that there is no higher-end technology than an advanced system of abstract intelligence, simple in its instructions and sensible in its performances.

Suprarural has a main structure based on the integration of these rules in a loop-based model that moves back and forth between systemic protocols and articulated projects. If rural systems are described as a detailed taxonomy of existing principles of organization, Suprarural projects are made up of the ways in which these principles distance themselves from the systematic documentation of the catalog through its intensive differentiation. Suprarural Architecture is no more related to the specificities of

tions and emergences. Clearly not a defined product, Suprarural Architecture is one design phase among many. Its visions are both bred in, and removed from, the statics of the rural; they are impelled towards the configuration of artistic territorial actions. Suprarural is, in that sense, the art of territorial activation.

**SUPRARURAL**
Pablo Gerson

These images of the agrarian landscapes of the Argentine Pampas and the American Midwest seek to emphasize the homogeneity and de-dramatization of territorial representation. At the same time, they express a certain artificiality—even strangeness—in the decomposition of their elements, thus producing an aligned visual archive. As a whole, the archive manages to reconstruct a productive territory and its imaginary through serialization and repetition.

# PROJECTS

# NOTES ON THE SECOND EDITION
## Stan Allen

*In the Old World, the nuances and differences be-*
*tween nations form the main focus of the picture.*
*In the New World, man and his productions dis-*
*appear, so to speak, in the midst of a wild and*
*outsize nature.*

*— Alexander von Humboldt, 1807*

Mies van der Rohe left Germany in 1937, arriving
in Chicago midway through what would come to be called
"the American Century." And while his later buildings reflect an optimism propelled by post-war prosperity, something of the darkness of a continent drifting towards war
and crisis remain present in his work. Mies's works in
Chicago, New York, and Toronto are a hybrid of Old World
and New, a vestige of European high-culture filtered
through the lens of American technological progress and
economic prosperity. Today, half a century after Mies's
death, the Mies Crown Hall Americas Prize celebrates that
hybridity, confident that even in the face of the leveling
effects of globalization and the unprecedented access to information, a specifically "American" identity persists among
architects working in North and South America today.

But what exactly do we mean when we talk about
"the Americas"? Can we talk about a character specific to
the vast and varied territory encompassed by North,
Central and South America, distinct from Europe, Asia, or
Africa? Is a sense of place still meaningful in today's global cultural landscape? It is a rich and complicated topic,
but the outline of the answer lies in two intertwined aspects, one cultural, the other material.

North and South America share a colonial history. A substantial part of the population of the Americas
comes from somewhere else and migrated here, as immi-
grants and colonists, or brought here forcibly by the slave
trade. These diverse populations came into violent conflict with indigenous peoples who were here first, but they
also interchanged customs and cultures. The culture of

the Americas is marked by this rich syncretism. The Europeans—and later others—who came here left behind their own history and confronted a radically "other" culture, a culture tied intimately to the land.

Ecology teaches us that mixtures are always more robust than pure essences, and it is the radically different blendings, from Canada, to Mexico, to Brazil, that give the Americas such complexity and vitality. We can also say that the modern state is a relative newcomer. It is a young state, still in construction. The Americas are a place of opportunity, where it is possible to experiment, and to reinvent oneself, or reinvent society. For a European modernist like Le Corbusier, Latin America represented a chance to implement his ideas on an empty slate, free of the weight of history. But in Brazil and Venezuela, (to mention just two examples) architects such as Lucio Costa or Raúl Villanueva assimilated those modernist ideas *and* swerved away from them, inflecting their buildings toward the local customs, climate and landscape in ways that Le Corbusier could never have imagined. These buildings feel fresh and original, but this is not invention *ex nihilo*. It is instead an intricate cross-cultural conversation where identity emerges out of the convergence of multiple histories.

But the other point—related of course—is that there is a fundamentally different relationship to land and territory in the Americas. North and South America form a vast continental landmass. The presence of this vast territory is deeply embedded in the American consciousness: "I take SPACE to be the central fact to man born in America, from Folsom Cave to now. I spell it large because it comes large here. Large, and without mercy," in the words of the poet Charles Olson.[1] You feel the vastness of the land out there, empty space always beyond the horizon. Nature has a different presence here: wilder, larger and more complex. The Americas are a young geology too, still in formation, and all this feeds the notion of possibility and self-invention.

The American imagination is deeply marked by landscape. The vast expanse of the North and South American continental landmass was both a daunting chal-

152

lenge and at the same time an open and unknown prospect to early settlers and explorers, among them Alexander von Humboldt, whose experiences traveling in South America upended prevailing theories of climate, nature, and geography. The New World was different from the Old in part for its expansiveness and its wildness; confronting and transforming the land helped to shape the national consciousness. Angel Rama's masterful book *The Lettered City* details this confrontation of the Old World's urban nexus of lettered culture and state power with an unruly landscape and population—a confrontation that transformed both the European culture of letters as well as the New World host.[2] Places are more than just geography; they are constructed in the imagination, and deeply embedded in complex histories.

It is not surprising then that one of the dominate themes among the MCHAP finalist projects is the relationship to ground and to nature. Climate plays a key role in South and Central America in particular. The *brise soleil* makes more sense in Brasilia than in Paris, and an extraordinary building such as Villanova Artigas's FAU could only be possible in Sao Paulo's temperate climate. At the FAU, the space of the campus flows seamlessly through the structure, converting an object-building into an infrastructural platform and constructed ground. Above all, we can say that the ground is an active protagonist in much of this new work, brought into close dialogue with the architecture, and blurring the boundary between nature and culture. And this is not necessarily a traditional notion of the ground either—not always green, it is a ground can be excavated, displaced, and reinvented as a new architectural material. Landscape and architecture live very close to one another in the Americas.

The Pachacamec Museum, designed by Patricia Llosa and Rodolfo Cortegana, is a building that is experienced not as object but as landscape: pathways that overlap, diverge and converge, rather than a collection of rooms. Outdoor spaces are as important as indoor, in keeping with the task of framing the monumental site that is both part of and apart from the Museum. The projects by Grafton architects in Lima and Michal Maltzan in

153

Los Angeles eschew conventional landscape references; they operate instead in a geological register. These are highly urban buildings, but in both cases, there are significant raised outdoor public spaces that function as platforms and connectors, leveraging the smooth connectivity associated with landscape to create new opportunities of gathering and meeting. The UTEC in Lima, in particular, reads as a constructed cliff, in dialogue with the characteristic geological formations of the Lima coastline.

Angelo Bucci's Weekend House in São Paulo develops out of the legacy of Artigas and Paulo Mendes da Rocha, in which robust structural elements redefine architecture's relationship to the ground and create unprecedented spatial and programmatic openness. But in swerving from that precedent, Bucci has created something highly original: he inverts the conventional logic of the country villa, folding garden, and house, together in an indissoluble blend. The house in not in the garden but the garden is not quite in the house either; it is impossible to disentangle house from garden, culture from constructed nature. Gardens are as much about time as they are about space, as Jorge Luis Borges's tale "The Garden of Forking Paths" reminds us. The memory of Borges lives on in Alberto Kalach's tower in Mexico City, where work spaces are suspended between a closed, labyrinthine garden at the street entry, and an expansive roof terrace that connects the building to the adjacent park and the landscape of the city beyond. Kalach is an architect of time as much as space, whose buildings seem to work in an anachronic register, deploying multiple time scales simultaneously: ancient and modern.

But this discussion of an "American" identify apparently runs up against a contradiction in the case of the winning project by the Japanese architects Sejima and Nishisawa. Grace Farms is a building entirely consistent with SANAA's larger *oeuvre*, and the specifically "Japanese" characteristics of their work have often been remarked upon: lightness, restraint, and the dialectic of transparency and opacity. But the building is inflected to its context in subtle yet consequential ways. In the first and most obvious instance, the building directly engages the New

154

England landscape of rolling hills and open fields. This is not a wild landscape, but one which bears the marks of human occupation. Cleared of old-growth forests as far back as the early 18th century, this rocky soil was farmed to exhaustion. Abandoned for richer soil and the open territory to the West, forests and meadows have reappeared, but now as a patchwork of rural, town and suburban development.[3] SANAA's building is literally fitted to this landscape, making the topography visible in all of its specificity—not as a natural landscape but as constructed ground.

     Grace Farms is ten minutes away from Philip Johnson's Glass House in New Canaan. Although Sejima and Nishisawa tend to minimize the connection, there is a clear relationship, particularly in the way the building meets to the ground. The inevitable comparison between the Glass House and Mies's Farnsworth House helps to clarify the kinship. Both are freestanding steel and glass pavilions on rural properties. Both are structured around a service core that allows the space to flow freely, and both are invested in a limpid clarity made possible by large expanses of plate-glass. But there is one aspect in which the two houses differ fundamentally. Johnson's Glass House—perhaps as an American response to Mies's European prototype—rests securely on a brick plinth embedded in the landscape, which in turn flows into the space of the house without interruption. Farnsworth, by contrast, floats, aloof from the ground, raised on steel columns that are the continuation of the house's primary structure.[4] The Farnsworth House models a standard form of steel construction visible in Mies' larger buildings: the house is a built fragment of the Lakeshore Drive towers, or the Seagram Building. It wants to function not only as itself but as a generalizable prototype, still marked by Modernist ambitions of standardization and reform. The Glass House is at once more modest and more ambitious. It accepts society and technology as given (even to the extent of mixing painted wood and steel on the exterior). The references the Glass House makes are not technological but cultural: it is a temple in the landscape, marking the ground, and concretizing a quasi-sacred space. If Farnsworth is a prototype, the Glass House is an archetype.

155

Grace Farms is clearly, in this instance, much closer to Johnson than Mies; although the white painted steel recalls the Farnsworth House, the structure at Grace Farms does not hover above the ground. Instead, it occupies the site, allowing the surrounding landscape to flow into and through the building. It could almost be seen as a mannerist exaggeration of Johnson's brick plinth, now set free to follow the topography of the New England Landscape. No longer a temple form, the building as discreet object has been dissolved into the field of the ground itself.

From Alexander von Humboldt to Alexis de Tocqueville and Charles Dickens or, in the twentieth century, the Swiss photographer Robert Frank, there is a long history of outsiders bringing a fresh perspective to the social and cultural landscape of the Americas. Sejima and Nishisawa can be counted in this company; their building remains at once their own, yet inflected to and inflecting it's found landscape. Differences matter, and it is diversity that enriches the culture and experience of the Americas. There are legitimate tensions between North and South, and important cultural, social and political differences. Perhaps today, instead of an exchange between the New World and the Old World, or North and South, it makes more sense to talk about a global exchange—less a binary opposition, and more of an activated network, based on differences and the possibility of shared ground.

156

1        Charles Olsen, *Call Me Ishmael*, (New York, Harcourt and Brace, 1947).
2        Angel Rama, *The Lettered City* (Duke University Press, 1996).
3        See William Cronon, *Changes in the Land: Indians, Colonists and the Ecology of New England*, (New York, Hill and Wang, 1983).
4        Of course the Farnsworth House is also elevated in response to the flood plain it occupies; but as Jeff Kipnis has argued, there are significant conceptual differences that go beyond this immediate pragmatic response to the site.

# WEEKEND HOUSE
## SÃO PAULO, BRAZIL

## SPBR ARQUITETOS

# THE POSSIBILITIES OF THE ECCENTRIC

SPBR is an architecture office located in the city of São Paulo and created by Angelo Bucci in 2003. Bucci has been active in the professional realm as well as in academia since 1989, and the balance between these environments has oriented the office's practice as it has evolved over time. SPBR's projects reflect a critical approach in regard to certain aspects of modern architecture. With this heritage as a starting point, they value the importance of the structure's conception, constructive solutions, economic viability and, above all, the understanding of the city as an open field where architecture projects engage in dialogue.

São Paulo is a metropolis of twenty million people and located about seventy kilometers from the coast. Its inhabitants spend a large part of their day sitting in traffic, especially on weekends, when the highways are full of thousands of people trying to get to the beach. The site of this house is located in the central area of São Paulo, between Avenida Brigadeiro Faria Lima (a major avenue) and an important infrastructure line (a highway and a railway) on the edges of Pinheiros River. The lot is also inside the conic projection area corresponding to Congonhas Airport, and all flights arriving from Río de Janeiro fly right over the house.

In order to avoid driving for long hours on the weekends, the clients developed an unexpected—but logical—program: a weekend house in the center of São Paulo.

A pool, a sun deck, and a garden are the key elements of the project. The rest of the program is made up of a small apartment for the house-sitter and a space to cook and receive guests. Since zoning dispositions allow a maximum height of six meters for this part of the city, and all the edges of the site had already been built up to that level, the decision was made to consider the last floor—the only one that receives natural light throughout the entire day—as the project's ground floor. The pool and the sun deck are placed on this level as parallel massing. In a one-meter opening located between the two of them, two columns separated by a twelve meter span are placed, which in turn become the supporting structure, through beams, of the pool and the sun deck. The inferior level—the only enclosed space of the house—hangs from the lat-

159

ter without ever touching the ground floor. Structurally, the pool works as the counterweight of the livable spaces. It's almost like making the sea bear the weight of the beach.

The ground floor was left free of any type of construction in order to achieve the largest possible amount of garden space. The end result is three different layers, each of them with a distinct atmosphere within the house: ground level (an introspective feel, with a garden), the first floor (interior sensation, floating), and the terrace (extroverted and open space).

When comparing this house and its program to other architectural projects, there are two fundamental differences that stand out. On the one hand, the metropolis becomes a place where it is possible to enjoy the weekend; and on the other, the elements of a house that are generally considered to be secondary are, in this case, the main building blocks.

160

| | |
|---|---|
| Architect: | SPBR Arquitetos |
| Partner in charge: | Angelo Bucci |
| Design team: | Nilton Suenaga, Tatiana Ozzetti, Ciro Miguel, Eric Ennser, João Paulo Meirelles de Faria, Juliana Braga, Fernanda Cavallaro, Victor Próspero |
| Square meters: | 270 m² (site), 183 m² (built) |
| Location: | São Paulo, Brazil |
| Years: | 2010–2011 (project), 2013 (construction) |
| Consultants: | Ibsen Puleo Uvo (structure), Apoio Assessoria e Projeto de Fundações (foundations), JDP Projetos de Instalações (installations), Engesolos Engenharia de Solos e Fundações (geotechnics), Raul Pereira (landscape), Reka (lighting), Móveis AEME (wooden shuttering), Carlos Augusto Stefani (metallic shuttering), STW vidrios (glass) |
| Contractor: | José Antonio Queijo Felix |
| Construction: | Theobaldo Bremenkamp, Reinaldo Francisco Ramos |

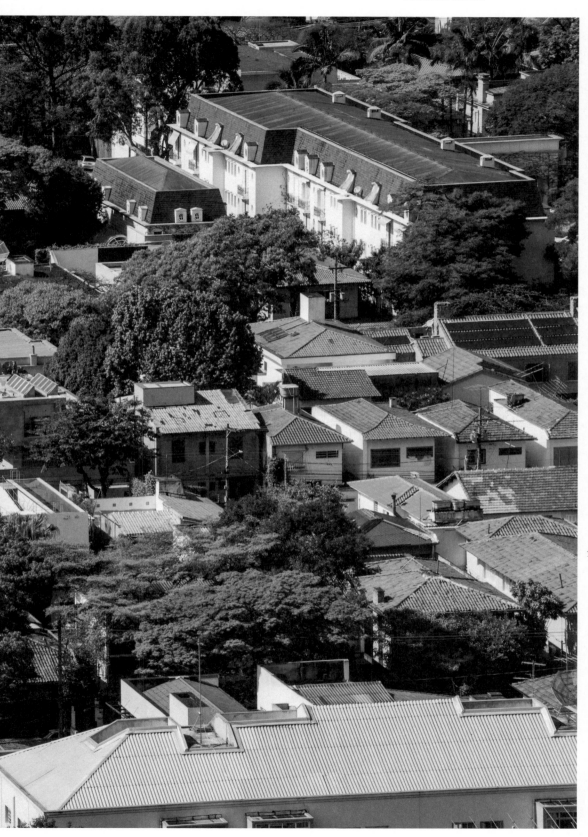

# COMMENT FROM THE JURY
## Jean Pierre Crousse

A professional couple from São Paulo, tired of the endless hours spent in traffic commuting from their city apartment to their beach house, decides to buy a lot in Pinheiros, a compact residential neighborhood in the center of São Paulo. They intend to build a pool and spend their weekends in their own city, free of the inconveniences of traffic. The site has a few problems: it is only 10 meters wide, and the adjacent 6-meter-tall houses cast unwanted shadows on the pool, in the morning and in the afternoon. The architect cannot find a way to solve this problem; he advises the owners to change sites. The owners decide to change architects.

It is at this juncture that Angelo Bucci's relationship with this couple begins. He proposes an atypical program, but one that carries enormous potential. Bucci's idea is to have the pool leave its traditional spot as a water surface located on the ground, and to elevate itself to the maximum height allowed in the area, 6 meters above street level, while in the process revealing its mass and weight, like a water tank. This strategy, which would allow them to avoid the shadow projected by the nearby houses onto their pool, is welcomed by the couple with enthusiasm, and opens up a world of possibilities that Bucci has masterfully figured out how to exploit.

Always faithful to his "Paulista" affiliation, Bucci defies gravity by elevating geometrically rigorous masses, suspended in the air with a minimum of support points. He uses exposed reinforced concrete as a material expression, as well as a structural possibility. This project, however, transcends these communal traditional characteristics that were initiated by Vilanova Artigas, and later perfected by Mendes da Rocha.

The traditional relationships that a house establishes with the land are inverted in this case: the program of the house becomes secondary, and the garden and the pool become the main focal point. The livable space is defined by the tropical garden, which in turn elevates itself through the adjoining walls of the site, and in doing so bestows a certain interior quality to the area.

169

The transition from city to inner domesticity is handled not through walls or fences, but instead through the artificial topography of the garden. As the visitor walks through the main entrance, he is confronted by a lush vegetation along a path that very quickly distances him from the urban and introduces him in a tropical landscape, while in the shadow of the suspended volumes that house the pool, the intimate spaces of the bedroom and the house-sitter's quarters. This last space also works as a counterweight to the pools' mass and frees the two only columns of any torque bearing efforts, which allows the slender vertical load bearers to visually disappear in the dense foresting.

As the visitor ascends towards the pool, he leaves the vegetation behind and reaches the roof of the private area, an irregular roof-terrace that appears as a multi-purpose sand dune right next to the pool. In this space, the urban landscape reemerges amidst the roofs of the neighbors' houses. The sky and the horizon are now visible. The elongated pool seems to indicate the direction of the airport; every seven minutes an airplane flies over the house and arrives at São Paulo.

The collaboration between Bucci and landscape architect Raúl Pereira was essential from the very beginning. In reality, the Weekend House is a condensed site, or, rather, a folded one, in a 10 x 25-meter-long, 6-meter-tall space. By walking the distance that separates the street from the pool, we encounter the same landscape that we might see on a trip from São Paulo to the coast, going through the Atlantic Mata to get to the beach and its horizon. The project not only dims the lines between territory, landscape, and architecture, but also generates a vertical stratification of microclimates, from a humid, shadowy and cool environment in the garden, to a sunny and hot one on the terrace-sand dune and the pool.

170

The Weekend House reinvents the relationship between the city and nature by proposing a critical view of the opposition between the city and the countryside. This new way of living in the city announces a more sustainable use of the territory, starting with its smallest component: a house. Its importance lies in its capacity to generate fundamental questions regarding the need for establishing a renewed relationship between architecture, city, landscape, and territory.

# NEW CAMPUS FOR THE UTEC
# LIMA, PERÚ

## GRAFTON ARCHITECTS

## RENEWED FORMS OF MATTER

Grafton Architects was created by Yvonne Farrell and Shelley McNamara in 1978. They both graduated from University College Dublin (UCD) and are members of the Royal Institute of Architects of Ireland, honorary members of the Royal Institute of British Architects, and chosen members of the noted Irish Art organization Aosdana. Between 1976 and 2002 they were a part of the UCD faculty. Throughout their career, they have been invited to lecture at the Academia di Architettura de Mendrisio, at the École Polytechnique Fédérale de Lausanne, at the Kenzo Tange Chair at Harvard's GSD, and at the Louis Kahn Chair at Yale University.

The new vertical campus for the University of Engineering and Technology (UTEC) sits near the Pacific Ocean in Lima, Peru. The city is located twelve degrees south of the Equator, where a cold-water current coming from Antarctica ensures constant pleasant weather with the temperature fluctuating between thirteen and twenty-four degrees celsius year-round. Amidst this microclimate, the new campus is set upon a small valley that stretches to the sea; to the north it is limited by a busy highway and to the south by a residential district called Barranco.

Drawing inspiration from their surroundings, the architects devised the building as a new type of geography, which they define as a 'man-made cliff.' The lower floors of the building, which are located alongside the highway, house the largest areas, such as the labs, while the smaller ones, such as the administrative and teaching facilities, are on the top floors. The roofs of the lower spaces are seen as cascading gardens from the opposite side. As well as providing green outdoor spaces, they recall the terraced crop fields from Machu Picchu and the outskirts of Lake Titicaca. They also modulate the vertical campus's façade, aligning it with the dominant scale of the residential area located towards the south. Due to Lima's favorable climate, outdoor circulation is used, which in turn facilitates a social and educational connection between students and faculty, strengthens the relationship with the ocean and the Andes, and fosters an experience where the ocean air breezes through sun-protected spaces. The only facilities

173

that have air conditioning are those that need some degree of special climate control.

The reinforced concrete structure of the building is organized by a 19.8-meter-long module and has an intermediate inner grid of waffle slabs of 9.9 meters on each side. Since the campus is located in a seismic zone, the upper part of the building was placed upon large seismic isolators, which are located underground in the parking area. Due to the curved form of the 358.6-meter-long plot, every structural module of 19.8 meters was adjusted along the outer edge. This way, instead of having a sole, continuous view, a number of interconnected spaces are created. The interiors of the research labs are presented as exhibition space and are a distinguishing feature of the university. Since they are located near the circulation areas, they are part of everyday life inside the school and help build an educational atmosphere that encourages interdisciplinary exchange while the students move about their day. The different areas and levels blend together in the horizon, with the hope that, in time, the vegetation and the wild life will integrate and enrich the life of this new academic community.

| | |
|---|---|
| Architects: | Grafton Architects (Yvonne Farrell, Shelley McNamara) |
| Architects of Record: | Shell Arquitectos |
| Square meters: | 67,000 m$^2$ (total), 35,000 m$^2$ (1$^{st}$ stage completed) |
| Location: | Lima, Peru |
| Year: | 2015 |
| Construction: | Graña y Montero S.A. |
| Consultants: | GCAQ Ingenieros Civiles (structure), Gutiérrez Cantillo Ingenieros (mechanics), AT Consultores (electrical), Equipo G (sanitation), Alvaro Mena (project manager), Paisaje Vivo (landscape), Rie Sakata (lighting), Jiménez & Moreno (acoustics) |
| Client: | University of Engineering and Technology UTEC |
| Budget: | $100,000,000 |

# COMMENT FROM THE JURY
## Ila Berman

The new UTEC campus in Lima, Peru by Grafton Architects is a complex architectural megaform that operates simultaneously as a synthetic topography, an infrastructural network, and a densely-stacked yet permeable urban fabric. Emulating the high cliffs that run along and separate the city of Lima from the Pacific Ocean and delineating the edge of a valley that diverges from, and runs perpendicular to, the water's edge, this project acts as an enormous artificial landscape molded out of concrete rather than rock. It conceptually functions as a lens through which to reimagine the extreme verticality and intense sectional topography that characterize the Andean geography of the region, as well as the traditional form of stepped terracing used in its acculturation. In this confluence of systems, as the geological infuses this layered yet highly-articulated built landform with continuity and a monolithic consistency reminiscent of the matter out of which the earth is made, the architectural intervenes to insert spatial intervals between the building's thick geomorphological strata, in order to aerate the campus—to render it not only inhabitable, but also permeable and legible to its adjoining urbanity. Rather than a horizontally-arrayed arrangement of separate buildings typical of a university campus, the programmatic micro-elements of UTEC—its classrooms, laboratories, and office spaces—are typologically reclassified by the architects as discrete sets of occupiable pixels that are laterally ordered, vertically stacked, and condensed into a single aggregate structure, whose differentiated, stratified section is used to negotiate between the two distinct forms of urbanism situated on either side of the site. The building's steep sheer 'cliff' face therefore abuts and buffers the busy thoroughfare to the north and is scaled to this area's dense, high-rise urbanity, while the more staggered and incrementally stepped terrain of lecture rooms and laboratories overlooks and mediates the adjacent Barranco neighborhood to the south.

The campus building not only skillfully responds to the configuration, rhythm, and shifting orientation of

183

these surrounding territories, but also acts as a framing device through which to reread and engage the city as each of its views, both proximate and distant, is carefully collapsed, absorbed, and inserted into the architecture's structural and circulatory web. Blurring the boundaries between inside and out, this extensive and continuous infrastructural network, which is internal to the building yet simultaneously operates as exterior space, also acts as a social condenser that contributes to the public space within the campus as it visually exposes and theatricalizes the activities on site. This network of circuitous concrete strands zigzagging through the building is used by students and faculty to traverse the campus as they might hike across a landscape or meander through the city. It organizes the enclosed functions of the campus as a street grid, delimiting the parcellation of city blocks, yet layers this urban fabric into a new mountainous topography, a synthetic three-dimensional landscape structured by perforated vertical concrete fins and crisscrossed by suspended streets that miraculously float above each other while framing sublime canyon-like spaces that enable light and air to penetrate the building and views to weave across the space. UTEC reinvents the architecture of the campus in a way that astounds. Blending city, infrastructure, and landscape, it deftly balances a form of urban monumentality appropriate to both the academic and civic aspirations of the institution and the deep geological and cultural history of the region, with a mode of informality indicative of the urban network within which it is inserted and the collective communal ground it is intended to support.

184

# PACHACAMAC MUSEUM
## LIMA, PERÚ

## LLOSA CORTEGANA ARCHITECTS

## MIMESIS AND HETEROTOPIA

Llosa Cortegana Arquitectos was founded in Lima, Peru in 2005 by Patricia Llosa and Rodolfo Cortegana. Both architects graduated from the School of Architecture and Urbanism of Ricardo Palma University. Since 2002, they have been part of the faculty at the School of Architecture of the Pontifical Catholic University of Peru. Throughout their career, their practice has received several awards and distinctions, such as the National First Place in the category Education at the XV Bienal de Arquitectura Peruana (2012), as well as numerous mentions at the Celima Award for Architectural Quality (2003, 2005, 2007, and 2011). Their work has also been selected for exhibition at the Bienal Iberoamericana de Arquitectura y Urbanismo (2016).

The Pachacamac Sanctuary is a place where Pre-Hispanic architecture is capable of making an impression through the power of silence and scale. Its paths are confined by walled structures that permanently guide the visitor to the worship sites. Its relationship to its surroundings is defined by a number of lengthy routes, those elements that throughout time have organized the occupation of the land. The Pre-Hispanic architects understood that architecture was a form of mediating between man and the worshipping of his gods. Profoundly rooted in their tradition, they allowed their buildings to function through the insertion of certain terrain-adaptive strategies. Through relevant innovation carried out according to the different conditions of the landscape, the constructional traditions molded the architecture.

The Pachacamac Museum's contemporary architecture seeks to reference Pre-Hispanic architecture; through its elements, it builds an alternative grammar that inhabits the symbolical-historical plain and that defines the different spaces that frame the preexisting sanctuary.

In light of the magnitude of the surroundings, the architects decided to give the new building a 'weak attitude.' In order to avoid forcefully imposing it on the territory, they searched for a scale directly related to the topography and the slopes of the site. The visitor can only sense the totality of the building once they arrive at the piazza. The museum's spaces and outdoor routes direct the visitor's views and reinforce a bond with the preexisting

187

structures. The masses fold, and a series of voids are interspersed among the different ramped routes, which have been designed to resemble the Pre-Hispanic roads used by those on pilgrimage to their temples, following lineal spaces marked by large walls that set the direction of the crowds.

The material aspects of the project also relate to the Pachacamac Sanctuary. The exposed reinforced concrete, the boarded shuttering, and the rustic finishing are associated with the Pre-Hispanic earthen walls, though thinner and with a lighter bulk. In this sense, its design does not look to compete with the preexisting structures through a striking composition of mass and void, but instead tries to build shadows and routes.

The project sets out to produce a conceptual approach in regard to the territory and the preexisting structures. The architects sought to design a building that displayed a profound respect for the sacred land on which it stands, while considering this action as just one more layer of stratification in the long transformative process of the sanctuary.

188

| | |
|---|---|
| Architects: | Llosa Cortegana Arquitectos (Patricia Llosa, Rodolfo Cortegana) |
| Design team: | Angélica Piazza, Daniela Chong, Llona / Zamora, Braulio Miki, Jorge Avedaño, Adela Zavala, José Ortiz, Solange Ávila |
| Square meters: | 7,518 m² (total), 3,028 m² (built), 4,490 m² (exterior) |
| Location: | Pachacamac Sanctuary, Lurín District, Lima, Peru |
| Years: | 2005–2013 (project), 2014–2015 (construction) |
| Construction: | Prisma |
| Budget: | $3,330,000 |
| Client: | Ministerio de Cultura del Perú |

195

196

# COMMENT FROM THE JURY
## Stan Allen

Designing an interpretive center for a major archeological site is a daunting challenge for an architect. To begin with, there is the question of scale; one cannot compete with the vast landforms of the 600 hectare Pachacamec site. Beyond considerations of scale, the site has become naturalized over many centuries, embedded in a deep historical time. Moreover, an unbridgeable cultural gulf is apparent: the civilizations that erected these monuments are only knowable in traces and fragments; the site will (and perhaps should) always remain enigmatic, strange and "other" to modern eyes.

Patricia Llosa and Rodolfo Cortegana, architects of the Pachacamec Museum, understand this very well. They have confronted these issues with tact and intelligence. Their Pachacamec Museum is a subtle building that defers to the site and its history while also reframing the visitor's experience and understanding. It is of its time, yet sympathetic to the past it confronts.

Three dominant spatial tropes area visible in the ruin itself: first, the pyramid, familiar form of pre-Columbian sacred architecture. But this was not only a temple site, it was an entire city that grew up around the rituals of worship, sacrifice, and pilgrimage. Counterpoised to the pyramid is the labyrinth; if the pyramid stands for clarity, singularity and vertical ascension –pure exteriority– the labyrinth is horizontal and dark: passages without exit, an endless interior. Complicating the classic opposition of pyramid and labyrinth is a third figure: the pilgrimage road, a linear pathway linking distant sites and affording communication. The road is a proto-modern space, enabling the slow passage of pilgrims, but also facilitating the movement of the runners who carried messages to distant sites, linking up time and space at a territorial scale.

All three spatial figures are present in the museum. There is a subtle recall of the eroded profile of the temples in the blind elevation that the museum presents at the entry. The material of the building itself belongs to the site, and there are no conventional windows or doors that might

197

signal modern scale and occupation. One of the building's most convincing spaces is the labyrinthine office accommodation. Patios and skylights provide ample light, and while these spaces are inward looking, there is nothing of the labyrinth's dark history here.

But it does not seem accidental that the road—the pathway—is the most dominant reference in the architecture of the museum. In different ways, both the pyramid and the labyrinth can be expressions of power; the path is a more optimistic space. In the Pachacamec Museum, it is multiplied and folded back on itself. The route presents choices: it reframes views and directs the movement of the visitor. It's possible itineraries include the didactic route through the Museum interior, but that is not mandatory, particularly for the repeat visitor. This subtle choreography of pathways and vistas is among the building's most successful accomplishments.

Within the precinct of the museum, these routes converge on a lower-level plaza where the conventional amenities (bookstore, café, restrooms) can be found. Here the view changes: no longer focused on the monumental horizon, but instead on the closed-in vista of water and trees that appear unexpectedly in the desert landscape. This secret garden reveals yet another astonishing fact of the site. The ancient cultures who transformed this landscape not only erected pyramids and constructed a sacred city, but they also excavated downwards to expose the water table, creating a kind of artificial oasis, an ojo de agua (eye of the water). It is an unexpected space that both perfectly complements the distant vistas and offers welcome respite to the visitor.

198

The success of the museum is precisely to work at the scale of landscape itself, and to capture spaces and experiences beyond the frame of its own modest footprint. This makes the architecture expansive, both experientially and intellectually. It is a remarkable achievement: confronted with such a monumental site to construct a complex and expansive architectural experience with modest means.

---

1        Denis Hollier, *Against Architecture: The Writings of Georges Bataille* (Cambridge, MA: The MIT Press, 1992). See chapter 4, *"The Labyrinth, The Pyramid and the Labyrinth"* pp. 57 – 73.

# TOWER 41
## MEXICO CITY, MEXICO

### TALLER DE ARQUITECTURA X /
### ALBERTO KALACH

### CHEATING TYPOLOGY

Taller de Arquitectura X is an architecture office based in Mexico City and run by Alberto Kalach. Throughout his career, Kalach has worked on numerous projects at different scales, from private houses to public buildings. His most significant building to date is the "José Vasconcelos Mexico Public Library," which was included in the group of Outstanding Projects in the first MCHAP cycle. Taller de Arquitectura X's projects have been featured in several publications and special monographic editions.

Kalach is also well known for his interest in urban and ecological issues. This concern has lead him to create the "Ciudad Futura" (Future City) group, alongside other important Mexican architects. This group later developed a master plan for the "Regreso a la Ciudad Lacustre" (Return to the Lacustrine City) project, an environmental hydrology proposal meant to rescue the Mexican Basin based on the idea of revisiting the virtues and benefits of a city that was built on water and still floats on it.

Tower 41 was designed by Alberto Kalach and is located on a strategic site in Mexico City with views towards the majestic Chapultepec Forest. According to the building's authors, "it presents itself to its immediate surroundings as a sculpture of light in the afternoon." The design of the inner space was determined by the structure of the building: two structural walls hold a series of steel mezzanines, which are reinforced by a secondary steel structure on the façade. This configuration facilitates free floor plans and flexible space for office use. There are seven office levels, a triple height lobby, vertical circulation located along the Northeastern wall, and a roof garden on the final level that establishes a direct relationship with the park.

In order to avoid air conditioning, cross ventilation was chosen as the bioclimatic strategy and Bi-folding windows were placed on both sides of the building. The architects also designed a garden, a noise-reducing wall, and some fountains on the ground floor to decrease noise pollution caused by the nearby streets.

201

Architect:          Taller de Arquitectura X / Alberto Kalach
Design team:        Gabriel Mancera, Iván Ramírez, David Martínez, Patricia Lazcano
Square meters:      270 m² (site), 1,820 m² (built)
Location:           Mexico City, Mexico
Year:               2012–2014
Client:             Teófilo Kalach

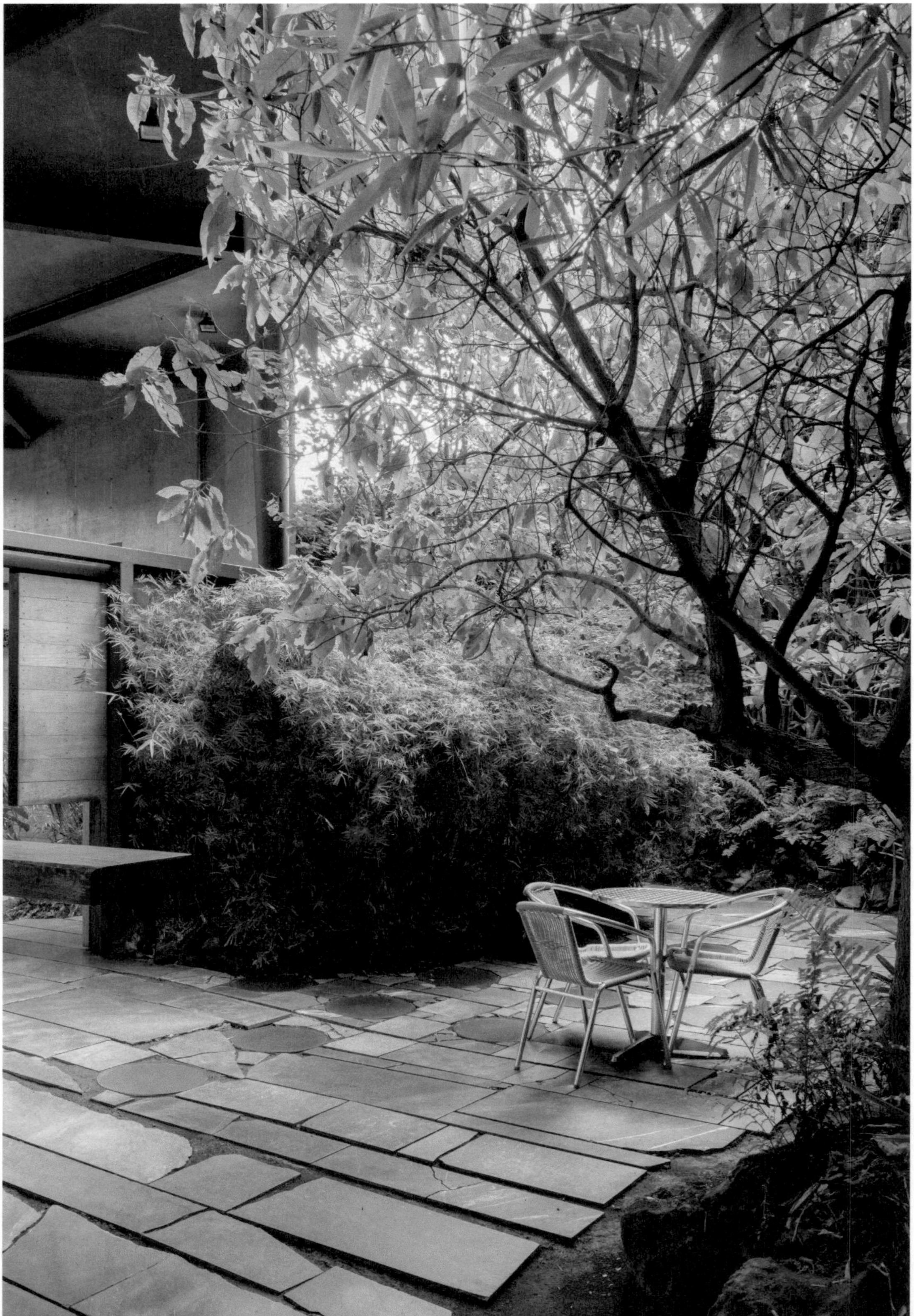

# COMMENT FROM THE JURY
## Stan Allen

There is a model in Alberto Kalach's office that perfectly explains the structure of Tower 41. The plot is an elongated trapezoid. On the short sides of the plan are two massive piers. Starting high above the street, steel trusses span between the piers, forming a bridge over the urban fabric below. It is a powerful statement of structural intent. The synthesis of these two elemental forms—tower and bridge—is the measure of Kalach's architectural imagination and structural intelligence. Yet the model, however useful, in no way describes or anticipates the actual reality of the building, either as an urban artifact or as a lived experience. This is not a failure on the architect's part but rather an affirmation of the transformative power of a fully realized work of architecture: the capacity to go beyond the simple registration of the architect's representational tools. The building functions in a complex and irreducible relationship with its urban context and the people who inhabit it.

The effect from the exterior, for example, is less that of a structural skeleton, and more a play of skins—surfaces of differing degrees of transparency, reflectivity, and density. The brown-tinted concrete of the piers visually blends with the bronze glass and the corten steel. The curtain wall stops short of the top and bottom trusses, partially revealing the structure. As a consequence, the building oscillates between a singular sculptural object and an assembly of parts, perhaps as yet unfinished. This is particularly true when seen from the north, where the curtain wall is activated by the presence of operable windows. The view from the primary street is angular; the observer never sees the idealized elevation of the "bridge" but instead always one pier and one curtain-wall face. These acute geometries break up the mass and exaggerate the verticality of the building. The building appears simultaneously heavy and light, earthbound and levitating at the same time. This is contrary to the usual quality of a tower as an arrogant statement, claiming dominion over its site; instead, there is something slightly fragile, provisional almost, about the presence of this tower located between park and city.

211

You enter the Tower 41 through a modest wooden door from the street. There is nothing of the monumental announcement of the building's presence so often associated with office towers. You might be entering the modest warehouse that formerly occupied the site. From there you climb through a garden, encountering an unsettling mirror/passage, a reminder that the garden is also the place of the irrational. The rationality of the engineered structure has made a place for the surreal. The symmetry of the structure is further complicated by the asymmetrical placement of the lifts and services to one side. As a result, the building is experienced laterally, always entering and moving from floor to floor, from the anchor of the back pier. Given the warmth of the surfaces, the tall ceilings and the close proximity of the window walls, the loft spaces created at each floor are at once generous and intimate. But this is not a space that monumentalizes the view of the park. Instead the inhabitant is poised between park and city, between nature and culture, mixing both realities. This is particularly true of the roof garden, where structural elements and plant materials exist side by side.

All great cities are fundamentally unfinished. Mexico City itself is a vast, dynamic metropolis, permanently under construction. It has a deep history, always present just beyond the surface. With the Tower 41, Kalach has perfectly captured the collective consciousness of the city where he lives and works. This is a building that could only exist in its time and place, embodying the dynamism of a city permanently under construction, while at the same time suggesting a culture that continuously recycles past architectures. Kalach is a rigorous modernist; but the optimism of his architecture is tempered by a dystopian overlay, distancing his work from the programs of an earlier European modernism. It does not seem far-fetched to align his architecture with the Latin American literature of magical realism on the one hand, or the work of contemporary Mexican film-makers such as Alejandro González Iñárritu or Guillermo del Toro. What they all share is a sense of a place where absolute precision coexists with the irrational and the inexplicable. Working within the constraints of a modest commercial project, Kalach's achievement is to create an architecture that evokes experiences we thought only literature and film were capable describing.

STAR APARTMENTS
LOS ANGELES, UNITED STATES

MICHAEL MALTZAN ARCHITECTURE

DISARMING THE URBAN BATTLEFIELD

Michael Maltzan Architecture is an architecture and urban design office created in 1995 in Los Angeles and committed to the creation of progressive transformative experiences, capable of drawing up new trajectories for architecture, urbanism, and public space. Their practice is constantly involved with the context and the community of the places where they work; they also strive to achieve interdisciplinary associations, in order to integrate architecture and sustainability. The office has been widely published and has received several awards, such as the Progressive Architecture Awards and the Rudy Bruner Foundation for Urban Excellence Gold Medal. They have also been runners up for the Smithsonian/Cooper-Hewitt Museum's National Design Award.

The Star Apartments project—built for the Skid Row Housing Trust—transformed an existing one-story commercial building, located in downtown Los Angeles, into a mixed-used complex with 102 apartment units for formerly homeless individuals. This housing complex, designed by Michael Maltzan Architecture, sets a new urban model that increases density through the addition of new community spaces and residential levels.

The six-story, 8,800 square meter building—which was built following LEED regulations—looks to expand upon the Skid Row Housing Trust's model of providing permanent supportive housing within downtown Los Angeles by incorporating a new type of shared public space within the building. Star Apartments is organized around three main spatial zones stacked upon each other: a public health zone at street level, a second level for community and wellness programs, and four residential floors above them. The building includes an onsite medical clinic, a health and wellness center, and the new headquarters of the LA County Department of Health Services's (DHS) "Housing for Health Division."

Not only is the integration of social services, community recreational facilities, and residential units a unique building program, but the project also utilizes an innovative new construction methodology. Faced with a limited budget and a tight schedule, the office decided to use prefabricated modules lifted into place over the existing

215

podium in order to help provide a higher quality of construction, meet tighter construction tolerances, accelerate construction time, and accomplish the project's ambitious sustainability goals.

| Architect: | Michael Maltzan Architecture |
|---|---|
| Square meters: | 29,000 m² |
| Location: | 240 E. Sixth Street, Los Angeles, USA. |
| Year: | 2014 |
| Construction: | Westport Construction (general contractor), Guerdon Enterprises (prefabricated contractor) Cowley Real Estate Partners and Anejo Development (building managers) |
| Consultants: | B.W. Smith Structural Engineers, Nova Structures Inc. (structure), Green Engineering Consulting Group, Inc. (installation engineering), KPFF Consulting Engineers (civil engineering), LEED for Home Platinum (sustainability), Valley Crest Design Group (landscape), Collaborative House (interior design), Michael Maltzan Architecture (lighting), Martin Newson & Associates LLC (acoustics), Curtis Fletcher (prefabrication), Arup (coding), GB Works (LEED consultant) |
| Client: | Skid Row Housing Trust |
| Budget: | $ 59,300,000 |

# COMMENT FROM THE JURY
## Florencia Rodriguez

Although Downtown Los Angeles was a consolidated and growing urban area a century ago, its development found its counterpoint already in the 1930s. The fifty-block road known as Skid Row, originally home to temporary workers, grew until it reached around 10,000 homeless people. For a long time, they were recurrent victims of acts that did nothing but reinforce their marginalized living, such as clearance programs, lawsuits, and raids.

Another factor that impacted the city development was the turn in the growth of many American towns since the Postwar. Los Angeles and its surroundings were affected by the urban sprawl fashion that led to its downtown shrinking. The combination of abandoned buildings, closed shops, and minimal pedestrian movement facilitated the growth of Skid Row as a point of congregation for homeless persons. Over the last few decades, there has always been an average of 5,000 individuals living on that street. The most lasting and touching image of this part of the city is the endless row of white tents they inhabit in contrast to the empty buildings and barren land. The street itself has been re-signified as a long and inadequate ephemeral building. Lately, Downtown LA has been going through a revitalization process that recognizes the identity and relevance of Skid Row's inhabitants. Most of them suffer several psychical and psychiatric problems that require medical attention. For that, the state offers economic support but doesn't guarantee any permanent solution.

In that context, the Skid Row Housing Trust has managed to design a public/private cooperation using part of the health budget for housing. Each home costs $200,000, the equivalent of two years of support for one individual. This initiative also provides medical control and constant social assistance posts to help reintegrate the people back into the community. Michael Maltzan Architecture has designed a group of very propositive projects for Skid Row Housing Trust, and Star Apartments is critical. This housing and mixed-use building has symbolically pointed to new developmental issues. Located right in the middle of

225

Skid Row, the project needed to resolve and interconnect several complex situations. For one, the ground floor had to be maintained not to lose already approved commercial permits. In addition to the 102 required apartments, the program called for a vegetable garden, multi-use rooms for communal activities, and a large kitchen, as well as medical and psychiatric attention posts. Thus, Maltzan's design addresses several relevant issues: urban form, the reconstruction of the grid, community performance, and functionality while creating a spectacular brutalist monument, an icon capable of elevating such a complex social program.

Not only the view from the building is mesmerizing. The feeling of entering a space of care, full of possibilities, while leaving a harsh and threatening reality behind, is evident when one crosses the door. The communal areas are neat and straightforward, and despite requiring very low maintenance, they do not feel precarious or temporary. The second floor, a big open and shared space, performs as a park, a meeting place that replaces the street while looking at it: it is a space of social resiliency.

Above, the prefabricated apartments stack heroically. The puzzling structure provides this part of the building with a series of thoughtful and unique characteristics. What used to be out of sight becomes visible, and that very gesture transforms the way we look at it. The units are placed around open voids providing those inside different views of the city and the interior space. The apartments are highly functional and have the right proportions: they are comfortable and allow natural light and ventilation. Residents are granted access to a home by committing to attend medical check-ups and group therapy. The experience of visiting some of them and learning from their struggle is difficult to translate into words, but what is clear is the pride they express in the conviction that they have reached a place that has changed their lives and given them the chance of happiness. There is certain reciprocity between the ephemeral architecture of the Skid Row infinite tent line and Star Apartments. The street is re-signified by the building, which as a silent monument offers new perspectives and a possible future to the homeless.

226

GRACE FARMS
NEW CANAAN, CONNECTICUT,
UNITED STATES

SANAA

THE FORM OF CONTINGENCY

SANAA is a Japanese office created in 1995 by Kazuyo Sejima and Ryue Nishizawa. Sejima graduated from Japan Women's University and, after completing her studies, she joined Toyo Ito & Associates. She has been a professor at Keio University, as well as a visiting professor at the École Polytechnique Fédérale de Lausanne (EPFL), Princeton University, and the Vienna University of Applied Arts. Nishizawa graduated from Yokohama National University, where he was also associate professor. He has been visiting professor at the EPFL, Princeton, and Harvard's GSD. Kazuyo Sejima was the director of the 2012 Venice Architecture Biennale.

The new building for Grace Farms Foundation is located in New Canaan, Connecticut, United States in a vast, undulating site, full of trees, lakes, and ponds, and surrounded by quiet suburban homes. Grace Farms is a foundation that supports initiatives relating to nature, art, justice, community, and faith and fosters participation at local, national, and global scales. It carries out all these activities through a series of facilities that are available to the public, as well as integrated programs that are open to any individual or nonprofit organization that wishes to join them in order to work towards the common good. The visitors may join in on walks through nature, attend lectures, concerts, art, and book discussions, practice sports, and participate in events and cultural projects such as screenings, conferences, and exhibitions. In addition to its scheduled programs, visitors can also come on site to enjoy ongoing offerings.

The program for the "River" building, designed by SANAA, joins an existent group of buildings on the same property: a former private residence, a number of pastures, and a barn. The proposal is based on a very long canopy that replicates the topography and floats in the middle of the forest, while allowing for the formation of certain closed areas and semi-covered spaces along its entire extension. The architects' goal was to turn the building into an indistinguishable part of the landscape and invite its visitors to enjoy the experience of nature and architecture in equal fashion.

The "River" has a total area of 7,700 square meters, of which 5,200 are covered and located along the 400

229

meters that comprise the length of the building. Their widths vary between 4.5 and 7.5 meters, and their heights between 3 and 4.5 meters.

The building employs a mixed structure of concrete, steel, and wood. All the vertical enclosures are made entirely of glass, and they vary in size, character, use, and distance between them. The separation between the five closed areas in turn generate several open spaces under the canopy, each of them with their own distinct atmosphere and diverse views of the changing topography. These enclosures house the following sequence: indoor amphitheater for performances and convenings, a library, containing resources available for research in the fields of justice, art, community, nature, and faith; a common area, where the dining room and living room are located; a pavilion, an information and welcome center; and the subterranean recreational and multipurpose space also used for performances.

The roof structure is made of wood laminated beams sustained by metal columns. The modulation of the columns varies slightly in order to accommodate the entire system to the topography. The roof's upper finishing consists of anodized aluminum panels of 2 by 0.60 meters. For the enclosures, insulated glass panels with a specially designed seven-millimeter separation and fritted edges to conceal the seal were used. The inner floors are divided into light concrete, similar in color to gravel, wood (red and maple oak), and grey brick, while the outside floors where done entirely in gravel.

230

| | |
|---|---|
| Architects: | SANAA (Kazuyo Sejima, Ryue Nishizawa) |
| Architect of Record: | Handel Architects LLP |
| Design team: | Kazuyo Sejima, Ryue Nishizawa, Shohei Yoshida, Takayuki Hasegawa, Tommy Haddock |
| Square meters: | 32 ha (site), 7,700 m² (total), 5,200 m² (covered space) |
| Location: | New Canaan, Connecticut, United States |
| Years: | 2013–2015 (construction) |
| Construction: | Sciame Construction |
| Consultants: | Paratus Group (project direction), Olin (landscape), Silman (structural engineer), SAPS (structure), McChord Engineering Associates (civil engineering), BuroHappold Engineering (mechanical engineering, lighting, sustainability, energy modeling), Langan Engineering (geotechnical engineering), Alderson Engineering (geothermic design), Client Grace Farms Foundation |
| Budget: | $83,000,000 |

# COMMENT FROM THE JURY
## Wiel Arets

We leave Manhattan, where one slim tower is built next to the other, climbing above the clouds, an energetic monumental metropolis. The green scenery horizon of New Canaan, Connecticut comes suddenly, winding roads gently guide our view toward a weak, soft, easy-going, slow experience: the sub-metropolitan Grace Farms. This is a project born out of multiple readings of the site; readings with no beginning or end, without hierarchy. A seemingly easy program, the opposite of singularly defined elements, is spread out over the terrain and assembled under the floating roof, softly folding the natural topography of the existing landscape. The reflection of the clouds appears in the lakes and wetlands, the most appealing elements of the scenery alongside the trees, their leaves changing colors with the seasons. The artificial intervention disappears into the setting with its shining aluminum-curved roof. Their horizontal appearance make the existing horse bars look like territorial markers; the architects employ them to create territorial references to the farming nature of the land.

When Thomas Demand[1] visited the office of Kazuyo Sejima and Ryue Nishizawa, located in a village-like neighborhood in Tokyo, he was inspired by their models. He was fascinated by their fragmented parts, which he reconstructed to build a new reality. When confronted with the two pieces he made, located underneath the glass-covered spaces of the roof (which the program calls the library), one gets another reading of the projects' multi-fold experience. Like all the other covered glass spaces, this spot enables everyone in the building to experience a new outlook of the site. It is a harmless orchestration, a seemingly romantic, natural view; a picture without a frame, a constantly changing perspective of the multiple readings of this country-site. It has been forever transformed by the decoded and coded work of SANAA, perhaps inspired by Demand's deconstruction of the architect's model-or vice versa.

The window view on the 86th floor of 432 Park Ave,[2] overlooking the model-like urban landscape of this overwhelming metropolis, feels harmless, quiet and slow.

239

It resembles a fairytale, overlooking the Gothic *carnava-lesque* crowning's of early twentieth-century buildings, the tallest ones in the world in those days. To recall the view from Philip Johnson's Glass House overlooking the valley is to feel the silhouette of an ever-changing nature.

Strolling through the landscape, a choir of angels performing in the distance, somewhere close to the lake, catches our attention. It was probably Susan Philipsz's idea, as she enjoyed the weather, to make the trees sing— and the wind truly teases us to wander around the lake and experience the property. It is a metropolis-like experience to be partly lead by the cantilevering wooden roof, while walking from the scattered indoor program to the outdoor one; it beckons us to return as much as possible, it challenges us to slow down—or perhaps speedup, depending on our expectations.

240

1        Thomas Demand is a German artist who photographed SANAA's models for the Grace Farms project. These pieces expand his earlier series, based on the models of John Lautner, from 2011.
2        432 Park Avenue is a building in Manhattan designed by Rafael Viñoly, the tallest residential tower in America. The MCHAP jury visited this site on the same day it visited Grace Farms and Philip Johnson's Glass House.

# MCHAP 2 PROJECTS

The MCHAP process begins with a global network of nominators: not only architects, landscape architects, and planners, but also writers, educators, policymakers, and even a chef. Approximately two hundred projects are nominated for the Americas Prize each MCHAP cycle, generating a significant catalog of contemporary architecture vetted by those with direct experience of the works and the impact they've had on their inhabitants and communities. All nominated projects are exhibited to the public in Chicago at IIT College of Architecture's Mies van der Rohe–designed S. R. Crown Hall.

During their first meeting, the jury discusses all nominees and develops a shortlist of outstanding projects: works that offer a quality, element, or approach that the jury believes merits special attention. In the 2016 cycle, MCHAP received 180 nominations and recognized 27 outstanding projects.

432 PARK AVENUE, New York, NY, USA
Rafael Viñoly Architects

ARENA DO MORRO, Máe Luiza, Brazil
Herzog & de Meuron

245

BILL & MELINDA GATES HALL, Ithaca, NY, USA
Morphosis

CERRADO HOUSE, Moeda, Brazil
Vazios /A | Carlos M. Teixeira

CERRITO CHAPEL, Asunción, Paraguay
Javier Corvalán

CÓRDOBA CULTURAL CENTER, Córdoba, Argentina
Castañeda, Cohen, Nanzer, Saal, Salassa, Tissot Architects

EDUCATIONAL PARK "ANCESTRAL KNOWLEDGE", Vigía del Fuerte, Colombia,
Lucas Serna Rodas, Farhid Alexander Maya Ramirez, Diana Herrera Duque, Mauricio Valencia

META MPK 20, Menlo Park, CA, USA
Gehry Partners

GUNA HOUSE, Concepción, Chile
Pezo von Ellrichshausen

HALIFAX CENTRAL LIBRARY, Halifax, Canada
Schmidt Hammer Lassen Architects | Morten Schmidt

KRISHNA P. SINGH CENTER FOR NANOTECHNOLOGY, Philadelphia, PA, USA
Weiss/Manfredi Architecture

248

M HOUSE, Rosario, Argentina
Estudio Aire

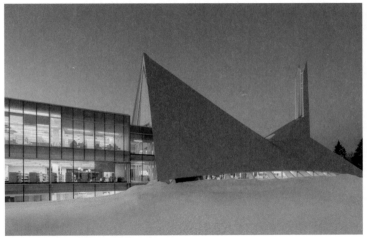

MONIQUE CORRIVEAU-LIBRARY, Quebec, Canada
Dan Hanganu + Côté Leahy Cardas Architects

OLYMPIC GOLF COURSE CLUBHOUSE RIO 2016, Rio de Janeiro, Brazil
Rua Arquitetos | Pedro Évora and Pedro Rivera

PEREZ ART MUSEUM MIAMI, Miami, FL, USA
Herzog & de Meuron

**PHYSICS DEPARTMENT BUILDING - UNIVERSITY OF TARAPACA**, Arica, Chile
Marsino Arquitectura

**REFORMA TOWER**, Mexico City, Mexico
LBR&A Arquitectos | L. Benjamin Romano

**SHOOTING RANGE IN ONTARIO**, Cookstown, Canada
Magma Architecture

STADE DE SOCCER DE MONTRÉAL, Montreal, Canada
Saucier + Perrotte Architects

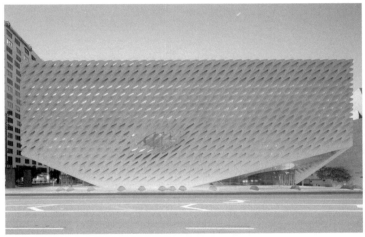

THE BROAD, Los Angeles, CA, USA
Diller Scofidio + Renfro

THE OHIO STATE UNIVERSITY EAST REGIONAL CHILLED WATER PLANT, Columbus,
OH, USA, Leers Weinzapfel Associates,

UVA EL PARAISO - SAN ANTONIO DE PRADO, Medellin, Colombia
Empresa de Desarrollo Urbano EDU - Taller de Diseño

VAULTED HOUSE, Los Vilos, Chile
Cecilia Puga

252

VENTURA HOUSE, Monterrey, Mexico
Tatiana Bilbao Estudio

VERTICAL ITAIM BUILDING, São Paulo, Brazil
studio mk27 | Marcio Kogan

VIK WINE CELLAR, Milahue, Chile
Smiljan Radic

253

WOOD INNOVATION AND DESIGN CENTER, Canada
Michael Green Architecture

AERONAUTICAL AND AEROSPACE INSTITUTE
OF PUERTO RICO
Aguadilla, Puerto Rico
JosÉ Javier Toro

AGA KHAN MUSEUM
Toronto, Canada
Maki and Associates

AGP EGLASS FACTORY & OFFICES
Lima, Peru
V.Oid | Felipe Ferrer CÁrdenas

ARCUS CENTER FOR SOCIAL JUSTICE
LEADERSHIP
Kalamazoo, MI, USA
Studio Gang Architects

ARGOS CENTER FOR INNOVATION
Medellin, Colombia
Lorenzo Castro Jaramillo

ASPEN ART MUSEUM
Aspen, CO, USA
Shigeru Ban Architects

AYELEN SCHOOL
Rancagua, Chile
ELEMENTAL

BARROQUINHA SLOPE
Salvador, Brazil
Gustavo Cedroni

BBVA BANCOMER TOWER
Mexico City, Mexico
LegoRogers (Legorreta + Legorreta and Rogers Stirk
Harbour + Partners)

BCI BANK
Santiago, Chile
Borja Huidobro, Sebastian di Girolamo, Cristian
Valdivieso, German Zegers

BIGWOOD
Ketchum, ID, USA
Olson Kundig Architects

BIOMUSEO
Panama City, Panama
Gehry Partners

BOREAS BUILDING
Rosario, Argentina
Martin Aloras

BOX 298 OFFICE BUILDING
São Paulo, Brazil
Andrade Morettin Arquitetos

BRUCE C. BOLLING MUNICIPAL BUILDING
Boston, MA, USA
Francine Houben / Mecanoo Architecten; Victor
Vizgaitis / Sasaki Associates

CALERA DEL REY
Calera del Rey, Uruguay
Gualano + Gualano Arquitectos

CANADIAN MUSEUM FOR HUMAN RIGHTS
Winnipeg, Canada
Antoine Predock Architect Studio

CASE WESTERN RESERVE UNIVERSITY;
TINKHAM VEALE UNIVERSITY CENTER
Cleveland, OH, USA
Ralph Johnson

CENTRO.
Mexico City, Mexico
Enrique Norten / TEN Arquitectos

CERO K. INDUSTRIAL BUILDING
San Carlos, Chile
Maximillano Noguera & Alejandra Marambio

CHAPEL OF THE NORTH AMERICAN MARTYRS
Carmichael, CA, USA
Craig Hodgetts and Hsinming Fung

CHICAGO HORIZON
Chicago, IL, USA
Ultramoderne + Brett Schneider

CHICAGO PUBLIC LIBRARY, CHINATOWN
BRANCH
Chicago, IL, USA
SOM | Brian Lee, FAIA

CHICAGO RIVERWALK - PHASE II
Chicago, IL, USA
Ross Barney Architects + Sasaki Associates

CHINMAYA MISSION AUSTIN
Austin, TX, USA
MirÓ Rivera Architects

CINETECA NACIONAL
Mexico City, Mexico
Rojkind Arquitectos

CIVIL ENGINEERING SCHOOL AND CUR
AUDITORIUM - FIRST STAGE
Rosario, Argentina
Caballero - Fernandez Arquitectos

CLAREVIEW COMMUNITY RECREATION
CENTRE
Edmonton, Canada
Stephen R. Teeple

254

CMN POP UP STORE
Mexico City, Mexico
AT103 | Julio Amezcua + Francisco Pardo

CONSTITUCION CULTURAL CENTER
Constitucion, Chile
ELEMENTAL

CORNING MUSEUM OF GLASS
Corning, NY, USA
Thomas Phifer and Partners

CORRUIRAS SOCIAL DWELLING
São Paulo, Brazil
Boldarini Arquitetos Associados

CUEXCOMATITLAN WATERFRONT
PROMENADE
Tlajomulco, Mexico
Ricardo Agraz

DE LA CRUZ CHAPEL
Santa Ana, Argentina
Estudio Cella

DEANS BUILDING SCHOOL OF COMMERCIAL
BANKING
Mexico City, Mexico
Taller | Rocha + Carrillo | Mauricio Rocha, Gabriela
Carrillo

DENVER UNION STATION HUB + TRANSIT-
ORIENTED DEVELOPMENT
Denver, CO, USA
SOM | Roger Duffy, FAIA

DEPT OF SANITATION GARAGE AND SALT SHED
New York, NY, USA
WXY Studio/Dattner Architects

DINAMARCA 399
Valparaiso, Chile
Joaquin Velasco Rubio

ECONOMICS AND BUSINESS FACULTY - DIEGO
PORTALES UNIVERSITY
Rafael Hevia / Rodrigo Duque Motta

EDIFICIO SEIS
Santiago, Chile
Franco Somigli - Felipe Moreno - Juan Sebastian
Lama - Mathias Klotz

EL MANGALETA WEEKEND HOUSES FOR RENT
Icho Cruz, Argentina
Marco Rampulla

EL RANCHO
Playa Hermosa, Uruguay
Mbad Arquitectos

ELEVATION 10
Rio de Janeiro, Brazil
Pedro Varella

ELMER A. HENDERSON: A JOHNS HOPKINS
PARTNERSHIP SCHOOL AND THE HARRY AND
JEANETTE WEINBERG EARLY CHILDHOOD
CENTER
Baltimore, MD, USA
Robert M. Rogers, FAIA

EMERSON COLLEGE LOS ANGELES
Los Angeles, CA, USA
Morphosis Architects

EQUESTRIAN PROJECT
Valle de Bravo, Mexico
Manuel Cervantes Cespedes / CC Arquitectos

FACULTY OF ARTS ACADEMIC BUILDING,
PONTIFICIA UNIVERSIDAD CATOLICA DE
CHILE
Santiago, Chile
Fernando Pérez -Oyarzún, José Quintanilla-Chaia

FLOAT
Fergusons Cove, Canada
Omar Gandhi Architect Inc.

FRIENDSHIP PARK
Montevideo, Uruguay
Arq. Marcelo Roux, Arq.
Gastón Cuña, Arq. Patricia Roland, Federico Lezama

GOLDRING CENTRE FOR HIGH PERFORMANCE
SPORT, UNIVERSITY OF TORONTO
Toronto, Canada
John & Patricia Patkau

GOLF HOUSE
Buenos Aires, Argentina
Luciano Kruik Arquitectos

GRAND HYATT PLAYA DEL CARMEN
Playa del Carmen, Mexico
Sordo Madaleno Arquitectos

GUADELOUPEAN CENTRE FOR INDIAN
CULTURE
Petit-Canal, Guadeloupe
Pile et Face Architects

HELIÓPOLIS SOCIAL HOUSING
São Paulo, Brazil
Biselli + Katchborian Arquitetos

HIDDEN HOME
Zaragoza, El Salvador
Ana Cristina Olivares de Guerrero

255

HOUSE IN BARRANCO 1915-2015
Lima, Peru
Oscar Borasino

HOUSE ON A DUNE
Harbour Island, Bahamas
Chad Oppenheim

INFINITA HOUSE
Babahoyo, Ecuador
Natura Futura Arquitectura

ISMAILI CENTRE, TORONTO
Toronto, Canada
Charles Correa

JOA CHAPEL
Rio de Janeiro, Brazil
Bernardes Arquitetura

JUST BE
Mexico City, Mexico
ARQMOV Workshop

KÄPÄCLÄJUI INDIGENOUS CAPACITATION
CENTER
Grano de Oro, Turrialba, Costa Rica
Entre Nos Atelier

KING STREET LIVE/WORK/GROW
Halifax, Canada
Susan Fitzgerald Architecture

LA BREA AFFORDABLE HOUSING FOR
FORMERLY HOMELESS LGBT YOUTH
West Hollywood, CA, USA
Patrick Tighe Architecture with John V. Mutlow
Architect

LAKE HURON RESIDENCE
Goderich, Canada
Hariri Pontarini Architects | Siamak Hariri

LANDSCAPE CANOPY
Guatemala City, Guatemala
Axel Paredes and Ana Aleman

LANDSTEINER CAMPUS TOLUCA
Toluca de Lerdo, Mexico
Gerardo Asali de la mora

LEARNING TO FLY
San Jose Villanueva, El Salvador
Jose Roberto Paredes

LIBERTAD STREET HOUSE
Montevideo, Uruguay
Pedro Livni and Karin Bla

LO BARNECHEA II
Santiago, Chile
Elemental

LOOKOUT SCAFFOLD
Merida, Mexico
Román Jesús Cordero Tovar and David Sosa Solís

LUSITANIA PAZ DE COLOMBIA SCHOOL
Medellin, Colombia
Camilo Avellaneda Valcárcel

LUTHERAN EVANGELICAL CHURCH
Lima, Peru
Oscar Borasino

MAPOCHO 42K: A GEOGRAPHICAL
PROMENADE
FOR SOCIAL EQUITY
Santiago, Chile
Sandra Iturriaga, Juan Baixas,
Paulina Ibieta, Francisco Croxatto

MARIA RIBERA (LA CUBANA)
Mexico City, Mexico
Javier Sanchez Corral

MERCADO ROMA
Mexico City, Mexico
Rojkind Arquitectos

MEZTITLA HOUSE
Tepoztlán, Mexico
Luis Arturo García Bazán

MINIMOD CATUÇABA
Catuçaba, Brazil
MAPA Arquitetos

MIRAFLORES HOUSE
Funes, Argentina
Caballero - Fernandez Arquitectos

MOHAWK RESIDENCE
Chicago, IL, USA
UrbanLab

MODERN ART MUSEUM OF MEDELLIN (MAMM)
EXPANSION
Medellin, Colombia
51-1 Arquitectos + CtrlG

MONT-LAURIER MULTIFUNCTIONAL THEATRE
Mont-Laurier, Canada
Les Architectes FABG

MUSEUM OF CONGONHAS
Congonhas, Brazil
Gustavo Penna, Laura Penna, Norberto Bambozzi

MUSEUM OF OUTDOOR ARTS ELEMENT HOUSE
Anton Chico, Las Vegas, NV, USA
MOS Architects | Michael Meredith, Hilary Sample

256

MUSEUM OF TOMORROW
Rio de Janeiro, Brazil
Santiago Calatrava

MUY GÜEMES
Cordoba, Argentina
Agostina Gennaro, María José
Péndola

NATIONAL EMERGENCIES BUREAU
HEADQUARTERS
Santiago, Chile
Teodoro Fernandez Larrañaga

NATIONAL SAWDUST
Brooklyn, NY, USA
Bureau V

NAVE PERFORMING ARTS HALL
Santiago, Chile
Smiljan Radic

NEW CITY HALL IN BUENOS AIRES
Buenos Aires, Argentina
Foster + Partners

NOVA CUMBICA STATE SCHOOL
Guarulhos, Brazil
Hereñú & Ferroni Arquitetos

ONCE UPON A TIME
San Salvador, El Salvador
Jose Roberto Paredes

ONE SANTA FE
Los Angeles, CA, USA
Michael Maltzan, FAIA

ORELLANA'S CULTURAL CENTER AND
ARCHAEOLOGICAL MUSEUM (MACCO)
Francisco de Orellana, Ecuador
Pablo Antonio Moreira Viteri

PAINEIRA HOUSE
Brasilia, Brazil
BLOCO Arquitetos

PARQUE FLUVIAL RENATO POBLETE
Santiago, Chile
Cristián Boza D., Cristián Boza W., Diego Labbé,
Eduardo Ruiz-Risueño, Michel Carles Tapia

PHOTO MUSEUM CUATRO CAMINOS
Naucalpan de Juarez, Mexico
Taller | Rocha + Carrillo | Mauricio Rocha, Gabriela
Carrillo

PICO BRANCH LIBRARY
Santa Monica, CA, USA
Julie Eizenberg

PIES DESCALZOS SCHOOL
Cartagena de Indias, Colombia
Giancarlo Mazzanti - El Equipo Mazzanti

POLIS STATION: TOWARD A COMMUNITY-
CENTERED POLICE STATION
Chicago, IL, USA
Studio Gang Architects

POLITEAMA CULTURAL CENTER
Canelones, Uruguay
Estudio Lorieto-Pintos-Santellán arquitectos

POMONA COLLEGE STUDIO ART HALL
Claremont, CA, USA
wHY

PORTMIAMI TUNNEL
Miami, FL, USA
ArquitectonicaGEO

PRECISION HEADQUARTERS
Santiago, Chile
GAAA: Guillermo Acuña Arquitectos Asociados

PTERODACTYL
Culver City, CA, USA
Eric Owen Moss Architects

PUBLIC LIBRARY OF CONSTITUCION
Constitucion, Chile
Sebastián Irarrázaval

QUINCHO TIA CORAL
Asunción, Paraguay
Gabinete de Arquitectura

REFUGE ON THE BAY OF FUNDY
Centre Burlington, Canada
Talbot Sweetapple

RENOVATION OF THE CHILEAN MUSEUM OF
PRE-COLUMBIAN ART
Santiago, Chile
Smiljan Radic

RENOVATION OF THE RENWICK GALLERY
Washington DC, USA
Westlake Reed Leskosky

RESTORATION OF THE IAP-SP BUILDING
São Paulo, Brazil
Silvio Oksman

ROCK CREEK HOUSE
Washington DC, USA
NADAA

RURAL SCHOOL ALTO DEL MERCADO
Marinilla, Colombia
Juan Bernardo Echeverri and Ana Elvira Velez Villa

257

RYERSON UNIVERSITY STUDENT LEARNING
CENTRE
Toronto, Canada
Zeidler Partnership Architects + Snøhetta

SANMARTIN 605 APARTMENT BUILDING
Barranco, Peru
Teodoro Boza Rizo Patrón, Violeta Ferrand Malatesta

SARANDI PRIMARY SCHOOL
Montevideo, Uruguay
Pedro Barran Casas, PAEPU

SAUL-BELLOW LIBRARY
Montreal, Canada
Chevalier Morales Architectes

SCULPTURECENTER
Long Island City, NY, USA
Andrew Berman Architect

SEAGLASS CAROUSEL
New York, NY, USA
WXY Architecture + Urban Design

SESC JUNDIAÍ
Jundiai, Brazil
Teuba Arquitetura e Urbanismo

SL11024
Los Angeles, CA, USA
LOHA | Lorcan O'Herlihy Architects

SOCIEDAD DE MAR, SUMMER DWELLING
Jose Ignacio, Uruguay
adamo - faiden

ST. JAMES RESIDENCE
Chicago, IL, USA
Margret McCurry, FAIA

STONE ECHO
Espita, Mexico
PLUG Architecture / Roman Cordero and Izbeth
Mendoza

STRUCTURAL ARCHEOLOGY
Belo Horizonte, Brazil
Carlos M. Teixeira

STUDIO MADALENA
São Paulo, Brazil
Apiacás Arquitetos

SUGAR HILL DEVELOPMENT
New York, NY, USA
Adjaye Associates

SUSTAINABLE HOUSING
Ciudad Acuna, Mexico
Tatiana Bilbao Estudio

THE CLARK ART INSTITUTE
Williamstown, MA, USA
Tadao Ando Architect, Gensler,
Reed Hilderbrand, Selldorf Architects

THE CLICK CLACK HOTEL
Bogota, Colombia
PLAN:B Architects

THE HIGH LINE (PHASE 3)
New York, NY, USA
Diller Scofidio + Renfro / James Corner Field
Operations

THE ISABEL BADER CENTRE FOR THE
PERFORMING ARTS, QUEEN'S UNIVERSITY
Kingston, Canada
Snøhetta

THE WAVE: PUBLIC PERFORMANCE SPACE
Valparaiso, Chile
Christian Hermansen Cordua

THE WHITNEY MUSEUM
New York, NY, USA
Renzo Piano Building Workshop + Cooper Robertson

TONGVA PARK
Santa Monica, CA, USA
James Corner Field Operations

TOPO HOUSE
Blue Mounds, WI, USA
Johnsen Schmaling Architects

UBC BOOKSTORE RENOVATION + EXPANSION
Vancouver, Canada
Steve McFarlane

UNITED STATES COURTHOUSE, SALT LAKE
CITY
Salt Lake City, UT, USA
Thomas Phifer and Partners

VALPARAISO PAVILION
Valparaiso, Chile
Sebastian Irarrazaval

VERSACE SHOWROOM
New York, NY, USA
SO - IL

VIA AT WEST 57TH
New York, NY, USA
BIG | Bjarke Ingles Group

VIOLETA PARRA MUSEUM
Santiago, Chile
Cristian Undurraga

258

VITRA
São Paulo, Brazil
Studio Libeskind

WEIN HOUSE
Costa Esmeralda, Pinamar, Argentina
Besonias Almeida Arquitectos

WICKER FOREST
Santiago, Chile
Grupotalca

WILD TURKEY BOURBON VISITOR CENTER
Lawrenceburg, IN, USA
De Leon & Primmer Architecture Workshop

WORKSHOP HOUSE - TECNOMEC
São Paulo, Brazil
PAX.ARQ

The Prize for Emerging Practice, MCHAP.emerge, is awarded to exceptional built work by a practice in its first ten years of operation. Each cycle, the jury begins by acknowledging a group of outstanding projects whose approaches and impacts deserve special recognition. This list is then narrowed down to four or five finalists. The finalist architects are invited to Chicago to participate in a day-long public symposium led by IIT students and faculty; the winner is named during an evening benefit at S. R. Crown Hall.

The authors of the winning project are invited to teach at IIT and given $25,000 toward research and a publication. In 2016, MCHAP received fifty-six Emerging Practice nominations and selected eleven outstanding projects, including five finalists. The Prize for Emerging Practice winner was Pavilion on the Zocalo, a temporary installation by the Mexico City-based firm PRODUCTORA.

PAVILION ON THE ZOCALO (WINNER), Mexico City, Mexico
Productora

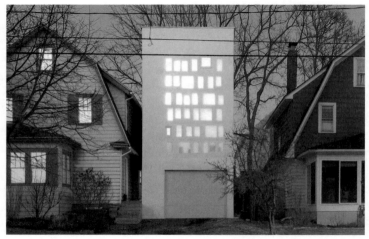

PARA PROJECT, Syracuse, NY, USA
Jon Lott, Haffenden House

OZ CONDOMINIUMS, Winnipeg, Canada
5468796 Architecture

C.I.D., Road to Ayquina, Chile
Emilio Marín & Juan Carlos López Architects

SAN FRANCISCO BUILDING, Asuncion, Paraguay
José Cubilla

263

BLUEPRINT AT STOREFRONT FOR ART AND ARCHITECTURE, New York, NY, USA
SO – IL

CASA SCOUT, BAAG, Ciudad Autónoma de Buenos Aires, Argentina
Buenos Aires Arquitectura Grupal

MULTIPROGRAM SHIP / SPORT AND CULTURAL PLATFORMS, Caracas, Venezuela
Alejandro Haiek Coll

TEQUILA CENTINELA CHAPEL, Arandas, Mexico
Estudio ALA Luis Enrique Flores - Armida Fernandez

VILA MATILDE HOUSE, São Paulo, Brazil
Terra e Tuma Associated Architects

265

TROIS-RIVIÈRES COGECO AMPHITHÉÂTRE, Trois-Rivières, Canada
Paul Laurendeau

5 HOUSES
Villa Carlos Paz, Argentina
Carlos Alejandro Ciravegna

AGUAS CLARAS HOUSE
Florida, Chile
Eduardo Castillo

AMBIENT 30 60
Santiago, Chile
Umwelt

ARQUITECTURA RIFA HOUSE G08
Montevideo, Uruguay
Martin Mitropulos + Facundo Álvarez

ART DECO PROJECT
Miami, FL, USA
Aranda\Lasch

BABYLON 1500 GALLERY
Rio de Janeiro, Brazil
Rua Arquitetos | Pedro Évora + Pedro Rivera

BAR RAVAL
Toronto, Canada
Partisans

BLOOM
Berkeley, CA, USA
Ronald Rael & Virginia San Fratello

BRICK HOUSE
Rosario, Argentina
Diego Arraigada

BRIDGE PAVILION
Los Molinos, Calamuchita, Argentina
Alarcia-Ferrer Arquitectos

CAVE OF LIGHT (SIFAIS)
La Carpio, Costa Rica
Entre Nos Atelier

CLAUDIA ANDUJAR GALLERY PAVILION
Brumadinho, Brazil
Arquitectos Associados

COMMUNITY DEVELOPMENT CENTER -
CERRO CORA
Luque, Paraguay
Oficina Comunitaria de Arquitectura (OCA)

COSTANERA LYON 2
Santiago, Chile
Simonetti-Stewart Architects | Eugenio Simonetti +
Renato Stewart

COURTYARD HOUSE
Aurora, IL, USA
Andrew Heid

DELTA CABIN
Tigre, Argentina
AToT - Lucia Hollman + Agustin Moscato

EAST OFFICE
Guatemala, Guatemala
PXParchitecture & Partners

FCA 2015
Mexico City, Mexico
Estudio MMX

FUNES TOWN HOUSE
Funes, Argentina
Pedrido Theiler Arquitectos

GABRIELA HOUSE
Merida, Mexico
TACO taller de arquitectura contextual

GHESKIO CHOLERA TREATMENT CENTER
Port-au-Prince, Haiti
MASS Design Group

GROTTO SAUNA
Georgian Bay, Canada
Partisans

HOUSE CS
Cachagua, Chile
Alvaro Arancibia + Sebastian Coll

HOUSE IN PARACAS
Paracas, Pisco, Peru
Tarata | Nicolás Kisic Aguirre

HOUSE PAINT PAVILION / "THEFIRSTONEIS-
CRAZYTHESECONDONEISNUTS"
Detroit, MI, USA
Nick Gelpi

INDUSTRIAL PARK / SOCIO PRODUCTIVE
UNIT
Barquisimeto, Venezuela
Alejandro Haiek Coll

LEVERING TRADE
Zapopan, Mexico
Atelier ARS° | Alejandro Guerrero + Andrea Soto

MAD BUILDING
Santiago, Chile
Max Nunez

MARGINAL STREET LOFTS
Boston, MA, USA
Merge Architects

MEMORIAL 27F
Concepcion, Chile
Ricardo Atanacio, Agustin Soza

266

MEZCAL DISTILLERY EL MILAGRITO
Santiago Matatlan, Mexico
Ambrosi | Etchegaray

NANCAGUA CITY HALL: A NEW PUBLIC
THRESHOLD
Nancagua, Chile
Beals Lyon Arquitectos

PUBLIC TOILETS AND KIOSKS ON
ECATEPEC-NEZAHUALCOYOTL BIKE
LANE
Ecatepec de Morelos, Mexico
LANZA Atelier

PUNTA SAN JUAN SEACOAST OBSERVATORY
Marcona, Peru
Jochamowitz Rivera Arquitectos

SAINT BERNARD'S CHAPEL
La Playosa, Argentina
Nicolás Campodonico

RESTREPO PLATA
Santa Elena de Piedritas School
Talara, Peru
Elizabeth Milagros Ananos Vega & Carlos Andres

SHADE AT THE FALLS
Isla de Yaquil, Chile
Cristian Felipe Palma Ramirez

SMF-TU - SOCIAL MEDICAL FACILITY
Las Toscas, Argentina
Baarqs

THE BEACH
Washington DC, USA
Snarkitecture

THE BROKEN LION HOUSE
Subachoque, Colombia
Lucas Oberlaender

TLP
Tijuana, Mexico
T38 Studio

TRANSMISSION CENTRAL
Santiago, Chile
Umwelt

WATER RESERVOIRS AS PUBLIC PARK AND
EQUIPMENT, UVA EL ORFELINATO
Medellin, Colombia
Colectivo 720 | Mario Fernando Camargo y Luis
Orlando Trombe

WINDHOVER CONTEMPLATIVE CENTER
Stanford, CA, USA
Aidlin Darling Design

ZERO 2016
USA
Community Solutions

267

# POST SCRIPTUM

The last part of the book puts together time-dispersed conversations and email instant reflections that 'From a Distance' add voices to the critical thinking of architecture, planetary culture, and nature, among other issues. It represents a symbolic opening of the discussions in this book to a broader community of designers. MCHAP intends to build a collaborative platform based on dialogues.

The recently deceased Jean-Luc Nancy corresponds with Florencia Rodriguez about the world, nature, religion, and a certain *fièvre rationaliste*. Isabella Moretti and Magdalena Tagliabue interview Graciela Silvestri about landscape roots, travel, and the Guaraní knowledge. When interviewing David Harvey, Mariano Gomez-Luque and Daniel Ibañez inquired about capital and urbanization.

After those dialogues, Juan Pablo Corvalán, Jeannette Sordi, Rodrigo Kommers Wender, Paul Preissner, Pedro Aparicio, Juliana Ramirez, Ana Rascovsky, and Todd Palmer email MCHAP to share some intimate thoughts and profound reflections distributed throughout the Americas.

Imagination, nature, artifice, ecology, environment, meaning, urbanity, care, and responsibility, are part of the glossary that is changing how we think and produce architecture.

In the last visual essay, Miguel de Guzmán portraits a black and white sublime and blurred New York City. The contrast with the rest of the images of this book is not accidental. On the contrary, after all the proposed expeditions and readings, it suggests diluting formal preconceptions about architecture, opening the idea of new possible futures.

# MIXED LANGUAGES:
# A WRITTEN EXCHANGE
# WITH JEAN-LUC NANCY
## Florencia Rodriguez

It was Nancy's idea to make this as a written interview via e-mail; it was our intention to reproduce it almost exactly as it happened—a proper epistolary exchange even though one wrote in French and the other in English. Words, either constantly used or intentionally lost, are here rethought of, their unstable meanings revealed: nature, global, politics. In this interview he argues that "Humanity today is both fetishistic and computational, it uses smartphones and sorcerers, it speaks with mixed languages stuffed with technical English, it drags along revolutionary Marxist tatters with trances of voodoo, democratic pretentions with cast or slavery systems, etc."

August 14th
Dear Monsieur Jean-Luc Nancy,

It is a great honor to be in touch with you and to be able to carry out this digital conversation. Thank you very much for your kind participation.

As Isabella told you in previous communications, our next issue is dedicated to the discussion and further understanding of what the idea of planet could be, or even what the 'world' might imply today. Many years ago, you were already writing about the concept of 'glomus' and this continuous, complex tissue that has wrapped and defined our planet. I would like to start our conversation by asking you about the contemporary pertinence of this idea.

A second part of my question is—to what do you think we are referring when we use the word 'nature' nowadays?

Please let me know what might be an approximate timeframe for your response.

Yours sincerely,
Florencia Rodriguez

August 14th
Ok I will answer ASAP!

August 15th
Dear Florencia Rodriguez,

Please find here my answers to your two first questions. I did not copy your questions in this file, I just put the main word of each as a signal. All the best on this 15th of August.

GLOMUS
I used long ago this biological and anatomical term to play with its sense of a game of 'boule' or 'pelote' with elements or entangled fibers in order to invoke, in contrast to 'globus,' a confused complexity, an indistinguishable melee. That which we call 'globalization,' coming from the 'global village' of McLuhan, has nothing to do with the beautiful sphericity of a globe: it is, rather, a skein, an interlacing, a labyrinth, and a brushy forest.

Such is at least the vision of the Occidental, which we still are even though the Occident is not only in Europe and the Americas, but also mixed in all cultures and all mores. Humanity today is both fetishistic and computational, it uses smartphones and sorcerers, it speaks with mixed languages stuffed with technical English, it drags along revolutionary Marxist tatters with trances of voodoo, democratic pretentions with cast or slavery systems, etc. etc.

But this grand melee is only a confusion for us who are perhaps old-fashioned, incapable of expressing ourselves other than according to certain organizations of rational thought, which we believe exclude any vicinity with the sacred, the naive, the magical. We ignore, in fact, how much of the humanity of the Occidental itself never ceased to be agitated by obscure passions, divinations, and irrational pulses. Newton alchemized and Einstein believed in god. Today the rationalist fever is such that it produces its own superstitions, idolatries, and delusions (all these words are anyway marked by a value of criticism that is imprinted by that which is called 'reason'): for example, transhumanism, indefinitely prolonged life, cloning, etc. At the same time, for billions of human beings around the world, the middle class that has been covering Europe and the United States for a long time, and that is gradually gaining ground elsewhere, through urban and industrial cells, represents an ideal or at least an enviable condition. The automobile, running water, available electricity, the urban spectacle as well as a minimum of freedom and equality—even formal ones—form a desirable whole that deserves either that we work to produce it where we are, or that we migrate to find it.

If some religious fanaticisms display a condemnation of this style of life devoted to earthly satisfactions, it is nevertheless clear that entire sections of the technic and so-called pleasures of the Occident are adopted or desired by the same sworn enemies of this Occident who see themselves as more and more Oriental, or more precisely, omnidirectional. All of this 'glomal' phenomenon, or better said 'glomalic' (cluster of capillary vessels), develops with a power greater than that which accompanies it—by way of mixed causes and effects—with very large exponential growth numbers: population, speed, transmission, calculation, communication and circuit-switching, information, deformation… everything happens on scales for which our mathematical habits are derisory. Billions of dollars are a subordinate unit, light years too, and the nanosecond or the micron are units of ordinary use.

The calculating civilization becomes itself incalculable, at the same that it continues to nourish the functioning of calculations, projections, and forecasts. But the paradox is that an increasing number of these calculations have to be employed to correct the inconvenient, or otherwise disastrous, effects of many technical interventions: depletion of fossil energy, depletion of soil, disappearances of living species and resources, etc. All of these 'repairs' require even more technical and economic means. At the same time, however, it is not certain that the system of increasing production does put itself in difficulty.

None of this can be said to be a simple certainty. No era is ever able to appreciate itself; and to repeat again, it remains to be seen if, today, the judgment of the old, tired Occidental is better established than the decided, young non-Occidental youth. One thing is certain: We are no longer able to plan for a determined future. The idea itself of 'progress' is in a very serious regression. We are re-learning the unpredictable, the absolute obscurity of all to come—and this could likely change the spirit of this "world without hope," according to the words of Marx.

NATURE
When we speak of nature, we are still most often captives of the representation of an autonomous order characterized by an internal purpose, in which come together the mineral, plant, and animal 'kingdoms' themselves coordinated into a cosmic totality. The internal purpose is that of the life that it produces and that reproduces itself. At the same time, we see it as a sort of vis-à-vis with man, who forms both an environment in which he evolves and an ensemble of usable resources. We observe as well that the human technic has agitated this order and that it is necessary to correct these disturbances.

But with this representation we leave out two important questions. The first: what is the exact relation of man to nature? The second: how can the existence itself of this whole, especially as it contains man, be thought? To the first question it must be answered that man belongs first to nature. It is an animal in which life has access to a status or a particular function. The more our knowledge has progressed, the more it has shown to us our close belonging to a kingdom of the living, and in it, all its chemical, electrical, and mechanical characteristics. If man distinguishes himself by language and by technic, it must be recognized that this distinction belongs to a continuing thread. It must therefore be thought that the internal purpose of nature extends into a purpose of excess: man is himself "the being of ends," as Kant said. Language—that is to say the possibility of conceiving, representing, and projecting—has a corollary in the technic, in other words, in the possibility of adding to nature new devices with their own purposes.

The disturbance, indeed the degradation of nature, is therefore itself linked to a natural source.

We thus arrive at the second question: if the ensemble includes nature and technic, or nature and culture, if it includes its own overflow and the emergence of finalities that can no longer be explained by the operation of a complete order in itself, how thus can its existence be thought?

Religions have proposed to think the ensemble as ordered—or 'subordinated'—by the divine powers whose divine purpose would be the pure and simple existence of a world devoted to periodic destructions and rebirths, modelling a kind of vitality or infinite game—so be it the pure glorification of the immeasurable power of god. In a sense, religions are well thought in the projecting of excessive, absolute regimes on the world of our experiences. In a certain way, humanity does nothing but put these projections into practice and push nature, through man, towards the supernatural and towards a recreation of the world.

The fact remains that if it is so, man can no longer be situated in relation to the aims or superior forces of the gods. He must situate himself in relation to himself, and to the scope of this indefinite overriding of nature. He must take back that which seems to be reserved for gods: the secret, the enigma, or the mystery of existence of all that exists...

August 16th
Dear Jean-Luc,

Thank you. I have never conducted an interview as an email conversation, and I must say that I'm enjoying this very much.

I will keep on sending the questions by email and you can work in the same word document. I don't want to abuse your generosity, so, if you agree, I will only send one more email with questions after receiving your answers to this one.

Here are my questions that are a mix of comments and spontaneous thoughts provoked by your answers:

I think the conceptualization of a rationalist fever (la fièvre rationaliste) is extremely appealing and appropriately represents an extremist faith in technics that has lately evolved into these ideas of the transhuman or even the 'posthumous.' Can we interpret this blind belief as one of the causes of our own degradation as humans/nature? And is it possible to live fully immersed in the enigma, the mystery of existence, absolutely doing away with the—collapsed—fantasy of eternal progress? So, in a kind of perverse way, may technology be emulating nature to desperately generate clumsy representations of that enigma that is in itself impossible to represent?

Sorry if there are too many questions together. Feel free to avoid any of them if they are not clear, or let me know if you need me to rephrase them. I also feel that my English might not be enough to express these ideas in a more transparent and sensitive way.

All the best,
Florencia

August 17<sup>th</sup>
Ok I will answer.

August 17<sup>th</sup>
voici chère Florencia

I think the conceptualization of a rationalist fever (la fièvre rationaliste) is extremely appealing and appropriately represents an extremist faith in technics that has lately evolved into these ideas of the transhuman or even the 'posthumous.' Can we interpret this blind belief as one of the causes of our own degradation as humans/nature? And is it possible to live fully immersed in the enigma, the mystery of existence, absolutely doing away with the—collapsed—fantasy of eternal progress? So, in a kind of perverse way, may technology be emulating nature to desperately generate clumsy representations of that enigma that is in itself impossible to represent?

The question is to what extent we can speak of a 'fever,' 'blind belief,' or 'perversity' as you have done—anyway, that is completely understandable because we are all forced to speak in this way since we must represent to ourselves a 'normality' or a 'naturalness,' or also a 'rationality' (without 'fever'), in human existence and in the world in which it appears. Yet we know as well that the human animal is an enigma to itself because it, precisely, has the ability to represent itself with a 'knowledge,' a 'truth,' a 'standard,' a 'norm,' etc. The very fact of speaking implies that I believe in what you have told me—and thus we can agree on certain meanings—and at the same time that I can think that you are mistaken or that you have concealed something from me. In other words, the 'truth' of what you say is not limited to the 'normal,' 'clear' meanings of your speech.

This is of course reciprocal, and it is also true of what you yourself perceive of what you are saying. You do not completely master the meaning, range, or resonance of your words. They can be insensibly (unconsciously) driven in directions that you ignore, and that I ignore as well.

For example, when you say that the enigma of existence is "impossible to represent": what makes you say that rather than "this enigma will eventually be explained" or "this mystery belongs to god"? You can assert that these two possibilities are excluded for you and have disappeared into the past. And yet some may still assert them…

Furthermore, what does 'impossible' mean? Why is there a limit to the possible? But if the possible is only thinkable from the already-given (as Bergson explains it), then the impossible could only be that which is not yet recognized as possible…

The word 'impossible' sometimes has (in Bataille, for example, where Lacan inherited it) designated that which does not belong to the register of 'possible/impossible'—which is that of the real/realizable—but more to that of the register in which it is not 'realizable,' but real in such a way that it is always already realized, or rather that it does not have to be realized because it already is. It has happened or it always happens (Wittgenstein: "The world is everything that is the case.")

Thus the "impossible to represent" could mean as well that which has not been represented because it is present in all representation: namely, that we exist, that the world exists.

In order to escape "clumsy representations" we must therefore learn to think this happening of the real given, poised, present in all presence. At least something is there that says "ergo sum," as Descartes says, and this proceeds any question of 'what' I 'am.' Kant says for his part: there is at least a real existence that interrogates existence, and that is enough to confirm that it exists.

We must now come to think 'that': not to the understanding of it scientifically nor mystically, but to think it—even as unthinkable. Here may be the direction for progress that needs to be made: a progress that can escape the progress of powers, of energies, of speeds, etc. I will stop, because otherwise it will become too long …

August 21<sup>st</sup>
Dear Jean-Luc,

I'm sorry for my delay in getting back to you. We had a holiday here in Argentina, and I had some family things during the weekend. I will send my question later today. Thank you for your patience. Florencia

August 21<sup>st</sup>
Absolutely not a problem!

August 21<sup>st</sup>
Dear Jean-Luc,

I'm sorry, I was trying to think of only one last question, but as I read and think, I feel the need to open the dialogue a little bit more...

You finished your last response with this comment:

"We must now come to think 'that': Not to the understanding of it scientifically nor mystically, but to think it—be it unthinkable.

There may be the direction for progress that needs to be made: a progress that can escape the progress of powers, of energies, of accelerations, etc."

My three last questions are:

- How do the new technologies, their impact on our way of living, and the complex political scenarios that we are immersed in, take part in the direction of the progress you are suggesting?

- There are some contemporary thinkers, such as Byung Chul Han or even Zizek, that theorize our society as one that has become 'pornographic,' and has lost a valuable distance or space in between that—as I interpret it—might be relevant to feel or to sensitively understand something about that presentation of the réel that you mentioned before. How do you feel about this?

- My third and last question is in direct relation to the central matter of our issue: how would you imagine an appropriate method of mapping and representing our planet today?

Thank you again!
Florencia

August 22nd
Here is my last answer—unless you want to ask a post-last question and so on: this is up to you!

*My three last questions are:*
*- How do the new technologies, their impact on our way of living, and the complex political scenarios that we are immersed in, take part in the direction of the progress you are suggesting?*

Our situation is very complex because technology and 'political scenarios' are not separable. That which you have called 'politics' is composed for the most part of techno-economic interests, including when it comes to interests of nations. In that respect, the United States today wants to protect itself from world deployment, and desires, among other things, to revive their production and use of coal. This accentuates their distance from ecological standards that seem necessary to all experts. But above all, this could lead to techno-logical and economic difficulties for the United States themselves: for example, in the competition between coal and natural gas, or in the production of electric cars. One starts from a political measure and immediately enters into an expert debate. Another well-known contemporary example: the lithium used in the production of smartphones requires an extraction of considerable amounts of water, which cannot continue without consequences in the regions or countries of exploitation. Yet smartphone producers are powerful companies, indifferent to the interests of these regions and capable of influencing the politics of the countries concerned.

One can continue indefinitely... At the same time, it is certain that our ways of life are already largely modified with regard to speed and the extent of movements, the capacities of information and calculation, and the general movement of book cultures and education from the invention of forms towards screen cultures, information, and the conception of performative forms rather than symbolic ones (I mean to say that an 800-meter high-rise building draws its meaning from performance, whereas an Egyptian or Mayan pyramid, a gothic cathedral, a palace, or a Chinese pagoda draw their meaning from that which one calls symbolism.)

One could venture to conclude this: we have entered in a sort of self-referentiality, the references, the guides, the resources of meaning find themselves with performative capacities. We can observe nano-organisms, send a probe to the sun, graft faces, etc., and that gives us our references. At an individual scale, this may be the use of Skype or the possibility of chemotherapy. Will this produce a general replacement of the symbolic? Of course, we are prepared to respond 'no.' But maybe we cannot know anything.

For millennia, humanity has lived by references to traditions, lineages, and totems—and that has already so profoundly shifted during the past ten centuries that today, without a doubt, for the majority of humans the reference of the technic accompanies, at least, or doubles, the symbolic reference. The smartphone and the wizard can very well coexist, like traveling by plane and believing in aliens or fearing the devil. By definition, one cannot foresee the future, and especially not in this register of the deep tendencies of the collective spirit. Think of Capitalism: who decided to start it? Who decided to invent the bank, the fiduciary money, the investment, the insurance? No one—it is society as a whole that pivoted slowly, that entered into a spiritual, symbolic mutation by transforming its practices, its codes, its interests...

*- There are some contemporary thinkers, such as Byung Chul Han or even Zizek, that theorize our society as one that has become 'pornographic,' and has lost a valuable distance or space in-between that—as I interpret it—might be relevant to feel or to sensitively understand something about that presentation of the réel that you mentioned before. How do you feel about this?*

'Pornography,' of which you speak, is the amplification of that which the Situationists have called 'spectacle,' which was itself the amplification of that which Marx has called 'commodity fetishism,' which was in turn the amplification of the condemnation of money by Greek philosophers and Jewish prophets. Yet if there is condemnation, it is because there is something to condemn. The Mediterranean world was very fertile in the development of commerce and all sorts of technics (for example maritime, but also financial) that prefigure capitalism. China has not been left out, especially in the period that follows, that of our 'Middle Ages,' but it had not yet embarked upon a mutation of its culture: it engaged with a prosperity that remained in reference to an altered symbolism, even transformed, but never to the point of becoming that what I have called the self-reference of the 276

Occidental's Capitalism development (of course, I am not speaking about modern China).

Pornography is the demonstration of that which shouldn't have been shown or even that which cannot be. Indeed, our world shows its appetite for performance, enrichment, unlimited production, and lack of recognizable finalities (Why there is more speed, more energy, more computation? ...). And it shows, at the same time, the physical and moral miseries to which ever more numerous populations are reduced. Yet all of that pornography does not create a revolutionary jolt. Some say that "the insurrection comes" (it is a phrase from the group calling itself in France Comité invisible (invisible committee)), but it is not easy to discern. Or instead it produces a reaction of rejection and withdrawal, which takes on nationalist and communitarian forms, and which would like to reanimate old symbols—but these pushes themselves continue to want to benefit from technical gains and therefore do nothing to move the levers of domination.

Demonstration. Indeed, self-reference is also a self-exhibition. But in order to understand that this display is obscene, it must be known how to think that which would be a new modesty, a new charm, and a new secret. A new intimacy. This is not invented. It can only come from the most profound movement of the real—of this real that this is men.

- *My third and last question is in direct relation to the central matter of our issue: how would you imagine an appropriate method of mapping and representing our planet today?*

The map and the representation are instruments intended for the mastering of movement, transportation, and a knowledge of themselves orientated towards intellectual mastery. However, we begin to figure out that all of these masteries encounter an unmasterable real. We can map the galaxies and the black holes just as well as the deforestations and the liquefactions of icebergs (which already shows that the map should be endlessly evolving), but it is rather to understand that the universe is not an object in front of us that we could master one day because it only exists in the movement of our knowledge production, and it obliges us, therefore, to think that all mastery operates against the backdrop of an unmasterable: of the enigma of existence. The enigma, or rather the dazzling clarity of this that is there without another reason for being, which is precisely an enigma itself.

This does not represent itself: it presents itself. A 'planet' means in Greek a wandering star. We are wandering, we have neither goals nor guides. No doubt, moreover, this truth was already there in all of the great religions and wisdoms (hidden, certainly, but not completely...); we have to invent a new symbolism, of new words, of new forms, for this unmasterable.

If, however, you really desire a map, I would propose to make an animated drawing in which the lands and the seas would change size, form, and color depending on the considerations of their territories, populations, and economic, strategic, and imaginary roles. It would reveal myriads of miniscule insects that would move in all directions and a shimmering bush of luminous or graphic signals. Finally, rains of question marks, exclamation marks, or ellipses, would arise stochastically in bursts. It would no longer be a sphere, but a flat two-sided expanse that would turn on itself like a Moebius ribbon.

August 23rd
Thank you again for your generosity. We will start translating and editing the exchange and will send you a draft for you to revise and approve. If something arises in this process, I will for sure accept your offer for a post-last question! Thanks again, Florencia

# PARADISE SOMEWHERE: A CONVERSATION WITH GRACIELA SILVESTRI
## Isabella Moretti, Magdalena Tagliabue

America has an immanent mixed culture. Argentinian architecture historian and cultural theorist Graciela Silvestri interrogates its fluvial geography to find clues in understanding its exceptional compound and imagination. The lines rivers draw are never permanent nor dividing but transient; they join, mix, and change. In this interview, she talks about her new book on the lowlands of the Paraná River and the Guaraní culture, her long-lasting research on landscape theory, and a constant concern on how political ecology cuts across concepts.

IM      The Mies Crown Hall Americas Prize (MCHAP) gives us cause to think about America in its territorial continuity and what that produces in architectural discourse. How can we think about a continental territory? You have dealt with the figure of water as a transversal and elemental subject that articulates territories from a geographic and discursive perspective. Water runs through, and delineates, regions. Does this give us an idea about how to approach the territory of the Americas? How has the region come up in your research?

GS      This is a problem that I ran into with my last book *Las tierras desubicadas*,[1] a book about the Latin American lowlands and the Paraná River. To begin with, we must look at the relationship between everything in what was called *Hispanoamérica* in the 19th century and what later came to be Latin America, which comes from a concept that is more French than Spanish because it includes the Caribbean. The territory is intersected by very different cultures.

For a long time, appreciation of South America and part of Central America was centered on the Andean zone. Undoubtedly, the cultures there were those that most fascinated the Castilian conquerors because of their heightened development. The lowlands remained, then, a place of wildness: they were considered people without culture, nomads, who lacked the status of the Incas, the Aztec, or the Mayans. According to some researchers, there existed a kind of Andean-centrism.[2]

The areas extending to the Atlantic Sea are, on the other hand, areas of great mixture. There, the class and caste systems are rather determined by money than by skin color. There are large cultural differences across the continent. That is why I focused on areas crossed by sea-bearing rivers. It is the geography itself that leads to this mixture, to this impossibility of defining its roots. I have to say that this, to me, is fantastic. I prefer mixture.

Anthropologists hold a key place in the study of these lowlands, especially from the 1970s onward. Anthropologists, and Claude Lévi-Strauss in particular, were looking for 'pure savages;' some isolated peoples still resist contact in the Peruvian-Brazilian Amazon. This anthropological gaze did not include indigenous people who lived in cities, because they were considered corrupted. This delusional idea aside, Lévi-Strauss and his disciples did a lot to rescue particular cultural subjects: Hélène Clastres, who wrote *La tierra sin mal (Land without Evil)* [1975] is one example. The Guaraní culture is represented as an anarchist and self-organized model of life, with no state power. Looking at that representation, a really interesting ecological and political question emerges, even if it makes reference to small groups of humans. This type of research helped to record this culture, which is, in actuality, several cultures. The name 'Guaraní' was created by the Jesuits, who transcribed the language. There is not much purity there, either.

MT      In your multiple efforts to define the identity of the territory and particularly in your book *El lugar común, (The Common Place)* [2011], the 'figure' appears as a form through which past, present and future are articulated, even as the representations help to define the landscape. Just now, you incorporated all the other elements needed to describe the concept of culture, and thus the representation associated with culture appears in the element of the figure. Besides representations, what other concepts or general elements are necessary to define landscape as a concept?

GS      I was interested in connecting words, which in the West are enormously abstract (especially the written word), with the visual image. The figure interests me because it is used both from a rhetorical and plastic point of view. In architecture, both are linked. We can take, for example, classical architecture—or what is understood as classical architecture. Leon Battista Alberti first wrote everything in Latin without using drawings, only later, illustrations were added to follow the descriptions; Vitruvius was also given to us originally with no images, that is, it was rewritten, reinvented. This relationship seems fantastic to me.

When the Jesuits arrive in this lower zone, they find a non-iconic people, a people without images. They did not have drawings, although they did have a way of making pottery that already bore some traces of decoration. But they learned very quickly. This is absolutely remarkable because they became superb artists and were to be highly sought after.

This brings me to the other question: Were they talking about landscape? No. Environment? No. The ideas of nature and culture were not even separate. We think that nature is everything objective and biological, while culture is a matter of arts and interpretation. This was much discussed following Philippe

Descola and Bruno Latour. In these places, however, there was no differentiation: the jaguar they hunted was considered a person like them, a person from a different family, but everything was within the natural world. The aesthetic distance created to enjoy the landscape did not exist.

Now, something very interesting happens for us architects. The Jesuits erected the famous Jesuit missions or Jesuit cities there, which had an overwhelming success in Europe. They were made up of the church, the plaza, the side pavilions, and the jungle. The Guaraní way of life was to open a clearing by slashing and burning. Those same ashes regenerated the jungle where they hunted. The pavilions caused a sensation: we have nature, there are no streets, there are pavilions, and there is a green heart in the middle of the square. Doesn't that sound like the basis of the modern movement? The neoclassicals knew this. For example, many kinds of hospitals mimic the ranch form of the Guaraní dwelling, in which several families lived together; it is just done from a hygienic perspective. The Jesuits allowed the Guaraní to maintain their own rituals. The Jesuits had already travelled through the Middle East, through China, and they knew that they had to adapt to local customs to evangelize, differentiating themselves from orders that took an inquisitive and harsh approach. Bartomeu Meliá, a Jesuit friend of mine, came to America as a young man and spent a year with isolated tribes. He thought of himself as the son of the Guaraní god Tupá. He brought together both religions, this can be traced back a long time. In these lowlands, mixing began a long time ago; the creation of some modern landscapes is rooted here. Especially in the flowering of the Jesuit city between the seventeenth and eighteenth centuries, at which time the Jesuits were thrown out.

IM    You have been one of the major theorists to work on visual culture in Argentina, restoring the image as formative for meaning and power, in parallel to the word. In that sense, you have built a very meaningful intellectual career around the theorization of 'landscape.' Landscape has allowed you to mix and match disciplines, combine sensitivities with hard data, contemplate connections and contaminations, and problematize nature-cultures. Twenty years after the publication of *El paisaje como cifra de armonía (Landscape as a Measure of Harmony)* [2001], do you still believe that landscape can be as provocative category? How do you all [together with Fernando Aliata, co-author of the book] think about it now?

GS    It's interesting; from a scientific perspective, human beings do not see 'reality,' nor do we see something totally invented; we see something skewed, blurred, because our minds are built to see certain things. We see certain colors and we don't see others, for example. There is a really great book called *The Order of Time* by Carlo Rovelli. Rovelli is a quantum physicist; he argues that we see only one sector of reality. While explaining quantum physics he offers complete verses of Horacio. The relationship between poetry, subjective interpretation, sensitivity, learning and the way we relate to things are quite well summed up in the word, 'landscape.'

Originally, landscape is country: *paese, paesetto.* A small country. One's little homeland. The word was reinterpreted later, in the 18th and 19th centuries, converting it to its strong impactful aesthetic version, which intersected with the social sciences and the hard sciences. Then it goes back into crisis, and one starts talking about 'environment' as if it were an objective question. It is also intersected by our own limitations in seeing, by our predispositions, by certain sensibilities that are taken up in the 1970s and connect social questions with ecological ones. Obviously, there are objective reasons, because for example, if global warming continues, the human race comes to an end. Yet, we still cannot not ignore the particular bias with which we see things, which we fail to interpret.

At the same time, architects trained in the *ecole de beaux arts*, like us, have what I would call a 'dry imagination.' The French landscape is a completely disciplined landscape where what is built is superior to what is planted. On the other hand, there is the Anglo-Saxon 'naturalist' movement, which gained traction in the United States. [It is a] view of landscape that is still naive about how it looks at that which they call 'nature.' The torch passed from England at the beginning of the 19th century to the United States in the second half of the 19th century with [the founding] of Yellowstone and other parks. The indigenous people who resided there were either evacuated or considered 'pure nature,' that is, they decided to ignore their cultural development and the territorial transformations that they had introduced.

In Argentina, on the other hand, the planted or 'green,' as we plainly call it in Spanish, was always disliked. I'll tell you an anecdote—a student of mine's doctoral thesis proposed the modification of a precarious settlement by incorporating hydroponic crops. The plan was not only to engage in rooftop cultivation and a kind of self-sustenance but also to make economic and sustainable development possible. The architects totally disliked it. It seemed to them a kind of false consolation to put something green inside an 'emergency' or precarious neighborhood, although, in reality, these were not emergency neighborhoods at all because they ended up being permanent living spaces. Now it is more accepted, but at that time everything green seemed feminine, and local architecture, in Argentina, is super masculine. It is in the vein of Le Corbusier, I would say, the brutalist lineage. This comes from a long French and Mediterranean tradition, where what is planted is inferior to what is built. Of course, we always build, even when planting, but this idea of growth, of things that came and went, fights the architectural feeling of building for once and for all. Which is not true either, because things collapse. But a thing built is different from a thing planted. That intersection interested me ...

For those of us who are going to die, who are human, there is a turning point between what is permanent—which remains for future generations—and something that fulfils a life cycle, short and finite. There must be things that maintain a temporality that endures longer than vegetation. To think about that which is useful and is permanent I always refer to Hannah Arendt, although there are many criticisms, of course. Richard Sennet, who studied with her, made very wise critiques.[3] She was very strong on the differentiation between that which is necessary, useful, and political discourse.

IM          There is also this strong feminist critique of Hannah Arendt, for the rigid division of public and private.

GS          Exactly. The domestic kingdom of the woman. We might recall the time at which Arendt was arriving on the scene. If you read carefully, she was not complacent when it came to the world of the necessary. Finally, in many ways, Arendt's own story is a feminist story. She was able to study and reach a notable status in the United States, where her theories really spread. Her book *The Human Condition* [1958] is first published in English.

One of the critiques made of Mies van der Rohe's houses is that it was all glass, transparent; intimacy was on display. I don't want that; I think that the intimate should be in some way isolated from the public. It is a subject to speak more freely on and not under the idea that "this is the feminine domain, that of intimacy." Arendt gave a great deal of importance to the domain of necessity. That was the foundation, right? If needs are not met there is no political domain; that is what she writes very clearly. But she thought that divisions should be maintained. It is an interesting subject to discuss, even more so in the world of architecture.

IM          At one point you argued that there are no studies on the role of travel in shaping the local architectural field. You began research on the subject and have theorized about travel and travel literature, taking example from Ulrico Schmidl's travels during the 16th century up through Mario Corea's in the 20th century.[4] This book and prize, *MCHAP 2*, specifically seeks to thematize the journey, from the South to the North, of a jury as it visits the finalist projects. Thus, we are interested in knowing how you have understood 'travel' as an epistemic and experiential category, because you have also organized and curated expeditions.

GS          Among other things, you know, I traveled the Paraná River. It arose from an old project that we had contemplated in the 1990s. It could not be done then because, among other reasons, tourist boats on the Paraná no longer existed. Years later, in 2008, Martín Prieto called me, who at that time was the director of the Spanish Cultural Center in Rosario (Argentina). He is the son of Adolfo Prieto, who wrote one of the best books on travel and landscape: on English travelers and Argentine literature. It is wonderful. It opened my eyes; it suggests that the Argentine landscape was written by the English. Isn't that great? He shows how Sarmiento, Alberdi, and all the Argentine founding fathers, for whom the landscape was very important, were building off the descriptions of these travelers who had a sensibility for nature that they wouldn't otherwise have.

Martín, Adolfo's son, then, proposes this trip to me. We found a boat that did the trip through the Pantanal, which is where the Paraná ends, and we modestly arrived as far as Asunción, Paraguay. From there, a group of us went to the Jesuit ruins on

Antes de la escisión [Before the Split], Daniel García. Courtesy of the artist.

the Paraguayan side. It was a wonderful trip. There I also went from the 'green' to 'water.' What happens in those areas, where the water is not pure? They are swamplands. Travelling the Paraná, one of the problems that came up is that water hyacinths got hooked on the propellers. New islands are constantly being formed and geographers cannot move fast enough. Two of my fellow travelers sat down with the captain and drew the new islets one by one. There was everything: wild boars, hyacinths, birds, monkeys ...

The Ecological Reserve of Buenos Aires is made up of that which makes its way down from the lands that descend from the Andes. When the Bermejo River enters the Paraná it suddenly becomes tinted; it is a wonder. One sees how these mixed lands also reflect a mixed geography, a trip ... In travel there is an inescapable mixture. Points of view intersect; the impact that has is the most interesting part. The anthropologist Irina Podgorny joined us on the trip, as well as astronomers—obviously you must look at the sky while navigating and guiding by the stars—, and cartoonists. The trip became a book based on the experiences of each participant.[5] There were also architects, poets, writers. We wanted a language that reached all audiences, so it was very important to us to think about who would participate. We wanted the book to speak to a culture that was not strictly academic. My own training as an architect has always made me reject the compartmentalization of knowledge, because the architect is always with the user (more abstract), or with the client (more concrete) with whom there is an exchange of ideas. On top of that process, there are specific needs, such as the availability of resources. It is teamwork in action that does not put the author at one level and the rest below. If a member of the group fails, the entire body of work fails ... We know that. This architectural idea could, in a way, recreate what Alexander von Humboldt did in the 19th century. He talked about everything: architecture, oenology, linguistics; he was one of these polymaths who were capable of giving the landscapes they described a kind of spirit. They wrote spectacularly, too. Humboldt, one cannot forget, did not only write, but he himself chose the illustrators that would, ever so carefully, reproduce his own drawings.

We were also excited to consider the travels of Ulysses, the novels of the Italian writer Roberto Calasso or *The Danube* by Claudio Magris. The theme of Ulysses' journey is the foundation of European culture. Above all, of Mediterranean culture.

MT The idea of "geographical imagination" also emerges in parallel to the trip, connecting travelers' stories with journalism, literary descriptions, and details from the natural and geological sciences. In the area of urbanism—and planning in general—we see an overlap of the idea of an architect and that of an engineer: how do you see the role of the architects being shaped around those dual possibilities today?

GS Geography is the measurement of the earth. It has a clear relationship to the beginnings of architecture. As early as the twentieth century, very notably in Argentina at least, there was an overlap between the figure of the planner and the architect. At the same time, in Germany, for example, a planner's education is more political than architectural-geographical. At the Universidad de Buenos Aires (University of Buenos Aires), the Institute of Geography is within the Faculty of Philosophy and Letters and what my geographer friends told me—Carlos Reboratti accompanied us on the trip—is that they had no cartographic training, because that was considered the domain of the military. For a long time, only the military had access to the maps and could not be in the public domain. Argentine cartography was formulated around

the idea of absolute and precise borders and, we should note, they were absolutely arbitrary. How can a border be set in a river when rivers change course and are constantly transformed? The river, on the contrary, joins, mixes; it does not divide. So where does the Río de la Plata end? What's the difference between the Río de la Plata and the Paraná? The Río de la Plata is the estuary of the Paraná. We have discussed this arbitrariness with many young geographers, like Carla Lois or Silvina Quintero, who worked on symbolic maps.

My first work on this topic was on the landscape of the Riachuelo River. I began to study it from an engineering point of view to understand how it was transformed into an urban landscape. Quinquela Martín and other painters were important parts of this transformation. Despite the river having a black color, they depicted reflections of colorful sheet metal and industrial constructions. The neighborhood of La Boca maintained that identity over the years. I was interested in the landscape as an industrial landscape.

When I presented my doctoral thesis on the topic, a geographer told me: "No, this is not landscape. Landscape is a part of nature." I replied that there were other types of landscapes and I brought out Georg Simmel, who really opened my eyes with his "philosophy of landscape." I continue to work with geographers and come up with interesting things, without us needing to depart from our specificities. I believe that in many social disciplines—in sociology without a doubt—aesthetic appreciation is persistently underestimated, as if it were secondary in our inhabiting the world. It is not at all. The first way of entering a relationship with nature is aesthetic, in the sense that it is sensory. One does not love nature because one knows its composition or its dangers; a child relates to nature when he begins to look at a flower or a butterfly. That knowledge is sensory and human. Jakob Johann von Uexküll, one of the great naturalists of the 20th century became known for contemplating how a blind tick knows that it must fall on top of a cow to suck its blood. They are other senses. Hence, Rovelli says that we look at only one part of the world. That is why I decided that the aesthetic question was going to be a fundamental point.

Going back to question of how to think about America, it is interesting to think that it's been shown that the journey from Bering to Patagonia was impassable by foot 15 thousand years ago. But we have records of humans being present in Patagonia that are twelve thousand years old, suggesting that the trip may have been made by boat. Another thing, potatoes and sweet potatoes emigrated before the Europeans arrived in Polynesia—how did they get there? By boat. Obviously, there is a journey. The notion of the trip and the boat are closely related. And I will make a third connection: Alberti was planning on writing a book on shipbuilding. The construction of boats and the construction of houses in the Riachuelo are directly connected: before doing it in sheet metal they did it with wood. The shipbuilders and caulkers were mainly Genoese or from other parts of Liguria. The ships that arrived at the port of La Boca brought sheet metal as ballast that they later exchanged for cows. There is a whole list of constructions to think about the future: why not live on a boat?

MT        The study of boat construction as a discipline is known as naval architecture.

GS        The moderns obsessed over boats; the level of comfort that can be reached in such small spaces. On a transatlantic voyage they would fit an incredible number of people aboard, which also moves … When Amerigo Vespucci arrived on the continent, he named Venezuela for "little Venice." The banks of the Orinoco were all occupied with floating stilt houses.

Fronteras [Borders], Daniel García. Courtesy of the artist.

That kind of palafittic construction would be taken up by the moderns together with rope construction. Traction bridges were not being made yet in Europe at that time. There is this beautiful drawing by Humboldt, who was a mining engineer and thus understood their behavior, that makes a proposal for a possible bridge. What does a bridge propose? The bridge in the landscape is another marvel. I am talking about the most elementary Heidegger: a bridge joining two shores gives the human that which otherwise would not make sense.

MT        Do you think it possible to approach a definition of a concept of identity via the notion of the movement associated with travel? If we take the strictly architectural point of view (the analysis of grounded projects) and the trip as a way of approaching a territory, two apparently contradictory forms are su-

perimposed on the notion of place: what is rooted and that which moves.

GS        An English traveler in the 19th century was exposed to real danger. He went into places still completely unknown, with little news, with nothing. They consulted chronicles to figure out where they could be of service. Darwin's chronicles are fantastic because they detail where in the city to purchase that which was needed to travel to unknown places. But then, later, the tourist trip is made possible, available not only to specialists, not only to people with means and resources, not only to governments, but to anyone. In some ways, when I travel, I am also bringing my own experience. Displacement was always fundamental for me, which contrasts with an idea of landscape as 'homeland.' The homeland does not move. A *paese* was a closed place between mountains, where one practically did not move in or out of, unless a traveler, a merchant came to sell. There is a nostalgia built into the word *paese, paisaje*, of going back to something in the past that in turn is impossible to recover or modify.

MT        The word nostalgia refers to returning to a place with pain, longing for the place from whence one came.

GS        Yesterday I read something on the BBC that was originally said among sailors, 'nostalgia for the land that is not there.' One would have to travel in that time, no? The ship is always something that triggers the imagination.

IM        Once you mentioned that during that expedition on the Paraná, you read a translation of Foucault's talks on heterotopias.[6] Instead of centering on the architectures of power and knowledge you underlined the 'happy heterotopias.' How is that? I imagine that the trip itself or the act of movement affected your way of reading that text.

GS        I graduated in 1979. By then a group of people who were in contact with different things and theories from abroad were introducing Foucault. But it was the Foucault of *Discipline and Punish* [1975] and *History of Sexuality* [1976]. In architecture, the panopticon became an elemental form … The point is that Foucault's heterotopias and other spaces were only published much later in Spanish by the Nueva Vision publishing house [2009], specifically as a part of the Hugo Vezzetti collection, someone who had introduced Foucault from the perspective of psychoanalysis. It was a radio conversation with architects. We realized that the spatial turn struck by Foucault was actually building on Bachelard; Bachelard's book *Water and Dreams* [1947] is wonderful. Foucault takes the issue of the significant importance of space as an active actor in human life that is not derived from history. This reading of heterotopias concludes with the idea that peoples with imagination are those with ships. It is wonderful because it is something that architects care a lot about … There is an imagination of going forward, out, towards the future, but also out of our own limits, our own borders. I loved that twist of Foucault, which we totally had. Many architects in the

1980s, in the post-dictatorship period, came together and taught us classes in philosophy. Carlos Altamirano, Beatriz Sarlo, Hugo Vezzetti, Oscar Terán, Jorge Dotti served as our guides for philosophical and literary questions. It was difficult, but architects are like that; our role is to coordinate different disciplines to shape a future architecture.

IM   Let's stay in the future but go back to your recent publication about the lowlands and the Guaraní paradise, the land with no evil. In a context of environmental catastrophe, do you think that paradisiacal imaginaries are necessary? As landscape has become an ambiguous concept that at once veils and exhibits the ecological crisis, do we need to imagine non-modern understandings of nature-cultures?

GS   In a land with no evil there is something very beautiful; Bartomeu Meliá explained to me that the Guaraní paradise is not transcendent; it is not outside the earth like the Christian paradise—it is a horizontal paradise. On the one hand, this has to do with travel, in some ways, with the search for a paradise somewhere. On the other hand, it brings about the discovery of a series of issues through an ecological impetus. Around the Guaraní villages there were gardens with native plants. Many of them are still unexploited. Stevia, a replacement for sugar, had a sad history. The Guaraní knew about stevia. But instead of being exploited by the Guaraní communities or by the Paraguayan communities, the Japanese came and brought it to the whole world. As with Stevia, there are hundreds of herbs, some medicinal, others nutritious, and other plants with properties still unknown to us.

   There are very serious ecological problems: livestock, agriculture, much larger than the emissions from transportation and the impact of constructed architecture. We are facing a global problem. Either we solve it together or it is not solved. It is not possible to say to South Americans alone, "take care of the Amazon" when in reality the energy crisis has been caused, above all, by the countries of the Global North. We are at an opportune moment because the pandemic either ends globally or it does not end. I would fight for a global dimension. In this sense, the statement of the Venice Architecture Biennale curated by Hashim Sarkis is very nice: "How will we live together?" The world of the necessary, going back to Arendt, is what we must take care of. The world of permanence also seems important to me because Arendt did not speak of immortality or transcendence but of permanence. Think of future generations. Talk to one other. Create, in some way, an environment for the time we have, make it the best possible environment for all. In this framework, architects must deal with the economy as a central issue. There is a very interesting speech by Enrico Berlinguer, a restorer of Eurocommunism, about *austerità*. It was later taken up in a book by Giuseppe Campos Venuti, *Urbanistica e austerità*, where, with the center of Bologna as an example, he suggests caring over demolishing. Now of course you must build, as well. However, what Berlinguer wonders in 1977 is how to do it in a world with such offensive wastefulness. We must reach out to the world. We must tighten our belts regarding things that are absolutely superfluous. I believe that once the question is asked, science can answer. You must ask the right questions.

MT   If we go back to the Guaraní case, we can think of it as a reason to study a territory and its culture, through historical research. However, at the same time, you were just recovering elements from the Guaraní soil that help us imagine possible solutions for specific medicine problems, for example. Having said all this, it is possible to argue for the relevance of historical research as an opportunity to think about the future.

1      Graciela Silvestri, *Las tierras desubicadas: Paisajes y culturas en la Sudamérica fluvial* (Paraná: Universidad Nacional de Entre Ríos, UNER, 2021).

2      Frank Salomon, Stuart B.Schwartz (ed.),"Introduction" in *The Cambridge History of the Native Peoples of the Americas* (Cambridge University Press, 2016), pp. 1-18.

3      See "Man as His Own Maker" in Richard Sennett, *The Craftsman* (2018).

4      Graciela Silvestri, "Alma de arquitecto: Conformación histórica del 'habitus' de los proyectistas del habitat" in *Registros* (11), 2014, pp. 72-97.

5      Graciela Silvestri (ed.). *Paraná Ra'anga: Itineracia 2011-2013* (Buenos Aires: Fundación OSDE). Available online at: https://issuu.com/artefundosde/docs/paran__rang_

6      Graciela Silvestri in conversation with FAN, available online: https://files.cargocollective.com/c689949/FAN_Parai-so-Guarani-.pdf

# ARCHITECTURE, CAPITALISM, URBANIZATION: AN INTERVIEW WITH DAVID HARVEY

### Mariano Gomez-Luque, Daniel Ibañez

David Harvey's writings touch a vital nerve for architects. They represent a robust effort to understand the dynamics of capitalism in spatial terms. His work is both an invitation to critically exercise our imaginative powers, and simultaneously a call to action—to find new socio-organizational forms that could challenge those already set, defined, and crystallized by the capitalist machine. During his last visit to the Harvard Graduate School of Design, we met with him to talk about the manifold relationships between architecture, capitalism, and urbanization.

MGL/DI    To begin with, we are particularly interested in discussing your relationship with the design disciplines. Somewhere in your recent work, you write: "As an urbanist, the whole question of architecture and the role of planning was never far from the surface of my thinking." Can you tell us more about your interest in, and involvements with, architecture?

DH    I have always been interested in the question of the production of space and have been writing about it for many years. The discourse has a long tradition; some people think that it was invented by Henri Lefebvre —whose 1974 book, The Production of Space, grounded much dialogue— but it was not. In fact, many urban planners from the 1960s, like John Friedmann, were linking planning with the production of space in parallel to Lefebvre's work.

'Spatiality' has a very expansive meaning for me: there are relative spaces, relational spaces, absolute spaces. These nuances are crucial to understand if we are to have a stronger connection with the ways in which things get shaped on the ground — this wall here … those steps there … a bridge over there … All of these relative spaces of the city are constantly being produced and reproduced. Then there are symbolic spaces, which have both a relationality and a meaning that are far greater than their mere physical manifestations. Many of these symbolic spaces have the power of a certain centrality, which we see exercised politically in cases like Tahrir Square in Cairo in 2011, or in the Occupy movement in New York. I'm interested in these manifestations, and of course, in the people who are making the walls—the engineers, the architects.

During the 1960s, many architects considered themselves urbanists. Even people like Rem Koolhaas (who I'm not a great fan of) were participating in exciting debates at the Architectural Association (AA) in London, where there was a social sense about cities. I gave some lectures at the AA back then and talked with architects —among them Richard Rogers— who were interested in the urban. Later, regrettably, people became exclusively concerned with building activity, and consequently forgot about the urban context.

Architecture is a world that I have always been close to, because architects have a view of space, although theirs is rather different from mine. Sometimes we have conversations in which we think we are talking about the same things, but we are not. It is a challenge, in the sense that there is something to be learned from this discordance.

MGL/DI    In your book The Enigma of Capital, you refer to your participation as a jury member, together with architects and engineers, in an international competition for a new city in South Korea. Could this episode be understood as your way of actively becoming an "urbanist"? Could you tell us more about that experience?

DH    We were in charge of making a judgment about the projects submitted to the competition. It was a very peculiar experience. I thought it was an opportunity to do something experimental. I had read a lot of what fellow jury member Arata Isozaki had written and was very attracted to his ideas about urban form. I was openly against creating determinations—spaces limited by fixed form and program; on the contrary, I wanted to see how different aspects and variables of projects interacted at the level of the social, and how they addressed nature, technology, production, employment, and political subjectivities.

In the end, the jury did not select a winner; instead, we selected a group of projects whose authors were supposed to continue developing and consolidating their proposals. It was an interesting learning experience, getting the engineers' perspective. I was a little shocked by what the architects on the jury had to say; they were mainly interested in a discussion about the symbolic qualities of circles and squares.

MGL/DI    Did you find a common ground for communicating with architects in the context of the jury deliberations?

DH    Everybody seemed interested in what I was trying to say, in the elements of my criteria for evaluating the projects. But of course, some people were horrified when I said that many of my ideas came from Marx. They said: "What!?" That's often a conversation stopper. People usually get caught in the ideological trap (whatever we may mean by that) when talking about Marx, often ignoring the power of his theoretical framework of understanding.

MGL/DI    Historically, interventions by architects and urban designers and planners have been circumscribed to what we traditionally call urban zones. However, as you —and others— have pointed out, the "urban" is undergoing a radical change of scale; it now operates at the level of the whole surface of the planet, both beneath and above it. What we call 'city', you have provocatively insisted, is the outcome of the process we call 'urbanization.' Your work has challenged divides like society/nature or urban/rural, opening up new spaces for design intervention beyond cities. Do you see emergent spaces where designers can effectively contribute to more socially-just and ecologically-sane environments? What do you think are the key problems to address—or illuminate—through new research?

DH        I am increasingly interested in the politics of daily life, to the degree that the qualities of daily life are partly embedded in the nature of the environments we construct. This entails a constructivist kind of approach. Without being environmental determinists, we could say that as we create environments, environments create us. This is part of what I call dialectical utopianism, a condition that I hope architecture practice can situate itself within.

MGL/DI        In Spaces of Hope, where you develop this concept ('dialectical utopianism'), you talk about the figure of the architect, in both a metaphorical and concrete sense, as an agent who can create and discover "spaces for new possibilities." One of the most contradictory dimensions we confront as architects is the fact that, regardless of our role as "creators of space"—perhaps a naïve claim after all—space is actually the outcome of forces beyond our control; that is, economic, political, institutional forces. How do you see this contradiction?

DH        Well, I don't know, that's for you to worry about! [LAUGHS] It is a real dilemma. I can, in fact, talk about the production of space, only to see later how what I say gets co-opted by capital. The same applies to architects, at least to those who have a social consciousness and try to work in a progressive way. They may see that their work gets co-opted by capital, and therefore may feel that in some way they contribute to the reproduction of this logic without wanting or intending to. And although architects are not alone in this, they do have an advantage, because they know what the implications are when a developer says you have to do this, which clearly exposes who is ultimately in charge of the process of the production of space. At that point, the creative architect, or what in Spaces of Hope I call the "insurgent architect," has to think about how to subvert this power relation: How can you use the knowledge and the technology at your disposal to achieve goals that are different from, or alternative to, capital's goals?

It is important to understand that given the power of capital in shaping the construction of the built environment, strategies of subversion are needed. In that sense, architects can be more confrontational; they can sit across the table from developers and oppose them.

MGL/DI        In the last 40 years, we have seen how, with the rise of neoliberalism and what you call 'flexible accumulation,' architecture has become a form of spectacle in itself—in other words, we have witnessed how buildings have turned into a luxury commodity proliferating within the sea of images, symbols and signs of contemporary urban space…

DH        It all depends on which part of the world you are in. Most of the so-called starchitects went to work to China because they thought that there were no constraints there. But Alejandro Aravena, for instance, is approaching the question of housing in a form that is more progressive than I have seen in other places. I think his idea of building a basic structure that you can later update, or complete more or less as you want, is a good idea. It is not radical, but at least it is open, and allows the participation of the inhabitants, mixing social governmental action with a more traditional self-building approach. That concept is not new, it came out of radical anarchist thinking, and is now being appropriated by the World Bank in what I think is another example of a good idea that gets co-opted by capital.

MGL/DI        Do you think that design disciplines in conjunction with social organizations and local communities can effectively articulate strategies of opposition and resistance to the relentless pace of capitalist urbanization?

DH        Yes. In Uruguay, for example, people have set up cooperatives to build their own houses, investing either through labor or with actual money, and they have produced very high-quality housing. They are now reactivating some abandoned buildings in downtown Montevideo, refurbishing them and turning them into housing. These are modest but very good examples of alternative ways in which communities can participate in the building process. You can see a clear connection between the logics of production and the politics of realization.

MGL/DI        Architecture seems to be an organic component of the capitalist tendency toward endless growth. What we mean by this is that it is still largely driven by building activity, by a process of construction understood in a positivistic way — building is always building anew, building more. But recently there have been attempts to rethink the agency of architecture in terms of "unbuilding" protocols—mechanisms of building subtraction and preservation. Do you see this idea as a potentially viable way of counteracting capitalist urbanization?

DH        Everything should be on the table. Today more than ever we need to think both politically and socially about the city; these dimensions have been buried under the process of urbanization, which is basically anti-city. This process works against public

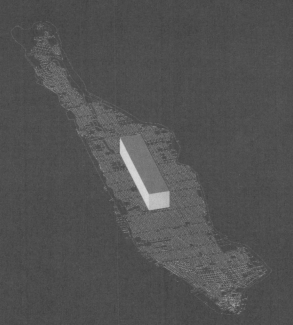

US — Cement: with the 4,500 million tons of cement produced in the United States between 1900 and 1999, a solid concrete block covering the area of Central Park and reaching 790 meters of height, could be built.

China — Cement: with the 6,500 million tons of cement produced in China between 2011 and 2013, a solid concrete block covering the area of Central Park and reaching 1140 meters of height, could be built.

US — Reinforced Concrete: with the 37,500 million tons of reinforced concrete produced in the United States between 1900 and 1999, a solid concrete block covering the area of Central Park and reaching 6600 meters of height, could be built.

China — Reinforced Concrete: with the 54,000 million tons of reinforced concrete between 2011 and 2013, a solid concrete block covering the area of Central Park and reaching 9500 meters of height, could be built.

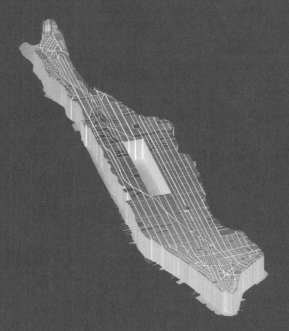

'Chinese' Manhattan: this drawing represents the volume of reinforced concrete consumed in China between 2011-2013, expressed in a hypothetical Manhattan built to reach uniformly a height of 1050 meters.

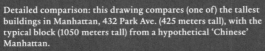

Detailed comparison: this drawing compares (one of) the tallest buildings in Manhattan, 432 Park Ave. (425 meters tall), with the typical block (1050 meters tall) from a hypothetical 'Chinese' Manhattan.

space and urban life in an effort to turn the city into a tool of capital. In this regard, there are various strategies to reconstruct the city on the ruins of capitalist urbanization. One is to create spaces that can assemble political expression, and which can liberate the public from typical strategies of enclosure.

Is it still possible to introduce various commons into the city, and if so, how? The objective here is to create a sense of the city as a totality that has both a social and a political meaning that people can act upon, feel comfortable with, and have dialogue and even conflict within. We should be open to new possibilities, as opposed to continuing simply filling in spaces, following an endless impulse for growth.

MGL/DI    Increasingly, design schools are in need of new frameworks of understanding in order to unpack the complexity of urbanization processes as a precondition to design intervention. At the GSD's Urban Theory Lab, under the guidance of Neil Brenner, we have been developing his (and Christian Schmid's) conceptual framework about "planetary urbanization." The theoretical discourse on planetary urbanization, building upon Lefebvre's hypothesis about the total urbanization of society —and, to a large extent, upon your own body of work— challenges the idea of the city as a distinct, bounded spatial entity. What do you think about the prospect of merging critical urban theory and design in order to address socio-spatial questions? Are multidisciplinary projects of this kind relevant to theorize contemporary urbanization?

DH    Yes, they are. To me, it is crucial to come to terms with the dynamics of urban processes as they exist right now. We cannot continue to think about the city as an isolated terrain, nor from mutually exclusive perspectives. It has been stunning to see social movements, like Gezi Park in Turkey or the Brazilian Spring, become system-wide, rapidly spreading to other cities—cases like the antiwar protests on February 15, 2003, when millions of people were in the streets in a few hundred global cities, opposing the Iraq War. I remember being in Athens the night of the occupation of Syntagma Square. One of their slogans was borrowed from the Indignados movement in Spain, something like: "Why is it taking you so long?" There is a kind of a contagion among cities, and an increasing global awareness about these movements.

Politically, the urban network is not only a capitalist construction; there is also a sense of the urban that is not clearly articulated, and we cannot know when it may be invoked or suddenly erupt. I don't think anybody could have predicted what happened on February 15, 2003. It was a shock, and it changed politics. We can now imagine that a project that we are undertaking in a particular place or city can have effects on other cities and places, through what we may call relational spaces. This relationality is intangible, or as

Marx said about value, "immaterial and supra-sensible, but objective." A lot of politics is intangible and supra-sensible, but has objective consequences.

MGL/DI    Your famous dicta "It is, in practice, hard to see where 'society' begins and 'nature' ends," and "There is nothing unnatural about New York City" have been very influential for urban political ecology. The work of scholars in this field engages with the long overdue task of reinserting questions of nature and ecology into the urban debate via a historical materialist analysis of urban flows, such as water. How can the analysis of a particular material flow help untangle the economic, political, social, and ecological processes that inform contemporary urban landscapes? How, for instance, can studying the consumption rates of cement, as you have pointed out, help scholars unpack urban complexities?

DH    At the beginning of Capital, Marx talks about "concrete abstraction," and so I thought that it would be interesting to talk about "abstract from the concrete." [LAUGHS] I think the purpose of the general theoretical frame is to create a cognitive map around what it is you are trying to do and how you are trying to do it. When you actually start doing these things, you often find that you can't possibly do them all. But there is a distinction between people who go and focus on details without having a general map, and those who struggle to create such a map.

In my work, I try to be conscious about how details connect with this cognitive map. William Blake said something like "the truth lies in a grain of sand," a notion in which everything converges. I see a big difference between students who deal only with the grain of sand, and students who focus on how the grain of sand is internalized within many other forces, even when you can't possibly track all of them. You have to contextualize your work. And you have to speculate. This can't be all hard science and hard information; you can get hard science and hard information about particular things you are working on, but those facts look different when you pull back the telescope and look at them in the context of the broader picture. This is the moment when the fun comes in, the moment of speculation.

MGL/DI    Indeed, our work is usually confined to the "grain of sand," whether we like it or not. Yet even the most discreet design intervention is tensioned and incorporated into myriad material, social, political, economic flows and forces. In this sense, we wonder where you think design agency lies in terms of facing the complexity of capitalist urbanization critically as well as operatively.

DH    I think designers have a great deal of experience in shaping environments and spaces in surprising, unexpected manners, or in ways that open possibilities that were not there before. In that sense, designers do have agency, but I think this agency is circumscribed by political and social context.

In the current conjuncture, for example, I don't think that the only valid form of intervention is related to organizing public participation. There are instances in which you have to be more subversive and underground, so to speak. Democratization is fine, but when you have a population that has only one thing in mind —like, "private property is sacrosanct and that's it"— and you are interested in talking about collective forms of design, you may not get away with what you want to do through public participation. Therefore, you may want to find ways to demonstrate how different collective forms of living or working have something to offer. You may have to go against prevailing public opinion. As Gramsci elaborated, there is "common sense" and there is "good sense." Radical social consciousness is good sense. We may find that very often the common sense of the population is neo-liberal, individualistic, private property-driven sense, and if you go with your idea of public participation, people may simply want to create something like an American suburb.

Agency is about creating, or opening, alternatives. People learn from experience: if you can create an urban experience that is radically different from that which is the convention, then the common sense over here will start looking at the good sense over there.

# FROM A DISTANCE

From: Juan Pablo Corvalán
Subject:A crack in the system

How is architecture changing?
Social space changes by definition and the architecture elite resist blindly.
In your opinion, what would define "the best architecture in The Americas"?
Architecture that avoids being co-opted by city marketing and commercial
forces. Has a renewed idea of nature impacted practices and ways of thinking
about architecture and the city? Only in a superficial way, to hide an agenda
of profit through space.

Is there a contemporary relationship between nature and technology in architecture?
It is very weak because urbanization is unequal and unsustainable

What do you think about the idea of autonomy?
Unpractical. Doubtful theoretically and doubtful architecturally, as compared
to what it promised to be.

Do you think topology is still relevant in a design process?
It is just a frame. Or even a tool. Barely a hypothesis.

What is the value of invention in architecture today?
Value as a capitalist line of measure for exchange seems a problem in spatial
issues. If architecture gets involved in the urban debate, it could approach
other measures and resist capitalist bogus means and reach for using space as
a creative mean of social expression.

The renewed question of spatial problematics of the city has been announced
several times through the unfolding of neoliberal forces in a planetary scale
by urban theory.
At the same time, architecture theory—and practice—seems superficial in its
avoidance of the urban diagnosis, fails in its attempts to provide "solutions," or avoids the issue completely in a closed, vicious, and elitist
circle. Throwing concerns of the city behind classroom walls and cocktails is
fine, but not enough. It's a new century. Why follow the same models that
proved unsustainable and unequal?

I still believe in architecture as a discipline that can contribute to civil
society. My bet: Academia as critical spatial practice.
As Alfredo Jaar would put it "A crack in the system."

From: Jeannette Sordi
Subject: Nature as Movement and Exchange

Until Anaximander invented the first cartographic representation in the 6th century b.c., nature was not a combined group of things but an ongoing perpetual process; nature was movement.1 After that, the organization of the world has followed a static and bi-dimensional representation of nature, one that could be confined within boundaries. The Americas as we know them today are the result of this anthropocentric representation at the continental scale. The name America itself derives from the first map that Amerigo Vespucci diffused of his discovery in the XVI century a.D.2 Sailing by sight, following river paths, and tracing new routes in the vast grasslands, a new territory was created; superimposing new boundaries and land uses over native ecosystems and indigenous communities. Nature became a commodity, a resource to be extracted, produced, cultivated, mutated.

Nowadays, the limits of this objectified view of nature are increasingly evident. Industrial agriculture and livestock are contaminating water and dramatically reducing biodiversity and forests; wood production is drying soils, reducing native vegetation, and causing more and more fires every year; coastal urbanization and tourism are severely compromising marine ecosystems that could mitigate the effects of erosion and floods. According to the United Nations' latest reports on climate change, attempts to ensure that fossil fuel emissions peaked in 2020 will fail.3 Rising sea levels, droughts, and fires will only worsen their effect in the years to come, leading to massive loss of biodiversity, population displacement, and migrations. However, despite the effects that these changes are having on mobility, housing, property, and people's everyday life, architecture and urban design too often still rely on an understanding of territory as bounded land and nature as a fixed object that can be manipulated and dominated.

Jim Enote, a Zuni farmer and the director of the A:shiwi A:wan Museum and Heritage Center in New Mexico, recently started an art project that aims to challenge the western understanding of place and nature. Between 1776 and 1887, over a billion and a half acres of indigenous lands were seized by the United States government.4 Executive orders were accompanied by atlases and maps that became unquestioned and lasting truths of ownership and identity. Partnering with Zuni artists, Enote is working to create maps that evoke the Zuni's sense of place, which prioritizes storytelling and shared knowledge over plots and boundaries.5 The award-winning Peruvian Pavilion, curated by Barcley&Crousse, presented a map of the Amazonia made of black and white pictures and sounds of the forest. The United States 2018 Pavilion, rephrased the notion of citizenship presenting histories of inequality and the violence imposed on people, non-human actors, and ecologies. At the 2017 Chilean Biennial, we highlighted those projects that addressed the Unpostponable Dialogues [Diálogos Impostergables] that affect contemporary cities; namely issues of vulnerability, resources, migrations, common space, etc. These are just some examples of art, architecture, and landscape design projects that are working on building a counter-narrative, one in which nature, cities, and territories are not just objects and lines on a map. The Best Architecture of the Americas should contribute to reestablishing an understanding of nature as movement and exchange, designing buildings and cities that are not just objects on a map but rather alive entities, in which plural populations, human and non-human ecologies, can interact and proliferate.

From: Rodrigo Kommers Wender
Subject: Narratives of Planetary Culture

There is an old mirage that reflecting back the image that we are intrinsically different and disconnected from nature, despite the overwhelming evidence from the fields of biology and ecology that we are intimately connected to everything. Since the advent of agriculture, and later, the creation of cities, we have experienced a gradual separation from the world around us. Modernity drew an even more precise frontier, to the point of splintering human production - the artificial - from that which surrounds it--the natural. Thus emerged contemporary atomization and hyper individualism, from which our models of life and our built environments determine forms of perceiving ourselves, others, and that which is beyond our small interior. Encapsulated in life-support technologies, connections and multiple interdependencies with the natural world seem too distant and extemporaneous to the choreographies of everyday life. The failure of modernism serves as a reply that this exterior no longer exists, and, therefore, that none of the elements necessary to sustain life as we conceive it - that inexhaustible support network capable of feeding and animating the artificial - can still be taken for granted.

Here there are no nostalgic glances seeking a return to an ulterior universe, no return to an imaginary past. Go back to what? Our bodies know that the modern notion of nature disappeared. The human/non-human, natural/artificial binaries are now part of Peter Sloterdijk's "great interior." It is not that the traditional categories of countryside and city, exterior and interior, wild and domesticated, technical and organic, even public and private, have been somehow overcome, as if it in some kind of sign of progress, but rather, in the words of Bruno Latour, they are "ignored to explore what kind of atmospheres we are all supposed to collectively survive in." And if we find ourselves disoriented in our search for alternatives to climate control, it is because this new world is defined by an inherently unstable heterogeneous ecosystem, continuously articulated, defined and constructed by man through political, cultural and scientific practices.

After the long obsession with the link between subjects and objects, we are now challenged by the conditions of the possibility of packaging, spheres, skins and environments. It is an inherently non-linear issue: a territory of expansion that requires tactical and strategic interventions, and confrontations between localization and globalization, between the personal and the common.

It is not by chance that the notion of landscape, which implies an expanded field, has taken on so much relevance in architectural discourses over the last decades. To the detriment of the idea of disciplinary autonomy, emphasis is placed on spatial and sensory experiences that converge in ambiguous ways, and the boundaries between subject, object and environment are blurred. From the artificial machine to the hybrid organism, from the notion of the border to that of atmospheric transitions, the condition of possibility for architecture is to contribute to this reinvention.

From: Paul Preissner
Subject: Kind of Familiar

Like (I suspect) a lot of people, I look at a lot of work and pictures and memes and art and photographs and images in magazines and books and the internets all the time now. I think I understand why there is this daily contest to supply the world with "the most interesting image" about architecture and how that seems to work into peoples' practice about creating their ideas for architecture. There's so much out there that it is difficult to have your thing be out there with any regard unless its somehow spectacular or oversaturated and alien or seems exotic, and I suppose: new. Our eyes are only human; peacocks grab our attention much faster than finches. But our attention is one of the few things we have left of ourselves, and rather than allowing it to be captured by others, we might want to keep it, for ourselves.

An idle attention creates the space for imagination, strange thoughts, and daydreams; it isn't being occupied with producing the immediate reaction required by the spectacular.

The remarkable and the sensational demand constant attention. As creative works, the striking is always needy; it is not interested in politics or opinion, just in capturing eyeballs in order to sell something. This need for attention frames a type of creativity dominated by capital at the expense of thought, turning the design process into an effort to make colorful novelty and fashion. This builds a type of architectural culture that can only serve capital, prioritizes the market of ornaments and turns conversations to the most banal things like, for example: decorative patterns, the influence of toys, or whether architecture is part of the ontology of objects.

The alternative (to propose one) might be to explore things which are not-interesting and somewhat boring (as opposed to spectacular), and seem familiar (as opposed to exotic). The stability of the familiar introduces a sort of place for real art and the confrontation that can only come from working with (and destabilizing) seemingly fixed and comfortable terrain. The alien is always experienced as theater and never taken seriously as a threat to existing order because the exceptional is always an exception. Developing a creative project that works with the familiar, uses anonymous history, and explores the nearly-normal might produce something murky and blurry and ultimately more subversive, introducing space for boredom and uncertainty into architecture.

Rather than racing to discover the gold in some new material, or calculating a minor variation on a very complex geometry, one should experiment with vacant feelings, sloppy composition, reckless order and dumb thoughts. This kind of architecture is a giant veto towards an idea of design focused on the novelty industry of amazement and makes a type of architecture that brings out deeper (and weirder) set of feelings and intellectual responses.

From: Pedro Aparicio Llorente & Juliana Ramirez
Subject: Off-Grid Architecture: Toilet Gardening

Architects know Ville Savoye: dates, myths, measurements, etc, but can we answer where its shit goes down? Yes, literally: where is the human waste it receives deposited or treated? Architecture will become contemporary once it engages in the ecologies produced by the human metabolism. What if architecture assumes responsibility over sanitary infrastructure? Meaning, can architecture integrate the demands that make urban life possible and bypass, or support, the need for large-scale water lines, sewage discharge, and waste management? Can architecture be off-grid?

To engage in the question of autonomy, one must revise relationships between architecture and infrastructure. In Accra, different elements that build a house, from a bulldozer to a front door, from a leather couch to a washing machine, are carefully organized, displayed and sold at the road's edge. This circulation of domestic space within a multi-use highway (both market and high-speed vehicle lane) presented two key similarities across the tropics: everyone wants to build a house; and zoning is never complete as zoning is always tricked. Similar to Accra, cities like Bogotá or Jakarta share an exponential growth in the last five decades, and with it, an increased demand for technologies of domestic space. By now, we recognize that much of the postcolonial public housing of the 1970-80s stands closer to radical ideas of collective form when compared to the neoliberal system of land developing that shape cities today. However, despite these efforts, cities across the tropics have built themselves and continue to do so, off the grid. In this regard, a roadside market of domestic elements is a precise self-portrait of a self-built metropolis, opening a fundamental question: if autoconstruction is a medium for housing, then who is building for infrastructure? More precisely, where are people dumping their own human waste? As architects, the idea of collective form must be understood beyond the human, making the study of sanitary infrastructure and the design for waste-disposal-flows a pertinent and contemporary spatial act.

Toilets are a central piece in the history of urbanization. Not only are they the basic interface between architecture and sanitary infrastructure, but also a central place where waste transformation becomes a question for design. The mismanagement of human waste leads to pollution of water sources, propagation of diseases, among other issues. While housing typologies have evolved, why is sewage still randomly dumped in lakes and rivers, burnt or buried? Some refer to this as the world's most urgent resource management crisis.

Understanding ground as live technology with learning loops provides an attempt to propose an architecture that participates in transforming human waste into potential energy. No longer can house and garden be seen as separate entities, we must give shape to an architecture thought of, and designed as an integral element of a garden where microorganisms work in the dehydration and decomposition of manure. An architecture that provides light and shadow for plants: indicator species that enable life within soils and make visible that well-managed human waste, is not waste, but compost. Perhaps it is about looking down to the ground, instead of automating things to magically disappear. In other words, toilets are not only about tile geometry and flush systems, but rather a complex device for redesigning how we conceive of, and inhabit, our metabolic processes.

From: Ana Rascovsky
Subject: Everything is Architecture

The fragility of the planet can bring new meaning to architecture: current
ecological, social and economic problems have created a generalized discourse
that has abandoned senseless practice and self-referential introspection
along with the pretense of a false autonomy. In connection to this "great
cause," a new architecture has emerged with varying degrees of commitment but
good intentions.

The lack of new challenges extending outside the disciplinary limits of architecture are notable: the society, the city, or the culture for those that
produce it. How is it possible that, in a region with so many urgent problems, these issues are not present in the architectural debate? Why does
architecture talk so much about issues intrinsic to the discipline when it
could be getting involved with current issues? Given that construction is one
of the factors that most influences the emission of carbon dioxide into the
atmosphere, why is this issue not a priority for architects? Why isn't
Plataforma Arquitectura full of projects with forests on the terraces? In a
region with so much inequality, why are there not thousands of projects circulating about the possibilities for the urbanization of slums? Why aren't
new, cheap, natural materials being investigated outside the commercial circuit? If doing architecture is to problematize an issue, what should those
issues be?

It is clear that in today's world the neoliberal policy based on maximum
profit has become so beyond grasp that political and economic disciplinary
interventions in these issues is complex. The space of architecture is limited to an intimate universe with a limited and domestic field of action.

Moreover, in Latin America, the vast majority of architecture is done by
private commission. The problem is everyday and framed in a family environment. And innovation has little place when profit must be secured.

But, on the other hand, just like in Lego Movie 2, (a difficult reference, I
know) where that which is pop and feminine is perceived as superficial and
banal but ultimately comes to underlines the sensitive and unprejudiced,
there is a new Latin American architecture that serves as an invitation to
contemplate that which is simple, essential, everyday; the small details that
define us.

Within this conceptualization, there are exemplar cases that have been able
to create dialectical links between architectural elements and relate few
existing resources with the beauty and cultural aspects of each region. They
may not be heroic, but instead, simple, understandable, and in resonance with
the signs of these times.

Now, once the concept of sustainability has been digested, made our own and
when we no longer discuss it but it informs our general practice, architecture regains its meaning. With a new concept of nature: hybridized and amal-
gamated within architecture: vegetation is one more material in a building.
Outer space is part of the program, of the landscape…

Meaning restores a lost glamor to architecture; it puts it back on the market. And that battle should not be easily conceded; real estate developers,
politics, art, should not be allowed to take over; architecture will then
continue to belong to architects.

From: Todd Palmer
Subject: Who Cares for Architecture?

Who gives architecture loving and watchful attention? Who maintains, guards, and stewards the built works considered most precious to the field? When otherwise fine buildings show evidence of strain or begin to fail—when siding peels, death rays singe the neighbors, foundations crack, insulation smolders, rafters burn, or plaster and stucco flake away --who are the men and women who care for architecture?

Do those who care for architecture—as embodied in the skills and expertise of custodians, plumbers, electricians, day-laborers, bricklayers, roofers, gardeners, window-washers, and carpinters—register to those who care about architecture, those who are empowered to speculate upon, vision and shape the physical manifestations and infrastructures that undergird our collective futures? Do those who care for architecture enter into the equation for those with the privilege of framing debate, arguing over authorship and policing boundary conditions between architecture and buildings, other disciplines, technologies and realms of expertise—from street plans, to power utilities, to aquifers and greenswards?

Certainly, wealthy patrons, government bodies, corporations, cultural institutions, systems of governance, from patriarchy to colonialism, all care about architecture. Indeed, a depth of care—an emotional commitment that exists on a spectrum ranging from concern to love—has long been devoted to this elevated register that elevates "mere buildings" and deems them "architectural." Certain edifices are ennobled and circulated as exemplary acts of construction through the attention given to their fine renderings, the conservation of their procedural artifacts and the embroidery of canny arguments, captivating origins stories, heroic narratives, and other kinds of capital-A architectural discourse.

In the physical artifacts of architecture and other buildings in cities large and small (not to mention isolated rural settlements, community-built barrios and other places people reside), one finds ample evidence of those who care for architecture. This care resides in the loving attention of ornament and structure, in the terracing and moating of grounds and in apertures and overhangs that define enclosure. Whether realized by industrial skilled labor, or autonomous craft, the loving care of collective eyes, hands and minds are touched and felt in balustrades and moldings, wrought in ironwork, bundled into cabling, uncovered in lathe, and etched into concrete. An intentional genius is infused into the programmatic delineations between the insides and outsides of all sorts of settings assigned to domestic, spiritual, erotic, communal or remunerative activities marked through partitions, lattices, curbs, pergolas and cubbyholes.

This is not the same as the fetishized care that is lauded in the commissioning of well-made details that embellish rarified weekend houses, private agoras and collector's museums. "Care" in this instance is the emotional commitment at the massive scale that is required to mobilize entire societies around culturally collective and ecologically resilient infrastructures. Defined by a mosaic of myriad inputs, amassing civic care for architecture may be as key to the survival of civilization as the communally sourced cathedrals once seemed to be to the "eternal salvation" that motivated medieval populaces. The question of who cares for architecture is implied and resonates for today in Le Corbusier's oft-digested early 20th century warning -- "It is a question of building which is at the root of the social unrest of today: architecture or revolution?" The story of what concerns architecture and who is concerned about architecture will matter to the future of the field in our own age of revolutions, driven by technologies of (divided) consciousness and (in)attention. Who cares for a discipline with such a tentative status (in the mass consciousness) is critical at this groundswell moment of great urgencies -- with radically changing climate and other pre-existing conditions of the otherwise "natural" states on the planet.

When care for architecture by a broader public is removed, the artifacts of architecture are readily swept away. Ignored, ridiculed, neglected and even hated -- it isn't a great distance from abandon, neglect and disdain to the rubbish heap. At their moments of pending demise, the Victorian mansion, Brutalist luxury tower, Edwardian rowhouse, Corbusian tower-in-the-park, Beaux Arts depot, or Sullivan-esque bank resembled little more in the collective imagination than the faceless and petty masks of powers withdrawn from more important concerns.

There is, today, ongoing work on the construction of the discipline and the design of buildings that includes other forms of knowledge and welcomes an intensive care for the labor, maintenance and ongoing custodianship of architectural spaces. These new narratives and constructions are open to the local and vernacular, to the peripheral, esoteric and sometimes, even the anachronistic. Like the love for anything that truly concerns us, this new architecture cares about who cares. It is relational, cooperative and emotionally relevant. It will signal that Architecture is constitutive of the civic whole – settings that guard, protect, shelter and maintain our noblest shared values – such as equity, sustainable ecologies, human rights, and the public good.

STAN ALLEN is an architect and George Dutton '27 Professor of Architecture at Princeton University. His practice SAA/Stan Allen Architect has realized buildings and urban projects in the United States, South America, and Asia. In 2016 he was one of twelve architects chosen to represent the US in the American Pavilion at the Venice Biennale, and his work was featured in the 2017 Chicago Biennial. His architectural work is published in *Points + Lines: Diagrams and Projects for the City* and his essays in *Practice: Architecture, Technique and Representation*. His most recent book, *Situated Objects* was published by Park Books in 2020.

PEDRO APARICIO LLORENTE is an architect and founding principal of APLO, a practice based in Bogotá that makes and researches buildings and landscapes. His work stems from ten years of experience in design and construction within the material practices and political ecologies of postcolonial tropical habitats. Aparicio holds an architecture degree from Universidad de los Andes and an MDes Urbanism Landscape Ecology from Harvard University Graduate School of Design, where he was awarded with the Gerlad M. McCue Medal for overall academic achievement. Other collaborations include positions as research fellow with the Canadian Center for Architecture in Montreal, the Kokrobitey Institute in Accra, and the Rujak Center for Urban Studies in Jakarta.

WIEL ARETS is an architect, educator, industrial designer, theorist, and urbanist based in Amsterdam, The Netherlands. He received his Master of Science in Architecture from the Technische Universiteit in Eindhoven and, in the same year, founded the internationally recognized practice Wiel Arets Architects (WAA) with offices in Amsterdam, Maastricht, Zürich, and Munich. Arets is currently professor at the College of Architecture at the Illinois Institute of Technology in Chicago of which he was previously Dean and Rowe Family Dean Endowed Chair. Prior to joining IIT, he was a professor of building planning and design at the Universität der Künste in Berlin and Dean of the Berlage Institute in Rotterdam. His books include *STILLS*, *Autobiographical References*, and *Un-Conscious-City*.

BARRY BERGDOLL is Meyer Schapiro Professor of Art History at Columbia University, where he has been on the faculty since 1986. He served as Chief Curator in the Department of Architecture and Design at the Museum of Modern Art (2007-14), where he curated exhibitions such as *Mies In Berlin* (2001, with Terry Riley), *Home Delivery: Fabricating the Modern Dwelling* (2007), *Bauhaus 1919–1933: Workshops for Modernity* (2009; with Leah Dickerman), *Latin America in Construction: Architecture 1955-1980* (2015 with J. Liernur, C. Comas, and P. del Real), and *Frank Lloyd Wright at 150: Unpacking the Archive* (2017). He has written on Karl Friedrich Schinkel, Marcel Breuer, Emilio Ambasz, and aspects of 19th century French architecture. He is currently completing a book on the history of exhibiting architecture.

ILA BERMAN is the former Dean of the School of Architecture and Edward E. Elson Professor at the University of Virginia and principal of Scaleshift Design. She is an architect, theorist, and curator of architecture and urbanism whose research investigates the relationship between culture and the evolution of contemporary material, technological, and spatial practices. She is the founding director of the Next Cities Institute, an interdisciplinary research center focused on the design of global urban futures, the editor of its book series, and the author of a number of books and publications including *Expanded Field: Architectural Installation Beyond Art*, *URBANbuild local_global*, and *New Constellations New Ecologies*, among others. Her design work and installations have been exhibited in many galleries and museums among them the 2006 and 2018 Venice International Architectural Biennales.

SOL CAMACHO is an architect, curator, and urban designer leading RADDAR, a design and research practice. She is currently leading the Pacaembu Stadium adaptive reuse project in São Paulo. From 2017 to 2022, she was the cultural director of the Instituto Bardi / Casa de Vidro in charge of curating exhibitions, cultural events, and coordinator of Lina Bo Bardi's archive. Amongst other curatorial projects is the exhibition Walls of Air for the Brazilian Pavilion for the 16th International Architecture Exhibition at the Venice Biennale. She edited the books *Walls of Air* (2018 - Fundação Bienal), *Glass Houses* (2019, Romano Guerra) and has written in various other publications such as *São Paulo Graphic Biography* (Yale Press 2017) and *Antarctic Resolution* (Lars Muller Publishers 2021). Sol graduated from Harvard GSD in 2008 and continues to be involved in academic activities teaching and lecturing on architecture, urban design, and heritage conservation in Latin America.

BEATRIZ COLOMINA is the Howard Crosby Butler Professor of the History of Architecture at Princeton University. She writes and curates on questions of design, art, sexuality and media. Her books include Sexuality and Space (Princeton Architectural Press, 1992), Privacy and Publicity: Modern Architecture as Mass Media (MIT Press, 1994), Domesticity at War (MIT Press and Actar, 2007), Clip/Stamp/Fold: The Radical Architecture of Little Magazines 196X–197X (Actar, 2010) with Craig Buckley, Manifesto Architecture: The Ghost of Mies (Sternberg, 2014) ,The Century of the Bed (Verlag fur Moderne Kunst, 2015) and Are We Human? Notes on an Archaeology of Design (Lars Muller, 2016) with Mark Wigley. Her latest book is X-Ray Architecture (Lars Muller, 2019). She has curated a number of exhibitions including Clip/Stamp/Fold (2006-2013), Playboy Architecture (2012-2016), Radical Pedagogies

(2014-2015), Liquid La Habana (2018) and The 24/7 Bed (2018). In 2016 she was chief curator with Mark Wigley of the third Istanbul Design Biennial. In 2018 she was mas made Honorary Doctor by the KTH Royal Institute of Technology in Stockholm and 2020 she was awarded the Ada Louise Huxtable Prize for her contributions to the field of architecture.

JUAN PABLO CORVALAN is an architect from the Ecole d'Ingenieurs de Geneve, Switzerland. He earned a Master of Excellence in Architecture at the Berlage Institute Rotterdam, The Netherlands. He is a doctoral candidate in Geography from the Pontifical Catholic University in Chile. He has lectured in Chilean as well as in foreign universities. His work has been published in various international media. He is a founding member of the critical discussion and research group Supersudaca. Today he coordinates Susuka.

JEAN PIERRE CROUSSE is a Peruvian architect. He studied Architecture at URP in Lima and at the Politécnico di Milano. Between 1999 and 2006 he taught at the Ecole d'Architecture de Paris Belleville. From 2006 on, he lectures at the Pontificia Universidad Católica del Perú (PUCP). In 2013 he earned a Master in Territory and Landscape from the UDP in Chile. In 2015 he was a design critic at the Graduate School of Design, Harvard University; in 2016 he was co-curator of the Peruvian Pavilion at the 15th Venice Biennale; in 2017 he became Director of the Master Program in Architecture at the PUCP; between 2019 and 2021 he lectured as visiting professor of Architectural Design at Yale University; since 2020, he is Professor at the University of Virginia.

DIRK DENISON is the Professor and Director of the Mies Crown Hall Americas Prize (MCHAP). He is an award-winning architect, educator, and supporter of the arts whose practice is defined by a close engagement with clients, communities, and artists. During three decades of teaching at the renowned Illinois Institute of Technology, Dirk has fostered the same engagement in his students both inside the classroom and through first-hand encounters with significant architecture in Chicago and internationally. Dirk's nationally recognized firm, Dirk Denison Architects, has developed its own modernist vocabulary in multiple scales of built works from New York to California. Homes designed in personal dialogue with clients are at the core of his firm's output. His first monograph, Dirk Denison 10 Houses, was released in December 2018. Beyond his work in architecture, Dirk has deep ties to cultural institutions in and outside Chicago. He has served on the boards of the Cranbrook Art Academy, Hubbard Street Dance, and the AIDS Foundation of Chicago, and formerly as board chair of the Architecture and Design Society and the Society for Contemporary Art at the Art Institute of Chicago. He is a member of the Mayor of Chicago's committee for public sculpture, and has also been an advisor to the mayor on landscape and planning.

URIEL FOGUÉ has a PhD in architecture (outstanding doctoral thesis prize 2014-15). He is professor at EPFL (Lausanne), ETSAM UPM (Madrid), and UEM (Madrid). He co-directs the architecture office Elii, which took part in the Spanish Pavilion at the 15th Venice Architecture Biennale (2016 Golden Lion award), has two works selected for the European Union Prize for Contemporary Architecture Mies Van der Rohe Award (2015, 2019), among other recognitions. He is co-author of the books: What is Home Without a Mother (2015) and Beyond the Limits (2020); co-editor of: Planos de intersección: materiales para un diálogo entre filosofía y arquitectura (Lampreave, 2011) and UHF.

MARIANO GOMEZ-LUQUE is an architect, editor of the New Geographies doctoral journal of the Harvard University Graduate School of Design (GSD), and co-director of FORMA, an office for general architecture based in Córdoba, Argentina. His research explores the intersections between the design disciplines and critical theory, with an emphasis on the status of architectural form under conditions of planetary urbanization. Mariano holds a Doctor of Design (2019) and a Master of Architecture (2013) from Harvard GSD.

DAVID HARVEY is a Distinguished Professor of Anthropology & Geographyat the Graduate Center of the City University of New York (CUNY), the Director of Research at the Center for Place, Culture and Politics, and the author of numerous books. He has been teaching Karl Marx's Capital for nearly 50 years. See davidharvey.com

DANIEL IBAÑEZ is a Spanish practicing architect and urbanist based in Cambridge, Massachusetts, USA. He is Doctor of Design from Harvard GSD, Director of the Master in Mass Timber Design, co-Director of the Master in Advanced Ecological Buildings and Biocities at the Institute for Advanced Architecture of Cataluya (IAAC) and member of the Urban Theory Lab. Ibañez is specialized in ecological urbanism and architecture, in particular how to frame the design disciplines in relation to broader socio-ecological interdependencies. He is author/editor of Wood Urbanism: From Molecular to Territorial (Actar, 2019) and author of ecological timber projects including the Fab Lab House (Madrid, 2010), Endesa Pavilion (Oslo, 2013), the Endesa World Fab Condenser (Barcelona, 2014), and prototypes such as the Tiny House o the Voxel (Barcelona, 2019-2020). Since 2018, he serves as senior consultant for the World Bank advising governments and international institutions on ecological, urban, and architectural developments.

RODRIGO KOMMERS WENDER is editorial director of PLOT magazine where he also served as editor-in-chief between 2014 and 2017. Previously, he was editor at Summa + magazine and in charge of the Portuguese edition. He collaborated in various publications as an illustrator and writer. He is an architect (cum laude) from the Faculty of Architecture of the University of Palermo.

SANFORD KWINTER is a New York-based theorist, writer, and editor and Professor of Science and Design at the Pratt Institute in New York. Kwinter has taught widely throughout the United States and Europe including at the University of Applied Arts in Vienna where he headed the Institute for Theory and History of Architecture and at the Harvard Design School where he co-directed the Master in Design Studies Programs. He was the recipient of the 2013 award for design writing by the American Academy of Arts and Letters. His current work addresses topics in neurobiology, ecology and indigenous knowledges and practices.

ISABELLA MORETTI is an architect and editor based in Buenos Aires. She is a doctorate candidate at the University of Buenos Aires where she also studied architecture. She holds a Master of Science in Design Research (Bauhaus Dessau Foundation / Humboldt Universität Berlin / Hochschule Anhalt). She has worked as a researcher at the Bauhaus Dessau Foundation and the City Government of Buenos Aires. Currently, she acts as editor-in-chief of Lots of Architecture –publishers and NESS magazine, and is also founding member of the collective FAN (Fantasías Arquitectónicas Nerviosas). Moretti is assisting professor at the University of Buenos Aires.

CIRO NAJLE is architect for the Universidad de Buenos Aires (1991, hons), and Master of Advanced Architectural Design for Columbia University (1997, hons). Until December 2021, he was Dean of the Escuela de Arquitectura y Estudios Urbanos at the Universidad Torcuato Di Tella, where he still teaches. He has previously taught at the Harvard Graduate School of Design, the Architectural Association, Cornell, Columbia, Berlage Institute, and the Universidad de Buenos Aires. He is the author of *The Generic Sublime* (2016), co-author of *Suprarural* (2017), and co-editor of *Landscape Urbanism, A Manual for the Machinic Landscape* (2004). Director of General Design Bureau, his research practice engages the convergence of digital culture, ecological thinking, and complexity theory in architecture at the age of globalization.

LLUÍS ORTEGA is PhD-architect by the Universitat Politècnica de Catalunya (UPC), MA in Philosophy by the Universitat de Barcelona and obtained his Master of Science (AAD) degree from Columbia University. He is cofounder and principal at JL-Arch, a practice based in Barcelona with Julia Capomaggi. He is author and editor of multiple books and was director of *Quaderns d'Arquitectura i Urbanisme*. At present, he is Research Professor Beatriz Galindo at UPC in Barcelona, Associate Professor at IIT in Chicago (on leave) and Visiting Professor at the Universidad Torcuato di Tella in Buenos Aires. He previously taught at UIC (Chicago), Universitat Politècnica de Catalunya, Universidad de Alicante, Harvard University, and at the Akademie der Bildenden Künste, Vienna.

TODD PALMER is a strategist, curator, and cultural leader of purpose-driven platforms at the intersection of design, public learning and spatial equity. As Director of the Diversity in Design Collaborative he is steering a group of design-focused organizations aligned to confront systemic barriers faced by Black talent in the sector. Palmer orchestrated the 2017 and 2019 editions of the Chicago Architecture Biennial as Executive Director, defining the emergent platform as a global catalyst connecting experimentation with civic urgencies. As Curator and Associate Director of the National Public Housing Museum, Todd facilitated grassroots efforts to rehabilitate a community site as a cultural framework for confronting poverty. Palmer has exhibited at the Studio Museum in Harlem, published in The Avery Review, and been a Critic teaching in RISD's MArch program.

PAUL PREISSNER is an architect and founder of Paul Preissner Architects; a pretty good practice located in Oak Park, Illinois. He is the commissioner and co-curator of "American Framing" at the Pavilion of the United States at the 17th International Architecture Exhibition – la Biennale di Venezia. Paul is a professor at the the University of Illinois Chicago and the author of *Kind of Boring: Canonical Work and Other Visible Things Meant to Be Viewed as Architecture* published by Actar.

ENRIQUE RAMIREZ is a writer and a historian of art and architecture. His work considers histories of buildings, cities, and landscapes alongside larger cultures of textual and literary production in Europe and the Americas from the Renaissance onwards.

JULIANA RAMÍREZ graduated as an architect from the University of the Andes and then focused on the development of social architectural projects, collaborative design strategies, pedagogy, and collective construction with vulnerable rural and urban communities. Though she has worked with semi-rural and rural communities in west Africa, the core of her experience is with rural communities in Colombia, deeply affected by poverty and violence due to Colombia's internal conflict. In 2017 and 2019 the Colombian Presidency's Agency for International Cooperation (APC) invited her to Ghana with the aim of training rural communities in earthen building techniques for composting toilets. In October 2019 her Toilet Garden Project was acknowledged with the Social Responsibility Award granted by the Colombian National Council of professionals in Architecture. She has been able to articulate her know-how to build along with indigenous communities like the inga that inhabit the Andean-amazonic corridor, the wayuus who inhabit the northern deserts among others.

ANA RASCOVSKY completed a master of excellence in architecture and urbanism from the Berlage Institute Rotterdam (Netherlands, 2002), a master (D.E.A.) in History of Urbanism from the Ecole d 'Architecture de Versailles (France, 2001) and a degree in architecture from the University of Buenos Aires, Faculty of Architecture, Design, and Urbanism (FADU-UBA, 1996). She is a professor at the University of Buenos Aires (UBA) and a founding member of Supersudaca - Think Tank of architecture and urbanism, which whom she received the French Embassy / National Arts Fund grant from Prins Claus Fonds. She co-directs studio PLANTA.

PATRICIO DEL REAL is associate professor of History of Art and Architecture at Harvard University. He works on modern architecture and its transnational connections with a focus on the Americas and explores the changing ideological maps and geographies of modernity, and the ways in which cultural and racial imaginaries have shaped the story of modern architecture. Del Real holds a PhD in Architecture History and Theory from Columbia University and a Master of Architecture from Harvard's Graduate School of Design.

FLORENCIA RODRIGUEZ is the founder and editorial director of NESS. Trained as an architect in Argentina, she has devoted her career to editing, writing, and teaching. She was a Loeb Fellow at the Harvard GSD between 2013 and 2014, where she is now a Lecturer in Architecture. In 2010, Rodriguez founded PLOT and directed it until 2017. Since then, from her platform NESS, she has continued making magazines, books, and other activities committed to the new forms of communication and criticism in the age of dispersion. Rodriguez has taught at the Universidad Torcuato Di Tella, Instituto Tecnológico de Monterrey, Boston Architectural College, and the Institute of Advanced Architecture of Catalonia, among others. She has received awards for her editorial work and published several articles in books and specialized media such as Harvard Design Magazine, Domus, Oris, summa +, Arquine, a+u, or Uncube. In 2016 she was part of the jury for the Mies Crown Hall Americas Prize (MCHAP) award at the Illinois Institute of Technology.

GRACIELA SILVESTRI is an architect and historian based in Buenos Aires. She has a degree in Architecture from the University of Buenos Aires and a PhD in History from the same university. She is a professor of Theory of Architecture at the National University of La Plata, and a Visiting Professor at the Graduate School of Design at Harvard University. Silvestri is the author of several books and articles, including *El paisaje como cifra de armonía* (along with Fernando Aliata, Nueva Visión, Buenos Aires, 2001), *El color del río. Historia cultural del paisaje del Riachuelo* (Editorial de la Universidad nacional de Quilmes, Buenos Aires, 2004), *El lugar común. Una historia de las figuras de paisaje en el Rio de la Plata* (Edhasa, Buenos Aires, 2011), and *Las tierras desubicadas: Paisajes y culturas en la Sudamérica fluvial* (Universidad Nacional de Entre Ríos, Paraná, 2021).

JEANNETTE SORDI is an architect and urban planner based in New York City. She is an adjunct associate professor at New York Tech and is a consultant for the Inter-American Development Bank. Until 2018, she was Associate Professor of Landscape and Urbanism at Adolfo Ibañez University in Santiago de Chile. Sordi earned a PhD in Urban Planning and Design from the University of Genoa (2013) and was a Doctoral Visiting Student at the Harvard Graduate School of Design (2011–2012). Her main publications include the books *Beyond Urbanism* (2014, 2017; List, SaCabana); *Andrea Branzi: From Radical Design to Post-Environmentalism* (ARQ, 2015), *The Camp and the City: Territories of Extraction* (List, 2017), *Part-time Cities* (ARQ, 2018), *NESS.docs 2: Landscape as Urbanism in the Americas* (LoA, 2020) and *Ecological Design: Strategies for the Vulnerable City* (IDB, 2021).

MAGDALENA TAGLIABUE is an architect (2015, Universidad de Buenos Aires) and an editor. As a Master's Degree Candidate in History and Critical Studies of Latin American Architecture (UBA), her research focuses on Publications concerning Latin American Discourses. She holds a Diploma on Editorial Politics and Cultural Projects from the Universidad de Buenos Aires (2018), and another on Architecture and Philosophy from the École Nationale Supérieure d'Architecture de Paris-La Villette (2016). She has worked as a curatorial assistant and researcher in Centro de Documentación Biblioteca M. I Net (FADU, UBA). She is a contributing editor in PLOT, Summa+, and NESS. She teaches History and Urban Project at the Universidad de Buenos Aires and the Universidad Argentina de la Empresa. In 2021, she got a grant from the Fondo Nacional de las Artes in Argentina to work on a project about Gender and Architecture.

MASON WHITE is Assistant Professor at the University of Toronto Daniels Faculty of Architecture, Landscape, and Design, where he conducts studios on the intersections between infrastructure and architecture. He received his B.Arch from Virginia Tech and M.Arch from Harvard Graduate School of Design. He is a founding partner of Lateral Office and a founding director of InfraNet Lab (www.infranetlab.org). His writing and work has been published in MONU, 306090, Detail, A+U, New Geographies, and Alphabet City, among others. In partnership with Archinect, InfraNet Lab has launched a new annual publicat ion called *Bracket*. He is a co-editor of *Bracket 1: On Farming* (Actar, 2010) and co-author of *Coupling: Strategies for Infrastructural Opportunism* (Princeton Architectural Press, 2010).

VISUAL ESSAYS

PABLO GERSON is an Argentinian architect, photographer, and documentary filmmaker who has built his professional practice on audiovisual production. His work focuses on issues related to architecture, urbanism, and landscape. Gerson studied photography at the International Center of Photography in New York. His work has been published in various media outlets and he has played an active role in a number of projects dedicated to the dissemination of visual disciplinary contents. In 2005, Gerson founded Estudiox (EX), a production house that develops educational and history-related content for film and television. In early 2017, Gerson joined forces with Florencia Rodriguez to develop the editorial platform Lots of architecture –publishers and -NESS. Gerson is a professor at the School of Architecture and Urban Studies at Torcuato di Tella University where he teaches Architectural Photography and Introduction to Expressive Media.

THE CANARY PROJECT was created by artist duo Susannah Sayler and Edward Morris. They use diverse media and participatory projects to investigate and contribute to the development of ecological consciousness. Their work has been exhibited in diverse venues internationally, including: MASS MoCA, The Cooper Hewitt Design Museum, the Walker Art Center, The Kunsthal Museum in Rotterdam, The Museum of Contemporary Art/Denver, the Museum of Science and Industry (Chicago, IL), etc. Sayler Morris have been Smithsonian Artist Research Fellows and Artist Fellows at The Nevada Museum of Art's Center for Art + Environment. In 2008-2009 Sayler and Morris were Loeb Fellows at Harvard University's Graduate School of Design. In 2016, they were awarded the 8th Annual David Brower Art/Act Award. They currently teach in the Transmedia Department at Syracuse University, where they co-direct The Canary Lab.

MIGUEL DE GUZMÁN is an architect and photographer. He founded ImagenSubliminal: Architectural Photography + Film based in New York and Madrid with Rocío Romero. ImagenSubliminal's photography has been published worldwide in print magazines as Architect, Dwell, El Croquis, Arquitectura Viva, A+U Japan, Domus, Casabella, Mark, C3, books, and newspapers. ImagenSubliminal: Architectural Photography + Film also collaborates with online media such as Archdaily, Dezeen, Designboom, and Divisare. Their film work has been displayed at MAXXI Rome, Centre Pompidou Paris, and Architecture film festivals in New York, Los Angeles, Budapest, Santiago de Chile, and Seoul.

DAVID SISSO is a photographer based in Buenos Aires, Argentina. Since 1993, he has been working as a photojournalist and editor at Rolling Stone magazine. Sisso was awarded two times with the Medal of Honor of the Society of Publications Design. Since 2001, he was part of many collective and individual exhibitions as of national and international fairs. In 2012, he was chosen the winner of the Repsol award in Lima Photo, Perú. In 2017, Editorial Planeta published his first book *Tierra Vacía*, with texts by Leila Guerriero and Esteban Feune. That same year, the homonymous exhibition was opening in Fola. The project includes photo, video, and an incidental soundtrack.

MCHAP 2 THE AMERICAS:
TERRITORIES & EXPEDITIONS

Guest editor: Florencia Rodriguez
Design: Mainstudio (Edwin van Gelder, Florian Schimanski)
Managing Editor: Isabella Moretti
Translation and proof-reading: Lisa Ubelaker Andrade
Editorial Assistance for MCHAP: Jayne Kelley
Printing and lithography: robstolk
Binding: Patist

Texts: Stan Allen, Wiel Arets, Pedro Aparicio & Juliana Ramírez, Barry Bergdoll, Ila Berman, Sol Camacho, The Canary Project (Susannah Sayler & Edward Morris), Beatriz Colomina, Juan Pablo Corvalán, Jean Pierre Crousse, Dirk Denison, Uriel Fogué, David Harvey, Mariano Gomez-Luque & Daniel Ibañez, Rodrigo Kommers Wender, Sanford Kwinter, Isabella Moretti & Magdalena Tagliabue, Jean-Luc Nancy, Ciro Najle & Lluís Ortega, Todd Palmer, Paul Preissner, Enrique Ramírez, Ana Raskovsky, Patricio del Real, Florencia Rodriguez, Graciela Silvestri, Jeannette Sordi, Mason White

Visual essays: The Canary Project (Susannah Sayler & Edward Morris), Pablo Gerson, Miguel de Guzman, David Sisso

Photographs of MCHAP Finalist Projects: (pp. 161-163, pp. 165-167) Nelson Kon; (pp. 164, 168) Pedro Kok; (pp. 175-182) Iwan Baan; (pp. 189-196) Cristóbal Palma; (p. 203) Yoshi Koitani; (pp. 204-209) Onnis Luque; (p. 210) Margot Kalach; (pp. 217-224) Iwan Baan; (pp. 231-238) Pablo Gerson

Photographs of MCHAP Outstanding Projects: (p. 245) Halkin Mason, courtesy Rafael Viñoly Architects; Iwan Baan; Matthew Carbone; (p. 246) Gabriel Castro; Leonrado Finotti; Gonzalo Viramonte; (p. 247) Alejandro Arango; Christophe Wu; Pezo von Ellrichshausen; (p. 248) Adam Mørk, courtesy Schmidt Hammer Lassen Architects; Albert Vecerka, courtesy Weiss / Manfredi Architecture; Walter Salcedo; (p. 249) Stéphane Groleau, courtesy clcarchitects; Leonardo Finotti; Iwan Baan; (p. 250) Felipe Diaz Contardo; Alfonso Merchand; Christie Mills; (p. 251) Olivier Blouin; Iwan Baan; Brad Feinknopf; (p. 252) Alejandro Arango; Gonzalo Puga; Iwan Baan; (p. 253) Pedro Vannucchi; Cristobal Palma; Ema Peter, courtesy of MGA | Michael Green Architecture

Photographs of MCHAP Emerge Finalist Projects: (p. 262) Lauro Rocha; Nathan Rader; James Brittain; (p. 263) Felipe Fontecilla; Luis Gallardo

Photographs of MCHAP Emerge Outstanding Projects: (p. 264) Iwan Baan; BAAG; Lab.Pro.Fab; (p. 265) Cesar Bejar; Pedro Kok; Adrien Williams

MCHAP
Dean & The Rowe Family College of Architecture Endowed Chair: Reed Kroloff
MCHAP Director: Dirk Denison
Program Coordinator: Sasha Zanko
MCHAP Fellow: Andrew Jiang

This publication and the Mies Crown Hall Americas Prize (MCHAP) are initiatives of the College of Architecture at Illinois Institute of Technology(IIT).

The Americas publication series reflects on the outcomes of each MCHAP cycle. This volume is inspired by discussions that took place in 2016, during the second cycle of the prize.

IIT College of Architecture students and faculty are crucial contributors to the prize's identity and activities, including through coursework that creates a dialogue with MCHAP finalists. Notably, in 2016, the MCHAP seminar was led by Adjunct Professor Keefer Dunn, with the participation of Alexander Campbell, Elliot Hilgert, Sumi Kim, Joshua Mac-Williams, Naila Opiangah, Sara Torres, and Jordan Widjaja.

MCHAP would like to thank those who seeded and developed the idea of the prize and its publication program, in particular Professor Wiel Arets, then dean; Professor and Master of Science Program Director Vedran Mimica, then Associate Dean for Research; Associate Professor Lluís Ortega; and especially Professor Alan Cramb, then Provost and subsequently President.

Finally, MCHAP would like to thank the clients of the 2016 finalist projects for their commitment to excellence in architecture: Mike Alvidrez, CEO, Skid Row Housing Trust; Eduardo Hochschild, chairman, Hochschild Mining; Teofilo Kalach, investor, Tower 41; Gloria Kalil Mayer and Sérgio Cardoso, clients, Weekend House; Denise Pozzi-Escot, director, Pachacamac Site Museum; and Sharon Prince, CEO and founder, Grace Farms Foundation.

Reed Kroloff, Dean and Rowe Family College of Architecture Endowed Chair, would like to thank our publishing partners, Actar and NESS; MCHAP Director Dirk Denison, MCHAP Coordinator Sasha Zanko, and MCHAP Fellow Andrew Jiang; and Florencia Rodriguez for her editorial directorship; in addition to all those who made the MCHAP program and this publication possible: the Lambert Fund, the City of Chicago, and the firms, institutions, and individuals that generously support the initiative, including the Canadian Centre for Architecture, the Alphawood Foundation, Kohler Co., and the Mies van der Rohe Society at Illinois Institute of Technology.

MCHAP 2016 CYCLE
(All positions listed were the ones current in 2016)

## MCHAP
Dean & The Rowe Family College of Architecture
Endowed Chair, Wiel Arets
MCHAP Director, Dirk Denison
MCHAP Coordinator, Sasha Zanko
IIT College of Architecture Associate Dean for
Research, Vedran Mimica
IIT College of Architecture Publications Director,
Daniel O'Connell
IIT AC Press Editor, Lluis Ortega
IIT College of Architecture Senior Designer, Travis Rothe
MCHAP Program Consultant, Tyler Waldof

## BOARD OF DIRECTORS
Wiel Arets, Dean, Board Chair
Frances Bronet, Provost, IIT
Alan W. Cramb, President, IIT
Dirk Denison, MCHAP Director
Helyn Goldenberg
David Hovey, Founding Principal, Optima
Phyllis Lambert, Founding Director, Canadian Centre
for Architecture
Dirk Lohan, Founder, Lohan Anderson
Victor Morgenstern, Trustee, Executive Committee, IIT
John W. Rowe, University Regent, IIT

## INTERNATIONAL ADVISORY COUNCIL
David Basulto, Founder and Editor in Chief, ArchDaily
Barry Bergdoll, Meyer Schapiro Professor of Art
History and Archaeology and Chair, Department of
Art History, Columbia University
Dirk Denison, MCHAP Director
Kenneth Frampton, Ware Professor of Architecture,
Graduate School of Architecture, Planning and
Preservation, Columbia University
Reed Kroloff, Principal, Jones/Kroloff
Jorge Francisco Liernur, Professor, Torcuato di Tella
University, and Researcher, National Scientific and
Technical Research Council, Argentina
Robert McCarter, Ruth and Norman Moore Professor
of Architecture, Sam Fox School of Design & Visual
Arts, Washington University in St. Louis
Vedran Mimica, Associate Dean for Research, Council
Chair
Dominique Perrault, Founding Principal, Dominique
Perrault Architecture
Martino Stierli, Philip Johnson Chief Curator of Archi-
tecture and Design, Museum of Modern Art, New York
Sarah Whiting, Dean and William Ward Watkin
Professor, School of Architecture, Rice University
Mirko Zardini, Director, Canadian Centre for
Architecture

## CHICAGO COMMITTEE
Zurich Esposito, American Institute of Architects,
Chicago Chapter
Sarah Herda, Graham Foundation for Advanced
Studies in the Fine Arts
Mark Kelly, Department of Cultural Affairs and

Special Events, City of Chicago
Lynn Osmond, Chicago Architecture Foundation
Zoë Ryan, Department of Architecture and Design, Art
Institute of Chicago
Pauline Saliga, Society of Architectural Historians
Jonathan Solomon, School of the Art Institute of Chicago
Edward Uhlir, Millennium Park Foundation
Steven F. Weiss, Mies van der Rohe Society
Antony Wood, Council on Tall Buildings and Urban
Habitat

## IIT FACULTY COMMITTEE
Carlos Bedoya Ikeda
Thomas Brock
Marshall Brown
Susan Conger-Austin
Keefer Dunn
Paul Endres
Martin Felsen
Frank Flury
Ron Henderson
Leslie Johnson
Sean Keller
Robert Krawczyk
Eva Kultermann
Peter Land
Richard E. Nelson
Lluis Ortega
Paul Pettigrew
Mauricio Pezo
John Ronan
Michelangelo Sabatino
Andrew Schachman
Agata Mierzwa Siemionow
Sofia von Ellrichshausen
Antony Wood

## IIT STUDENT COMMITTEE
Saly Alzraikat
John Baldwin
William Carlson
Louise Leite
Brianda Mireles
Rolando Rodiguez
Jorge Serra de Freitas
Daniela Sesma Espinoza
Jenna Staff
Cosette To
Alina Tompert

PUBLISHED BY
IIT Architecture Chicago
IIT College of Architecture
Chicago, Illinois, USA
www.arch.iit.edu

-NESS
Pablo Gerson, Max Rohm, and
Florencia Rodriguez
Buenos Aires / Boston
hello@nessmagazine.com
nessmagazine.com
Actar Publishers
New York / Barcelona
www.actar.com

Distributed by:
Actar D, Inc.

New York
440 Park Avenue South, 17th Floor
New York, NY 10016, USA
+1 2129662207
salesnewyork@actar-d.com

Barcelona
Roca i Belle, 2-4
08023 Barcelona, Spain
+34 933 282 183
eurosales@actar-d.com

Printed in the Netherlands
ISBN: 978-1-63840-014-1
LCCN: 2021947597

A CIP catalogue record for this book is available from
the Library of Congress, Washington, DC, USA

BLUR NY
Miguel de Guzmán / Imagen Subliminal

Miguel de Guzmán's images portray a city in which reality is perceived though fiction. Built as it exists in our memory, this unreal city nevertheless is reminiscent of New York. The images are composed by applying three operations: first, by photographing fragments of the city while avoiding singular elements and recognizable icons; second, by recomposing the fragments in new urban configurations; and finally, by dissolving their silhouettes through motion blur in order for fine textures and details to disappear and volumes to fade.